Harry Bonsall was a young man with an extraordinary vision, who knew where he was heading. God had given him a goal.

The training was arduous. Huge obstacles lay on the running track, and other athletes unexpectedly dropped out of the race.

What lessons did he learn along the way? How did he survive? Would he ever make it? "On Your Marks!"

'Don't miss the opportunity to read about this amazing servant of the Living God. I have met thousands of Christian leaders around the globe and Brash was among the most unique. 35 years ago, my wife and I came to the UK when *Operation Mobilisation* was just being born. Brash was one of the first Christian leaders to back OM 100% and from his college came men and women into many different aspects of OM.

'Pass this book on to others or get extra copies to give away. I'm reading Billy Graham's autobiography right now, and believe that especially for the UK, this book is just as important. GO FOR IT!'

George Verwer
International Director,
Operation Mobilisation

RUNNING FOR REVIVAL

The Life and Times of Henry Brash Bonsall

Ruth McGavin

Christian Focus

I dedicate this book to
Murray, David, Andrew and Carrie,
who are a constant joy and encouragement.
The story is their legacy. I dedicate it to them.

ISBN 1 85792 522 X

© Ruth McGavin
First published in 1999
by
Christian Focus Publications
Geanies House, Fearn,
Ross-shire, IV20 1TW, Great Britain

Cover design by Owen Daily

CONTENTS

A COMPLEMENT TO THE BIOGRAPHY

ACKNOWLEDGEMENTS

Hundreds of contributors have been involved in the making of this book, to whom I am absolutely indebted. Students, staff, and friends from different parts of the world, many of whom are included in this story, but not necessarily named. I would like to thank you all, personally. Happy memories!

To Meng Cheng Wan (now in Sydney, Australia), who really started it all with his amazing series of tapes, winkled out of my dear father over many pleasurable weeks!

To our dear friend, 'Brother Andrew', who wrote a warm and memorable Introduction so readily, and George Verwer, also a special friend of many years, who picked up my book at the other end and wrote such a challenging Book Review - both of whom have extensive and hectic world ministries. Thank you!

To the writers: Richard Massey (present Principal of BBI), Bob Dunnett (ex-Vice-Principal of BBI) for their excellent chapters; to Jim Stevenson-Berry, for his invaluable contribution to the 'NBI' section and the BBI College Council over so many years; with student leaders Peter Horne and Peter Conlan taking on the 'Two Peters', Vincent Rudman of post-war All Nations (South Africa), Anneke Companjen (BBI/Holland) and Audrey (Herbert) Johnson (early BBI) - who 'filled us in' on so many aspects of student life. Also to my brother-in-law, Ian 'Marathon Man' Hancox,   and our children David, Andrew and Caroline for their chapters. Thank you all!

To Melvin Donald of IVF Canada, who so kindly allowed me to use his excellent book 'A Spreading Tree', to fill in the details of my father's early student days, and the fascinating student links between Britain and Canada.

To Leonard Miall (ex-BBC war correspondent) and Christine Nixon, with Bob Hunt (Vice-Principal of All Nations Christian College), who helped me recall the All Nations history in Taplow, where I spent the first seven happy years of my life. My grateful thanks.

Then, of course, I am indebted to those wonderful secretaries, computer experts and 'readers', who helped me to produce and shape this biography to its present form. At first, Vivienne Jones and Sherilyn Leck...later assisted by Graham Pegg - with a huge bulk of the book picked up and carried by Helen Fearnley. A very special ministry!

I would like to thank Rob, Rupert and Gail for their patience and photocopying skills. My warmest thanks also to Stewart Anderson and John Muir for the invaluable role they played at the final hurdle.

As for the eight readers (some already mentioned) I am so grateful for their expert advice and encouragement...Marion Stroud, Frank Gosling, David Page, Peter Horne and my brother Charles Bonsall. To my dear husband, Murray, who has never failed to advise, enthuse and encourage, when the running was hard going, regardless of so many challenging medical commitments to other needy parts of the world. His excellent editorial skills were rigorously and consistently put to the test over a very long period of time. You deserve a medal!

To my friend, June (Coxhead) Dooney, of London Bible College days, who flew over from New Zealand and gave one highly significant week to sorting me out on the book front. A great friend at all times!

My warmest appreciation and thanks to William and Carine MacKenzie and the excellent team at 'Christian Focus', for their encouraging support. To Malcolm Maclean, Ian Thompson, Jonathan Dunbar, Alister MacInnes and to Owen Daily, for his superb cover design. Thank you all!

Finally, a very special tribute to our son, Andrew S.B. McGavin, who devoted three months of his university holidays and his own particular literary skills, helping his mother to reach the finishing line of another kind of marathon!

Andrew played a most strategic role in the final construction of this biography. I owe a *great* deal to him!

WHY THIS BOOK?

In 1984, my father had been startled by an unexpected request. *Meng Cheng Wan*, a Christian businessman from the Chinese Church in Birmingham had an idea. Keen for a positive response and anticipating my father's objections in advance, he approached him with a proposition:

'Mr. Bonsall, would you mind telling me your life story, with a view to writing a book? True humility dispenses with modesty. We need your story for the benefit of posterity!' 'Why did I feel this?' he later wrote. 'Well, I was over-awed by his giant intellect. Brilliant anecdotes and illustrations that were so original and instructive in their clarity. Also, his remarkable economy with words ... and the years of painstaking effort and discipline it must have taken just to gather and record them.

'Secondly, his age and experience, spanning the lives of many outstanding and godly Christians. He had such a large heart and that holy presence about him. He, of all people, was well-qualified to comment on his times and contemporaries. Your father was very, very interesting, but at first he didn't think there was anything to his life that was of interest to others. He told me so. I think he initially agreed to my request just to humour me! He wasn't all that keen in the beginning. It meant another hour of his time taken up by an inquisitive young man each week – and I am almost certain he did it out of kindness to me.

'But gradually he warmed to it, so each Wednesday evening we would have a session together. First, he would brew the tea for the two of us and we would wait for the tea to 'infuse' (he was very fond of that word ... and a bit of a connoisseur with different brands of tea!). Mrs. Bonsall would appear with delicious home-made cakes or biscuits, and then we would begin in earnest.

'As the interviews progressed Brash Bonsall's life's work impressed me more and more. Unfortunately, in the early days, he worked almost single-handed. It wasn't that he didn't delegate. He did. But his volume of work was so enormous – and his disposable funds so little, that I marvel, today, at how much he was able to achieve.

'You know, he never had an unkind thing to say of anyone (and I was not a gullible young man). True, I was over-awed, but all those years as a church leader and life insurance agent taught me to test the words of others to see if they "rang true". I never detected any sham on his part. He led a life of utter simplicity that spoke louder than words.'

In the end, my father himself became enthusiastic to continue – and Meng Cheng Wan passed the pen over to him.

Now, as his daughter I pick it up and do my best to share a little insight into his life ... from the beginning ... to show how God can use *anyone,* just given the opportunity!

Ruth McGavin

FOREWORD

Question: *'Why is it that God sometimes seems to pour so much singular talent into a single person that even a long lifetime is not nearly enough to bring out even one percent of it?'*

I don't know.

But there simply *are* a few of these people around and one of them is the man about whom this book is written.

I remember, during one of our meetings together, when I visited the Birmingham Bible Institute (where, by the way, two of my closest and most appreciated colleagues have been trained), that we were discussing BBI – its existence, its size and its purpose.

During the conversation I asked Mr. Bonsall: 'How many students do you have now?' and he replied: 'About eighty.' That, incidentally, is twice the number that they used to have at the WEC Missionary Training College in Glasgow and I thought our family was really growing too big! It took me about a year to get to know everyone, but when I mentioned this to Mr. Bonsall and said: 'Well, eighty is a great number. Why not put a ceiling there?' he almost burst out: 'Andrew, I don't *want* to stop at eighty. I want to go on to *eight hundred*!'

I stood there like a little boy. Facing a man with a vision much bigger than that College, much bigger than mine too. A man who would never be satisfied with any limitations, physical or otherwise ... of age, college numbers, money, or whatever.

Vision! Vision and faith are twins ... and the combination of the two is prayer.

I knew him to be a man of prayer. Maybe that is why his study was not so tidy; every time when I look at the neat rows of books in my own study I think of Brash Bonsall. He had so much in his

11

own mind and brains and heart and spirit. He was a creator, not a consumer ... and that is where *prayer* comes in.

I remember the last time when I spoke at BBI. There they were, that wonderful couple, sitting on the platform just behind me. My ex-student colleague, Johan Companjen, and I were sharing, when I noticed that Mr. Bonsall was 'in prayer'. I was impressed.... until I reached the close of my address ... and he kept on sleeping! Then I knew that there are limits. There is a time when you have taken in enough. There was no need for him to listen to a young missionary who was spending his life on the cutting edge in communist countries. There also comes a time when you have given out enough; influencing hundreds, if not thousands of students and tens of thousands of conference visitors, with untold numbers in meetings and rallies – and all over the world through his books. There is a time when you have given out enough. Then the goodness of God shines clearest and He stoops down to His little earth and picks the nice flower.

But I tell you, it is still hurting us. I still miss my good friend Brash Bonsall: my teaching visits to the students and the College: my visits to his home and acquaintance with the family, particularly with Ruth and her husband in Afghanistan. But also because of the wonderful book he wrote: 'What Every Young Christian Should Know'. I just love that title and feel very privileged that this old saint, this old warrior who never tired of doing good, wrote a book for *young* people.

People like Brash Bonsall know what the *real* price is. They know that perseverance, effort, decisions, sacrifices, prayer, faith and total dedication to the cause of Christ, will *have* to come in our lives before we are going to see a change. And a change we *did* see in Eastern Europe. That is what the whole battle of faith is about. We do not live for ourselves, nor die for ourselves. But for the world, a changing world, that will change anyway for better or worse. Only Christ can change it into what God wants it to be, through our influence and through our likeness to Jesus

... a place that is open to the preaching of the Gospel of the Lord Jesus Christ.

That was one of the passions in the heart of Mr. Bonsall and, with many others, I still echo: 'We miss him, and yet life goes on.' Others will take his place, but I am grateful for this biography that will stir up many more to go back to his writings, consider his sayings, follow his teachings and make a new commitment to Jesus Christ for themselves, 'Whom to know is life eternal, Whom to serve is joy unspeakable.'

Brother Andrew

Brother Andrew van der Byl is President of Open Doors International. He first travelled to Eastern Europe more than forty years ago. Since that time, numerous Bibles have been taken in, and precious links have been forged with the 'suffering church'.

1

TORCHBEARER

It was June 1990. Staff and members of the College Council filed on to the platform of the large auditorium in Hockley, Birmingham. The hall rapidly filled to capacity, a buzz of anticipation sweeping the room as graduates prepared themselves for this landmark event in their lives.

One man stood slowly to his feet, with some difficulty. Tall and broad-shouldered, with distinguished features, penetrating brown eyes, moustache and a shock of snowy hair, there was a distinctive air of quiet authority about him.

For this man, a moment of history had arrived. The handing over of a great commission, that had carried him from the shores of British Columbia to a country on the brink of war.

Beside him sat a woman, once tall and straight, but now white-haired and bent, with a beautiful face that glowed with a quiet inner serenity. With her indomitable faith and strength of character, she was the perfect partner in a remarkable team.

Now it seemed, their moment had come. Speeches, tributes and prizes were presented with great bursts of applause, and gales of laughter. This was clearly a large family occasion, hugely enjoyed by all – particularly the couple at the centre of the proceedings, who knew and loved each one.

As the memorable evening drew to a close, refreshments were announced and the man again stood up to make his way to the adjoining hall. Without any warning, the whole audience spontaneously rose to its feet, with a tumultuous standing ovation that seemed to go on and on and on!

Henry Brash Bonsall started to move slowly across the platform, supported on either side by two staff members with their black academic gowns flowing. It was a scene reminiscent of the Old Testament patriarch as he stood on the top of the hill, held up on either side by Aaron and Hur!

As the clapping and cheering carried on, so did the fire and vision, long after their beloved Principal had left the stage.

What was there about this unusual and gentle man to mark him out for a special mention? He would say, 'Nothing.' As far as he was concerned that day, the next part of the proceedings was tea in the adjoining hall! He would never anticipate, or look for any kind of honour or applause. Not many days later, he finally reached the end of his race. But the flame had been kindled ... and the torch passed on.

2

BEGINNINGS ...

It was a typical, bustling Saturday afternoon in July, 1899. Scruffy children played tag and small, wooden carriages bumped along outside the department store of John Brash (JP) in Cheapside, Lancaster. Henry Bonsall, a striking man with a flowing moustache, stepped nervously onto the pavement, walked up to the window and peered intently through the glass. She was there. Gertie Brash, a strong-willed and vivacious young woman of 26, with the bluest, twinkliest eyes you ever saw, was working as manageress of the 'mantle' section in her father's store, and was engrossed with a customer on a busy Saturday afternoon. Henry was also in the clothing business, as buyer and commercial traveller for Thomson and Williams of London – and quite a musician on the side. He was also charming, with a ready joke and a gift for witty conversation – all part of his trade. On this particular day, however, he was suddenly at a loss for words.

Pausing to regain his composure, he took a deep breath and strode purposefully through the door. Elsie, Gertie's sister, looked up to greet the new customer, but seeing who it was, rushed breathlessly into the showroom.

'Gertie, I must speak with you. Do be quick! Mr. Bonsall has come and wants to see you.'

'Mr. Bonsall?' she asked, 'What on earth does *he* want? Tell him I'm engaged and am likely to be so for an hour or more.'

Elsie left as quickly as she had arrived, and Gertie, waiting a few minutes, eventually peeped round the corner, hoping the coast would be clear. 'Has Mr. Bonsall gone?' she whispered. Mr. Bonsall had not gone. Gertie and Elsie were ushered into the dining room, where the determined suitor was sitting quietly. As soon as they entered, he rose gingerly and shook hands, at which point Elsie left the room, much to her sister's discomfort. Taking chairs at opposite ends of the long, wooden table, they sat in uncomfortable silence as the long clock ticked loudly in the corner. Gertie broke the silence.

'Well then,' she said, 'What do you want to see me for, in the middle of a busy Saturday afternoon?'

He looked at her hard, but said nothing for some time. Then he spoke, quietly but with purpose.

'May I write to you?'

'No!'

'May I send you flowers?'

'Yes, I love flowers. But Mr. Bonsall, I must tell you, I never intend to be married – and what's more, I don't want to be married.'

John Brash would have none of it either. He liked Henry Bonsall very well but when he began showing an interest in his daughter, he quickly changed his tune! Henry, nearly twenty years her senior, was 'too old', he said. If he really loved Gertie, he must prove his worth and not see her or speak to her for the space of a year.

In her desire to escape further romantic episodes, Gertie left her work at the store, and embarked on a nurses' training course at Brownlow Hill Hospital in Liverpool, determined to forget her embarrassing afternoon. Henry was broken-hearted, but equally determined not to give up. Obeying her father's request, he did not see her or speak to her, but made sure that one red rose was delivered to her door every day of that year! Every day on the wards, just as faithfully, Gertie wore her rose.

It was a marvellous day in March 1903, shared with 700 friends and well-wishers at Centenary Congregational Church,

Lancaster, when Henry claimed his bride – and their joy was increased, when a son was born in Preston on September 10th 1905 – Henry Brash Bonsall.

It was a difficult birth. Margaret, Gertie's authoress sister and bridesmaid, made an entry in her journal to mark the event:

'Baby Bonsall was born that September – and till Christmas it seemed that he scarcely would live. He was such a little skeleton, but he took a right turn at Christmas and flourished.'

Harry, as they called him, never looked back. From that day on, as an only child, he thrived on the love and prayerful devotion of his parents, which was to play a highly significant role in days to come.

3

ADVENTURE!

It is 4:30 pm one Sunday afternoon. The date, May 9th 1913. A slim child, with a thatch of blond, curly hair and dark penetrating brown eyes stands with his parents on the deck of the SS Virginian, enthralled, as the huge Allan Liner steams up the St. Lawrence Seaway into Montreal, Canada. A great commotion on the deck makes him look round, and he collapses with laughter at the sight of one immigrant housewife on board, who has tied all her household belongings into a white counterpane, which breaks as it is being hoisted into mid-air. The stevedores below are showered with kettles, irons and brooms. He watches, fascinated, as the French-Canadian longshoremen take control of the ship, all jabbering away in French like so many buccaneers, while the crew who have travelled with them for so long seem to melt into thin air. For seven-year-old Harry, this is the start of an incredible adventure.

It was Gertie, always full of pluck and sparkle, who had somehow got it into her head to emigrate. Nothing would dissuade her. In fact, she was so determined, that she had quietly put aside the princely sum of £700 from her household budget towards the passage. Henry was astonished. In 1912, £700 was a fortune! Henry was already well into his fifties when they set out from Liverpool docks and Harry was bursting with excitement at the prospect of the journey.

Harry's heroes
Harry never forgot his first impressions of this exciting new world – so vast in comparison to the island of his birth. It was an

exciting time to reach North America and Harry had no shortage of heroes. Only a few years earlier Jean Francois Gravelet, the great Blondin, had astounded crowds of 40,000 and more on Table Rock, as he carried a man, one and a half times his own weight, across the Niagara Falls. Blondin's playground was 1,000 feet of narrow rope strung out between the Canadian and American borders. Charlie Chaplin, the little gentleman tramp, with his twirling cane, bowler hat, tight jacket and baggy pants was also thrilling audiences everywhere with his slap-stick humour and his touching combination of comedy and pathos. When they finally reached their destination, Vancouver, Buffalo Bill was in town! Colourful posters everywhere advertised Cody's Wild West Show – Indian fights, round-ups, stage robbers and buffalo hunts, with stars such as Annie Oakley and Buck Taylor. What more could a young boy want! The romance of the place fired his imagination and never left him.

Vancouver
As Canada's second port, Vancouver – surrounded by water and overlooked by mountains, with its mild climate and fast growing metropolis – was soon to become a world leader in grain exports. At the same time, the export of coal and ores to Japan attracted many Japanese immigrants and their families, who worked at the Celtic Cannery and the local fisheries nearby.

Young Harry, who always loved walking, would wander along by the banks of the Fraser River, chatting to the Japanese fishermen and watching the large fishing vessels pulling in and out. His parents opened their home to some of these families and Harry grew up with a special concern for his friends, the Japanese.

The sea
Harry's boyhood years were surrounded by the sea. Exhilarating sea views were everywhere! False Creek with its beautiful new

sandy beach was just around the corner. Great ship-building yards, lumber and paper factories, sugar and petroleum refining plants and textile manufacturers were all within easy reach and the fish were plentiful and delicious, particularly British Columbia salmon from Vancouver Island. The rugged coastline was broken by deep fjords and bays, mountainous and heavily forested, and Harry liked nothing better than a walk or a cycle ride with a picnic at the end of it! Gertie was especially good at these and often invited friends for the outing.

Canadian school

Of course, life was not simply an endless holiday. Fortunately, academic subjects were never a great problem to Harry. With his love for learning, it soon became clear that he was a budding scholar. In fact, he always seemed to share the top four places with the same three girls! From the first, teachers remarked that there was something special and unique about Harry. He was an unusual and sensitive child, with a thirst for knowledge, a highly colourful imagination and an extraordinary memory. He seemed to look out on his world through a series of windows, full of poetic pictures and vivid illustrations of life. Stories he heard, people he met, scenes he had witnessed, tragic or funny, seemed to make an indelible impression on his mind ... and he wrote it all down. Carefully, he started compiling a quaint book of poems, essays and plays to present to his mother.

In 1914, the small family moved from 748 Bute Street (Vancouver's 'West End') to a twenty-roomed three-storey house nearby, at 1021 Georgia Street. That was a happy house! Henry worked hard to support his wife and young son and Gertie rented out extra rooms, keeping house, as well as scores of chickens and ducks (not to mention ninety-four rabbits!).

Harry had everything he could wish for, with his own garden plot and tool set. He spent hours in the carpenter's shop constructing things. Often he cycled happily around the city streets on his own, exploring, or taking a trip to the beautiful Stanley Park with its huge, ancient trees. Many times he would stand on tip-toes peering over the black, stone railway bridge, hoping for a glimpse of the great, thundering steam trains, then pause, breathless with excitement, as the engine passed right beneath him. Throughout his early childhood and teenage years, Harry was absolutely fascinated by trains and the romance of the Canadian railroads that played such a major part in everyone's life in those days, including the Indians, and the hobos who would follow the tracks to their next destination.

At this stage Harry seemed quite happy with his own company, his own family and their adult friends. In his spare time he read prodigiously (particularly history, classical literature and Charles Dickens) being drawn to the graphic and funny descriptions of people and Victorian life in the poorhouse. Little Nell of 'The Old Curiosity Shop' was his favourite. Dickens appealed to the journalist/historian in him and Harry always had a tender heart for the under-dog. If a story particularly moved him, he would quietly weep in sympathy, or laugh till the tears rolled down his cheeks when something tickled his humour.

At other times, he would turn his hand to poetry, even attempting the classical style at a very early age. A sadly-wise little poem describes the loss of his favourite chicken who wandered the home happily at will – until one day it met its fate at the untimely opening of a door!

THE CHICKEN'S DECEASE

He died on the morn of Christmas Day,
Died in a tragical, sad little way,
When all the world was happy and gay,
With Christmas cheer, and love sincere,
And all had something merry to say.

He died in the prime of his early youth,
Died in a manner, strange and uncouth,
Under our cheery household roof,
When the fires were set, and the knives were whet,
And trouble and sorrow held aloof.

On that fated morn his knell was rung,
E'en while the churchbell swayed and swung,
Its massive frame and iron tongue,
His senses darted, and departed,
Leaving him the dead among.

Thus we learn through pain and sorrow,
Life is very short and hollow;
And the wine of death we swallow,
While our laughter, shakes each rafter,
And we think not of the morrow.

Harry Bonsall, aged 12
(Published Vancouver Daily Province, December 29th, 1918)

Another source of great pleasure was music. At Georgia Street the piano was constantly in demand, although in fact Henry's favourite was the organ. Harry loved the organ too, with his natural flair for improvising and composition, which no doubt stemmed from his gifted parents and the fun they all used to have at the Brash family musical soirées in Lancaster.

War ...

Life was secure and wonderfully happy for Harry, but suddenly, in 1914, World War I burst like a bombshell into his comfortable existence. Clouds of war hung heavy over Canada and in October of that year 33,000 Canadian troops sailed for Europe, many of them never to return. More divisions followed to become allied shock troops on the Western Front, where casualties were staggering. Well-informed and sensitive to people's suffering at the best of times, young Harry had to reckon with the stark realities of life and death at a very early age.

The trauma of war, however, highlighted the need for a deeper security and anchor in life. With four generations of Methodists on his father's side, there was a deep family consciousness of eternal issues; and like a sponge, Harry soaked it all in from his surroundings. He had always taken the truth of the Bible for granted and despite the war, never questioned the goodness of God, the love and sacrifice of Jesus, the presence of the Holy Spirit or a heaven to follow. One little poem, jotted down on the back of an old exercise book, expressed a young man's understanding of his goal in life.

A Poemlet   (H.B.B.)

One yard forward,
One yard more;
The race is almost finished,
And we're nearly at the door.

One leap further,
Yes... we're there!
The golden gates wide open clang,
We're in the City fair.

In fact, even before they ventured out to Canada, Harry, at the tender age of five, had been preparing his own sermons! He took it *most* seriously. Every Sunday afternoon he had gone with his parents to the Avenham Lane Mission, Preston, where he prepared a sermon to inflict upon a forbearing congregation of about ten, never forgetting to take the collection! This preparation of sermons would continue each Sunday afternoon until he was almost sixteen when he started taking his own Sunday School class of boys. Delivering sermons in those early days was a tremendously serious affair for him. He prayed and agonised about them!

Henry and Gertie faithfully supported and prayed for their budding preacher and never laughed at his efforts, although they must have been sorely tempted on occasion.

4

THE GREAT DIVIDE

It was a warm summer morning in 1917, the Vancouver sun shining down brightly on 12-year-old Harry as he sat gazing out over the sparkling water of False Creek. The mountains rose majestically on either side, and his eyes drank in the surroundings, as a gentle breeze played with the curly blond hair that hung over his forehead. 'The world is so beautiful,' he thought to himself. 'How can it be possible that men are dying in agony in fields of mud only a few thousand miles from here.' He paused for a moment, then took out the family newspaper and opened it carefully, taking care not to smudge the print. Although so far from the scene of conflict, the young boy's brows furrowed as descriptions of war raced through his thoughts. Already in a serious frame of mind, he flicked through the other pages looking for interesting local news and within seconds a headline caught his eye:

One wrong turn and boy is dead. He had to read on...

> *'Yesterday, a 12-year-old boy was bitten by a rattlesnake in Nelson town. Life-saving serum was available in Seattle, Washington. His parents waited anxiously, as a motorcyclist raced from Seattle with the serum. After arriving at Elliot's Corner, the courier had two choices – left to Vancouver, right to Nelson. At the crucial crossing, he took the wrong turn and thundered on at 90 miles an hour – in the wrong direction. The boy died.'*

Harry read the report again with shock. Twelve years old, just like him. *One* wrong decision and a life was over. 'It could have been me,' he thought, his mind numbed.

The impact of this tragic story played increasingly on young Harry's mind. 'It could have been *me*.... What if it had been *me*?'

August 26th 1917

Shortly afterwards, school started once more, and when work had finished one afternoon, Harry came rushing out into the playground with all the other pupils, dozens of excited children all pushing and jostling to get out of the door at the same time. When he finally got through he stopped and stared for a moment. A man seemed to be chalking something on the pavement. What was going on? Again the jostling began as the children crowded round to see. It was Frank Miller, the American children's evangelist.

'Come along children. You're all invited to hear what I've got to say. It's just over the way, right opposite your school,' said the man with a twinkle in his eye.

That afternoon 400 children, including Harry, flocked to the meeting. As he listened to the message, he began to understand the Gospel of Jesus Christ in a completely new way and he realised that he had a choice to make. In his mind's eye, Harry pictured a little mountain stream that he had once seen with his parents on a breathtaking ride through the Rocky Mountains. Their train had screeched to a halt near Banff, right alongside the Great Divide, where the mountain torrent reached a small neck of land. At that crucial point, each drop of the torrent had to make its own decision. If it veered to the left, it would flow into the Kicking Horse River, on into Columbia and eventually the Pacific. But if it turned right, it would go coursing into Bow River, then the Saskatchewan and finally on into the Arctic Ocean, literally thousands of miles from its counterpart at the Great Divide. Once that choice was made, there was no going back. Harry now knew this was the moment of truth. Then he thought of the young boy who had died, and asked himself again, 'What if it had been *me*?' His mind was made up. He made his choice. From that time on, Harry knew that he was committed to living for God and serving Him. He was not only sure of his relationship with Jesus, but he was also quite clear that God wanted him to be a minister – and a minister with a particular mission in life.

An excited Harry raced home, his thin legs working as hard as they could to get him to his destination. He burst through the door to greet a surprised mother with his happy news. Gertie said nothing, but her eyes shone as her only son gave intricate details of the afternoon's proceedings. Two days later she presented him with a Bible, having written in the fly leaf a verse from Psalm 63: 'Early will I seek Thee.'

Peace ...
One year later, in November 1918, Harry sat at the small, wooden desk where he normally did his homework. His diary lay open before him, his pen poised thoughtfully as he relived in his mind the amazing events and excitement of the previous week. He began to write ...

'It came so suddenly. First a succession of German defeats, the capture of German prisoners by the Americans and the allies and then the end. I well remember the time, that is, as it appeared to Vancouver. The day before it happened was Sunday, November the 10th ... and we smiled whimsically as we saw the hoarse-voiced newspaper boys selling their papers right and left. Every rumour, everything extra, warranted the printing of a paper. Father satisfied his unbearable curiosity and sacrificed ten cents in the purchase of some two 'hextras'.

That evening we went to bed as usual. At about 12 o'clock

29

we heard the booming of the 9 o'clock gun. Once, twice, thrice, to twelve times. This was the appointed signal and we knew what it meant. At the same time it seemed, a terrific row broke out from the direction of Randell Street. We got up, dressed hurriedly, and went out. Everything was confusion. It seemed as if the city was alive. Two men played cornets outside the Hotel Vancouver. To their accompaniment we sang, or rather shouted, The Marseillaise, Rule Britannia, The Star-Spangled Banner, and God Save the King. One lady rattled two saucepan lids, another beat on an old bread-tin with a stick. Almost every auto, and there were hundreds of them, trailed a garbage can, three or four oil cans, or something tin and handy. You can imagine, but faintly, what a din there was. Every klaxon honked, everyone yelled and laughed. The streets were quite light, resplendent with waving flags. Two gentlemen we observed with alarm-clocks tied on the top of a pole and ringing furiously. The clock chimed two, and still the incessant din kept on. All next day, and practically all the day after, the rejoicing has continued.'

Harry laid down his pen and gazed from his window into the dark, but calm, expanse of night sky that lay over Vancouver. He picked it up once more to add a final thought.

'Only when one has felt over four years of war, shortage and sorrow, can one realize the real value of the word, and even more its meaning – Peace.'

Black Flu

The joyful celebrations that followed the war were short-lived, however. In 1919 a terrible 'flu' epidemic struck, and nearly 20 million people died throughout the world – more than in the war itself! Apparently spreading from the rat-infested trenches of France after the war, it worked its way relentlessly westwards until, a month later, it hit British Columbia. Like the bubonic plague and black death of earlier ages, people turned black after dying of it. All schools and theatres in Vancouver were closed for three months, and worst of all for the Bonsall family, Henry contracted the deadly illness. After some time it became clear that he would survive, but it was also evident that he would never work again. Despite this huge setback, the family were thankful, knowing that only the hand of God and the nursing of his wife had saved him. Harry had always taken life seriously, but the prospect of losing his beloved father meant that from this time on he had to make a particular effort in doing all he could to help his mother and support his father.

At one point, this included earning money by taking a summer job on a Japanese raspberry-picking ranch. Hours were 7 am to 1 pm, then 2 till 6 pm and he was treated very well, with first-class accommodation. The ranch, situated on the Fraser River, was at least 30 miles from Vancouver – and home. He was allowed to eat all he wanted, so Harry worked the rows of raspberry bushes, diligently pursuing the principle of 'pick one, eat one'. By the end of a typical day, he was often not only violently sick, but desperately missing the family he had left behind in Vancouver. One evening, after a long, hot day, he sat down exhausted on his bed and wrote one short entry in his diary:

'I've never been so homesick in my life.'

About this time, the family moved house once again to Kitsilano, a residential suburb of Vancouver, separated from the West End by False Creek. Harry's new home, 2154 York Street, had a large garden where he spent many happy hours jotting down his observations on anything that interested him, ranging from an imaginary conversation with his favourite cockerel (King Chandelier), the unwelcome visits of a certain Dr. Jordan (a bit of a rogue), to a mini thesis on carpentry (different kinds of wood and tools), and spiritual issues! Meanwhile, he kept fit by joining a YMCA gym and a huge, lively Boys Club nearby.

Life was fun, but Harry hadn't forgotten that God was with him through the good times and the bad, and it was this strong awareness that brought him to one of the most important events of his teenage years – his confirmation on Palm Sunday, 1920, when he was still fourteen. As he knelt in St. Mark's Church, Vancouver, Archbishop de Pencier laid his hands on the boy's head and Harry was suddenly aware that something significant was occurring. From that time on, he was conscious of what he would come to describe as *a prophetic gift*, which seemed to give fresh sparkle and life to all conversations about Jesus. It was quite unexpected and came quietly, rather like a ship that docks in the night.

5

HARRY THE STUDENT –
TRAINING THE MIND

'Sing a song of "Education '26" at U.B.C.
From the peaks of Pedagogy we descend, O Varsity.
To proclaim our worthy station – for each student will
agree,
That the future of the country will depend on such as we!'

September 1922. Someone was calling. 'Harry. Harry.' A slight
stirring was detected beneath the bedclothes. 'Harry,' the voice
repeated. This time, wavy blond hair was seen to emerge from
the covers. 'Come on, Sonnie Boy. Time to get up.' A faint groan
was heard as two sleepy, brown eyes blinked over the edge of the
blanket. Then he remembered what day it was.

The time had come for University, and Harry, at the tender
age of sixteen, was about to embark on a four year Arts course in
Classics, leading to a BA degree at the University of British
Columbia. Nervous excitement reigned, as last-minute
preparations were made for this first day of a new era in his life.
'Don't forget to pack enough pens,' Gertie fussed, handing him
yet another writing pen, just in case he ran out. Arriving at the
site, Harry took in his surroundings with keen interest.

It was a very young University – founded in 1908, in the
Fairview District. By 1922, when Harry joined, 1,176 students
were housed in the grounds of the Vancouver General Hospital,
with classes being held in very original surroundings – tents,

shacks, nearby homes, attics and even a church basement! Conditions had bordered on the intolerable, hopelessly crowded and extremely run-down. Although the provincial government had set aside 3,000 acres of land at Point Grey for the University in 1911, construction of buildings had been interrupted in its early stages by the outbreak of World War I.

For ten long years the only evidence of the University at the appointed site was the skeleton frame of the Science building and the beginnings of some barns. In fact, Gertie and Harry, out for a cycle ride one day in 1915, had unexpectedly stumbled on this large unfinished building in a clearing. At the time it had seemed strangely out of place, but later it was to become the new University Library. It was estimated then that university students in the Agricultural College were wasting some 6,000 hours going to and from their fields at Point Grey!

Despite the difficult working conditions, Harry loved his studies and threw himself into them with great energy and enthusiasm – as with everything else he tackled! Responsibilities and concern at home increased as his father's health grew worse, and for a while Harry wondered if he would have to give up University in order to find a job. However, the resourceful Gertie set herself up as a piano teacher, earning more income through lesson fees than her husband, so that her son could continue his studies.

Summer months for Harry were also occupied with money-earning activities. In fact, the great proportion of students in the Twenties did tough manual work during the vacations and despised those who only lay around in deckchairs! They never dabbled in studies but devoted themselves to their summer jobs and usually came back as brown and strong as bears, with an ability to do hard study which would never have been possible otherwise. All through those summers, Harry worked at the Dowling Furniture Factory in the east end of Vancouver, learning the carpenter's trade. The first summer in 1923 was hot and dry. Forest fires were everywhere and Harry stood amazed at the sight of countless mother birds dying on their nests with their wings spread out to protect their nestlings rather than leave them. Deeply moved, he thought, 'If God put such love into a few ounces of bird flesh, what love must exist in His own heart?'

Back at the University, Harry was a natural scholar and determined to give his best, but one aspect of student life was to make studies very difficult at times.

Canada in the 1920s had changed. Belief in the basic truth and inspiration of Scripture seemed to be a thing of the past. Most of the Presbyterian, Methodist and Congregational Churches had moved a long way from the good, solid, evangelical position of the pre-war years, and in the mid-20s Canadian churches joined together as one United Church of Canada. At first it looked like 'progress' and Harry and Gertie signed up to join, along with so many others, not realising until later that it preached a gospel of modernism. They soon changed allegiance when they understood just what this unity meant!

Life at home had been blissfully secure and sheltered. Now, on attending university, Harry suddenly came up against a barrage of strongly modernistic and liberal trends which were utterly hostile to him.

Isabel Miller (Kuhn), a fellow student at the University of British Columbia, who would later go on to become a missionary in China, described an English lecture in which her Professor paused to remark, 'Of course no-one in this enlightened age believes any more in the myth of Genesis.' Facing the large freshman class who were hanging on his words, and pulling his face into gravity, he asked, 'Is there anyone here who believes there is a Heaven and a Hell? Who believes that the story of Genesis is true? Please raise your hand.' He waited.

Up went Isabel's hand bravely as he waited, plus one other, amongst a hundred or so students. The Professor smiled pityingly and commented, 'Oh, you just believe that because your Papa and your Mama told you so.' He then proceeded with his lecture, assuming once for all, that no thinking human being believed the Bible any more.

It was in this atmosphere of hard work, combined with a sceptical, even derisory attitude towards Christianity amongst students, that Harry found himself. Slowly, almost imperceptibly at first, the young student started relying on his own abilities and strength in his daily life. Even though he was seeing God at work, notably through the evangelistic campaigns of Charles Price in 1923, Harry became more concerned with 'doing' Christian activities than deepening his relationship with God. Only the saddest event of his twenty years was able to bring things into the right perspective.

6

HEAVEN

'Today, on January 20th 1925, my father died in our arms.'

They had seen the end coming on relentlessly for the last year, like the walls of a room closing in on them with no escape. Henry Bonsall sat peacefully between Gertie and Harry in their glass-panelled sitting-room, gazing out onto Kitsilano Beach and the magnificent sight of a sunset over the Pacific. Harry felt stunned, almost unable to take in the enormity of the loss that was about to rock his life. He clutched his father's arm even tighter.

As this family trio, who had come through so much together, held each other close, Harry was aware of a very strange sensation as he looked around the room. It was as if all his university textbooks (on Geology, Biology, Classics and so forth) stood up on their shelves and looked down on them, saying, 'You are now coming to the River of Death. He must cross over to the Country Beyond. We are all true, but we belong to *this* side of the River, and we cannot help you for what belongs to the *other* side.' At that moment, it was as if God Himself was speaking in that room. He said, 'I come from the other side of the River, and am good for *both* sides of it.' John 11:25 seemed to come alive: *'I am the Resurrection and the Life. He that believes in Me, though he were dead, yet shall he live.'*

Suddenly Henry's eyes caught something amazing. 'Oh!' he exclaimed. It seemed so bright, his face was all lit up. They looked at the place where his eyes had seen it, but saw nothing. 'What is it? What do you see?' But he was with Jesus ... and they were on holy ground. How *near* heaven seemed! Both of them felt as if they had come to the very gate and longed to enter in.

That night Gertie lay alone in her bedroom for the first time and fervently prayed that she would sleep through the night without waking as usual at 4 am. For the last few months of Henry's illness she had woken up at the same time every morning and been unable to go back to sleep. Well, at 4 am exactly she woke up. Wide awake, too. She switched the light on to see the time, and groaned. She said, almost aloud, 'Father, I asked you not to let me wake up now, and here I am, wide awake!', then switched off the light. Suddenly she saw an amazing sight. The whole of the wall facing her bed was lit up as if it was on fire. Startled, she sat up, clutching her pillow.

At 7 am Gertie, still breathless with wonder, ran through to Harry's room and started shaking him gently. He rolled over and opened his eyes slowly, but rapidly opened them wider as he saw the unusual excitement on his mother's face.

'Harry. He was here. I saw him.'

'Who?'

'The Lord Jesus. He was in my room.'

'What? How do you know?'

'It was Him. There's no doubt. He stood in the centre of the room – so bright and shining, so full of sympathy and love – I was only able to gaze at Him. It wasn't a hallucination. It really happened. He spoke to me, Harry!'

'What did He say?'

'He said, "I have got your dear one safe. Take up your cross and follow me." Then He was gone, and the wall was the same as before. I got out of bed and felt for cracks in the wall – felt if the wall was hot and examined it closely – but there was nothing unusual. Then I got into bed and fell asleep immediately. I looked at the wall again a few minutes ago but there was nothing. For a few moments I tried to deceive myself that this was a fancy, a figment of the brain, but it was not so. I *saw* Him. Oh Harry, I'll never forget the loveliness of Him and the command He gave me.'

Nothing more could be said for a while, as mother and son reflected on what had happened. Jesus had come in person when they needed Him most.

Two weeks later Harry was getting into bed, and as usual, knelt down to pray, when an audible voice distinctly said, 'If you were to die like your old father, where would you go?'

He replied, 'He's gone to heaven, and I would too.'

'How do you know?' came back the Voice.

'Because I've never done any harm and I hope to do a lot of good,' said Harry, and quickly added, 'I've been christened and confirmed, too!' but as soon as he said it, he saw clearly that *that* wasn't good enough, and cried out, 'What shall I do?'

Instantly the Voice repeated words from John Chapter 3: 'God so loved the world, that He gave His one and only Son, that whoever believes in Him, shall not perish but have eternal life.'

It was all very well to accept the first part of that verse with the head only, just because it was a historical fact (lots of people could do that quite easily) but it was really the last half – the believing and receiving bit, that was so vitally important if anything was to become of it. It all sounded so simple – but Harry struggled! It was hard for this intelligent young man to let God be in control. Suddenly he realised that since his experience at Frank Miller's crusade eight years earlier, he had shifted his ground. One foot had been standing on what Christ had done for him, and the other on what *he* was doing to earn his own salvation. 'All my church-going,' he thought, 'It just doesn't count for anything! There's nothing to prove. It's already done.'

All at once, he saw that he just couldn't reach God through climbing the ladder of self-effort to find Him on the topmost rung. In order to find Him he actually had to start at the bottom! The words of Jesus sprang to his mind, '*I tell you the truth, unless you change and become like little children, you will never enter the kingdom of heaven*' (Matt. 18:3).

39

Despite a real awareness of God's presence with them, Henry's death had left a gaping hole in the close-knit family circle, and times were often lonely at home for the two left behind. Both were absolutely devoted to each other, but Gertie was also fiercely protective of her young twenty-year-old son, not realising, perhaps, that he needed the freedom to make his *own* relationships outside the home.

Harry was feeling particularly pensive one late summer afternoon in 1925. It was coming up to his fourth year of university studies and a rucksack of books lay beside him in the long grass as he sat, hunched up on a flat outcrop of rock, gazing out over the ocean.

As he went back in his mind over the events of the last few months – his father's death; his mother's needs; his new-found friends – God suddenly spoke to him quite clearly in the silence about one particular girl who seemed to stand head and shoulders above the rest. It was Juliet, a pretty dark-haired student, who was not only a brilliant musician but an evangelist at heart. In fact, she seemed to share the very goals and priorities that meant so much to Harry. As they joined in the fun and challenges of campus life, the two young friends were strangely drawn to each other and shared many a conversation over coffee after lectures on the things that *really* mattered in life. More and more, Harry felt convinced that they could be a great team together. The voice in the silence seemed so clear a confirmation of the friendship, that Harry decided to broach the subject with his mother.

Gertie, a strong character at all times however, had other ideas! One day Juliet came to call on Harry at 2252, West Third Avenue, Kitsilano…and Gertie showed her the door!

Harry was devastated. He had to make his own decision over the friendship right there, knowing full well that God had already spoken. Being a devoted son, he listened first to Gertie and, with a heavy heart, decided not to pursue the friendship. It cost him many sleepless nights and hours of recrimination.

40

7

THE FUNDAMENTALIST SOCIETY

'Little is much if God is in it
Man's busiest day is not worth God's minute.'

In the autumn, Harry returned to his fourth year of student life. It was the year of 'The Great Trek', when the University of British Columbia moved in a great procession to the new, but long-awaited site of Point Grey. Students took to the streets, shouting:

'We're through with tents and hovels! Point Grey! Point Grey!'

A great float with the theme of 'The Old Woman Who Lived in a Shoe' paraded the area. For those who looked closely enough, Harry could be seen peering out of the toe.

Although the site had changed, however, some things had not. Modernism and scepticism were still rife, and it was in this atmosphere that a number of Christians from different denominations, led by James Duncan, put an announcement on the notice-board.

> *Those interested in the formation of a Fundamentalist Society, meet in Lecture Room 202 on Thursday at 12.00pm and bring your lunch.*

Harry, along with his friends Eugene Cameron, Fred St. Denis, Esther Denman and others, waited in the room, having no idea who would appear. But as other students filed in,

exclamations of surprise went up from all around. One student who had just entered the room looked around with an open mouth. 'Doug Honeyford? I didn't know you were a Christian. And Bob Birch. That's terrific!' Within seconds, the happy sound of laughter and conversation could be heard from Room 202, and firm friendships were being formed that would last a lifetime.

So, the Student Christian Fundamentalist Society was born – 1925 forerunner to the Canadian Inter-Varsity Fellowship of Toronto (1928). The Inter-Varsity group at UBC would go on to have the longest continuous history of any university Inter-Varsity Fellowship group in Canada. In very difficult circumstances, these young men and women had learned the vital importance of being *seen* to be different. God blessed all those who stood out boldly in public and 'came out of their caves' to face their fellow students. Within three years, twelve of the original fifteen in that group would go on to become either ministers or missionaries.

1926: Henry Brash Bonsall B.A.
Finally, graduation day arrived. As Harry spent a good deal of time at home helping his mother, he didn't allow himself a wide variety of extra-curricular activities, but thoroughly enjoyed the friendship of his special circle within the newly formed Fundamentalist Society. At twenty he was still quite shy to take a lead unless he felt passionately about anything, but he certainly knew what he wanted in life.

The 1926 Totem Yearbook summed him up:

Henry Brash Bonsall
Though very young, Harry has finished with distinction each of his four years at college. Academically speaking, he has but one consuming passion – classical languages. It is strange, but true, that he finds a great source of pleasure in a

43

Greek or a Latin dictionary! For diversion, Harry attends the meetings of the University Classics Club. Of a quiet nature, he is known intimately, perhaps, to a small circle of friends only. His vocation in life will be the ministry of the Church of Canada.

Who would have guessed that this quiet, reserved and committed young man would become such a colourful character and achieve so much for God in his lifetime?

8

'YOU HAVE BEEN FAILED, MR. BONSALL'

The next two years were even more challenging – juggling three courses at once. An M.A. in Classics at U.B.C. (1926-28); an extra-mural one year Theology course at Knox College, Toronto; and yet another course in Hebrew at the United Church Theological College of Vancouver. Harry seemed to thrive on hard work and a challenge, always wanting to do things in style! Latin and Greek were his 'majors', studied in small specialist classes with three excellent professors, who taught Harry the vital importance of strict accuracy in translation.

Everything *seemed* to be going well. Harry's thesis was on *Rome and the Jews in the First Two Centuries of the Christian Era,* using Flavius Josephus as his main source and 'The Jews in the Time of Jesus Christ' by Emil Schivier as his principal text. However, there was a fourth professor who couldn't stand Harry's quiet determined faith. He would often try to lower him in the eyes of the class with such remarks as, '*You go to your Bible School, Mr. Bonsall*' or '*You go to your prayers about it.*' So, quite early, Harry was persecuted for Christ's sake. As time advanced it was more marked. He had worked hard, *very* hard, and was actually looking forward to receiving the mark for his thesis. Then, the night before Convocation, he received a phone call ...

'Could I speak with Henry Bonsall, please.'

'Yes, speaking.'

'Mr. Bonsall, I have some news regarding your thesis.'

Harry's heart jumped. He tried to appear calm. 'Oh, right. Do you actually have the results?'

'Yes, I do, Mr. Bonsall. I'm sorry, but you have been failed.'

Silence. It seemed as if cold steel had cut into his heart.

'Mr. Bonsall, are you still there?'

'Uh, yes, yes I am. I'm sorry, sir, but are you sure that is correct?'

'I'm afraid so. You were, in fact, passed by three of your professors and only failed by the fourth. Apparently your thesis was badly typed. I'm sorry.'

'Uh, well, thank you for letting me know, sir.'

He hung up the phone.

Stunned, Harry wandered in a daze into the living room, said quietly, 'Mother, I've been failed,' and walked out again. Gertie rushed after him. 'What do you mean you've been failed. You've never been failed before. You worked so hard.'

'Three of them passed me, but the one who's always made fun of me in class said my thesis was badly typed, so I've been failed.' He went slowly into his bedroom, closed the door and slumped onto his bed, trying not to think of a whole year's work wasted. 'Oh God, how could you let this happen?' he thought.

Gradually, time brought new perspective to this awful setback. Harry was even able to tell his mother, 'Don't worry. I'll do it all over again, and I shall be all the better for it. Besides, a year will soon pass.'

However much he tried to put a brave face on it, though, life at this point was *tough*. The thesis post-mortem was gruelling. Chapter by chapter, sentence by sentence, with his kind professor Harry T. Logan, formerly of Oxford. All through the summer of '28, week by week, he would walk over to his house in Point Grey, spend all evening and walk back in view of the ocean, sunset and forest-covered mountains.

Clumsy English? Bad typing? Little or nothing was added to that thesis, frustrating and vexatious as it was. But the whole exercise taught Harry to write books the hard way, with a discipline and technique of marshalling and presenting his material. In the end, it turned out to be a blessing in disguise, repaid a thousand-fold in years ahead. That study of Greek helped him to observe accurately, to develop reasoning powers, to remember attentively and to get to the heart of the original meaning of the Scriptures, something he loved to do.

When the time came for Harry to sit his exams once again he passed with 98%, but at the Convocation in the autumn, it was Gertie who went alone and picked up his M.A. Diploma and his hood. It seemed strange that this should have passed by so quietly and so unobserved. He had done so well, and the honour was really his. But God was with them both and prospered them.

They started giving the first of everything to Him. If Gertie had a new piano pupil, then the whole of the first lesson ($1.00) was His. New work was the same. They had always given a tenth, but soon 15 cents on the dollar was given, then 25 cents. Then it was 50/50 – half of their goods to the Lord. For Gertie and Harry, it became a thrill to be part of God's work like this, and the more they gave, the greater the joy and freedom.

At only twenty-two, Harry started teaching Greek at the newly-opened Vancouver Bible School before going on to Knox College, Toronto. As he taught, Harry's University lectures were still fresh in his mind and he loved the fine Principal, Rev. Walter Ellis, with his wonderful group of students, staff and council members. Not so long before, Isabel Kuhn had enrolled there as a night student, before going on to Moody Bible Institute and then to China.

Here, Harry, as a young teacher, learned valuable lessons and met outstanding men of God. Men like Gypsy Smith, and Rev. L. Legters, a tremendous character who later played a large part in the founding of the Wycliffe Bible Translators. All along the road, Harry would meet dynamic men and women like these. Kindred spirits, who taught him valuable lessons on life. These were his training years. He would need them more than he could ever have imagined.

A new venture

It was not easy to say goodbye. Knox College, Toronto, was a hundred times further away than the Japanese raspberry-picking ranch had been and this was not simply a summer job. A few days before Harry left, mother and son were both baptised by immersion in a tiny Free Methodist Chapel in Mount Pleasant. Gertie had been attending services conducted by Rev. W. Robertson in Vancouver, where the congregation used to meet in a theatre, so the facilities did *not* cater for such events! As Harry and Gertie sat in the barely-padded seats of the tiny Chapel, the peaceful atmosphere was suddenly ruptured by the sound of clunking, scraping and splashing.

'What's that?! I hope that's not going to be carrying on through the service,' whispered Harry to his mother.

'Surely they can't be doing repairs now,' she whispered back.

Rev. Robertson, sensing the concern on their faces, walked over to them with a sheepish grin on his face. 'Sorry about the noise. Just filling the tank, you know.' Thus, the clunking, scraping and splashing stopped in due time, Rev. Robertson conducted the baptism, and the whole occasion was a very meaningful step of dedication and obedience to God.

Shortly afterwards, Harry took a further great step – nearly three thousand miles eastwards. Leaving his mother in Vancouver, he boarded the Trans-Canada Express of the Canadian Pacific Railway – for Toronto. He was so close to his mother that leaving was a tremendous wrench, but it was the right thing to do. It would be many a long day before he saw her again and the golden sunshine of a Vancouver day.

As the steam train chugged out of the station, Gertie's lonely figure became smaller and smaller, finally disappearing from sight as the locomotive rounded a bend. Harry fell back into his seat, not sure whether to be excited or miserable, but it wasn't long before his thoughts were taken up with the magnificent scenery all around him.

Nothing could quite capture the thrill of the old Canadian railroads and those massive trans-continental locomotives. The train was almost a mile long! Night and day it never stopped for more than fifteen minutes every three or four hours, when the engineers checked all the wheels with a hammer and attached the new locomotive. Each window had three thicknesses of glass and the train stopped for 30 minutes for workers to clean them at Winnipeg. General Higgins, successor to General Bramwell Booth (founder of the Salvation Army) was travelling on board and jumped out at Winnipeg to address a huge crowd of some 300 Salvationists and passers-by. It was most impressive!

At midnight on the last night, the train screeched to a halt and divided; one half going to Toronto and the other to Montreal. Finally, at 8 am, three days and four nights after leaving Vancouver, the mighty Trans-Canadian Express rolled into Toronto station. The young Theolog had arrived!

9

INTER-VARSITY –
CHRISTIAN STUDENTS ON THE MOVE

'History is a continual dialogue between the past and the present about the future' (Bishop Leslie Newbiggin)

Harry was fascinated by the stories of university students who really meant business with God. To pass the time on that mammoth train journey to Toronto, he had started to read the latest news on the history of the Inter-Varsity Fellowship, and became increasingly inspired by the story of those who had gone before him.

In autumn 1884, seven outstanding and popular Cambridge students caused a national sensation, by offering their services to the China Inland Mission. Hudson Taylor was Founder and Director of C.I.M. and C. T. Studd (one of the seven) was probably the best all-round cricketer in Britain between 1881 and 1884. Later he founded the Worldwide Evangelisation Crusade (W.E.C).

Before sailing to China in 1885, Studd and his friend Smith (only twenty-three) made a dynamic tour of British universities ... with dramatic results. In fourteen years (1881-94) one hundred Cambridge graduates became missionaries! Victorian complacency was profoundly shattered.

By 1905, the Student Christian Movement (S.C.M.) was born from the other keen student movements in Britain. Their leaders were on fire for Christ and evangelism. But already the winds of European continental theology were blowing hard throughout Britain. Increasingly the liberal, rationalistic professors in the theological colleges were calling into question the deity of Christ, the virgin birth, the atoning death, the physical resurrection – and the reliability of the Scriptures. A split began to appear amongst the leaders and sadly, in 1910, C.I.C.C.U. (Cambridge Inter-Collegiate Christian Union) leaders decided to 'go it alone', leaving the 'doubters' with the S.C.M. (Student Christian Movement).

When World War I erupted, the colleges emptied, but by 1918 ex-servicemen began to stream back to the campuses once more.

By early 1919, Norman Grubb and Godfrey Buxton arrived at Cambridge, both with military decorations for bravery and recovering from war wounds. Buxton became President of C.I.C.C.U. and Grubb its Secretary. One Noel ('Tiny') Palmer, a freshman from Oxford and briefly Secretary of the Oxford S.C.M., was also recovering from war wounds in Cambridge. Norman Grubb invited him over to meet the C.I.C.C.U. men and he became a Christian.

Noel's life was revolutionized. Back at Oxford the rumour went around that Tiny had 'religious mania'. So he said goodbye to his secretaryship with speed! In Cambridge, Norman remembered:

'In my room in Trinity College, God gave me a clear vision of the I.V.F. that was to be. I saw that not only must there be this witness in every university, but that God *was* going to do it.'

December 1919
This was to be the year of the first 'Inter-Varsity Convention for all University Men' ('Inter-Varsity' being the title of the annual rugby match between Oxford and Cambridge), so Norman and Noel began by 'jellygraphing' scribbled notices to all students who believed that the gospel should be preached in their universities. That December Norman Grubb left Cambridge to join C. T. Studd in Africa.

1925

Just as the New Fundamentalist Society had emerged at Harry's university in Vancouver, Eric Liddell[1] (1924 Olympic Gold Medallist and hero of the film *Chariots of Fire*) had also launched a full-scale Mission at Edinburgh University in Scotland.

Later Norman Grubb married C. T. Studd's fourth daughter, Pauline, while his friend Noel Palmer married Josie (Josephine Booth-Clibborn, daughter of Katherine Booth, 'The Maréchal', and grand-daughter of General Booth) and ended up in Toronto! Hence ...

The Canadian connection

Early March 1928
Dr. Rowland Bingham, Canadian pioneer statesman, visits Cambridge C.I.C.C.U. in England. Rowland Bingham, at only twenty years of age, was

(1) founder of the Sudan Interior Mission (S.I.M. 1893),
(2) founder of the 'Evangelical Christian' magazine, and also
(3) founder and director of Canadian Keswick (a large Christian convention).

Bingham was keen. He saw how the modernistic Student Christian Movement in Britain was still trying to maintain its grip, in the face of the warmth of the Cambridge group, as their evangelical fervour permeated universities in other parts of Britain Bingham also saw 'the dead hand of modernism' at work amongst Canadian students and how the Canadian Christian Movement had fallen into the hands of a group who 'deliberately plotted the extermination of all that was evangelical....' There

---

1. Post-university, this same Eric Liddell would share a bachelor flat with David McGavin, father-in-law of the author, when both young men went out as Scottish missionaries to China.

were delegates from sixteen Christian Unions at High Leigh and the dynamic Dr. Bingham exclaimed to the C.I.C.C.U. leaders, 'You have something so wonderful here. Why shouldn't you share it with Canadian students?'

The same day in April 1928, an equally dynamic Norman Grubb arrived at the High Leigh Conference. Straight from Africa, and a winter mission deputation tour in Canada, Grubb was urgent. Graphically he described the needs on the Canadian university campuses, where there was *no* organised evangelical witness, apart from one exception – Harry's University of British Columbia! With passion and missionary fervour Grubb challenged these British undergrads.

'Send a deputation to Canada,' he urged.

Douglas Johnson was the first secretary of the committee, and has been described as 'the mastermind behind the British I.V.F. and unsung hero of post-war resurgence of Evangelicalism.' He wrote:

'At the end of Norman's tour de force, he more or less *ordered* the youthful committee to send out an apostle (like the elders at Antioch in Acts 13) to the Canadian campuses. There was a dead hush. Then somebody said, "I think we ought to do it in faith." But who?'

Howard Guinness, a medical student, was working for his October finals, when Douglas Johnson apparently deflected his mind from his textbooks and confronted him with the Canadian challenge! 'How about *you*?'

A cable to Canada followed: 'Response 100% positive!' Bingham's reply: 'If Guinness is missionary-minded, send him!'

Once the decision was taken, things moved fast. The IVF magazine read:

53

Delegate to the Canadian Universities
Dr. Howard Guinness, after qualifying at St. Bartholomew's Hospital, finds that 5 months are to elapse before he can hold a House Surgeon's appointment ... He has therefore offered to devote this period to visiting the Canadian universities on behalf of British Evangelical students.

Howard was fortunate to have special family links in Toronto, with his Aunt Geraldine and Uncle Howard Taylor (Hudson Taylor's son) ... and was treated like a missionary, sent out by a youthful committee of mostly 2nd or 3rd year students.

'Norman Grubb gave Guinness a heavy Canadian winter overcoat, suitable for the rigours of a Canadian winter. And, at the last minute, when the inexperienced students' committees realised their rookie missionary would need some funds ... some of them sold off tennis racquets, books, etc. which provided Howard with £14 pocket money for the trip.'

His passage to Canada was booked for October 27th, 1928. His aim:

> *'My first duty to the student in Canada is to lead him out into the fulness of the Holy Spirit's power.'*

Now that Harry was in Toronto, he eagerly looked forward to meeting Howard Guinness in person.

10

KNOX COLLEGE, TORONTO (1928-30)

Toronto was a *very* different world for Harry. As Canada's second city, it was a buzzing financial and industrial metropolis, boasting a wonderful setting; surrounded by the Don and Humber River valleys, and set on a series of ravines near to Lake Ontario, with a scattering of lush islands.

Knox College, at 75 George Street, was Harry's new home for the next two years. Built on the site of the campus of Toronto University, Knox was generally considered one of the most beautiful works of architecture in the whole of Canada. It was set in a lovely avenue of shady trees where branches met across the street to create a perfect overhead railway for numerous squirrels who would scamper backwards and forwards and distract the students.

Harry filed in with the rest of the new students for his opening class and drew back his chair, which scraped noisily on the floor. He quickly sat down and prepared himself to take notes.

The professor greeted the class and began his lecture, but at such a whirlwind speed that many, including Harry, struggled to keep up. He scribbled away in a desperate attempt not to get behind as frantic glances were exchanged between the harrassed students. By the end of the hour, Harry's hand was aching badly and the relief in the room was palpable when the professor finally dismissed the class. Something had to be done!

That night, Harry worked out his very own system of abbreviation, such as VB for Virgin Birth, or Dam for Damascus. From that time on, he wrote out a new card of abbreviations each day, and in this way Harry mastered forty new terms a week and five hundred by the end of the first term. A master stroke for quick note-taking, and a personal shorthand repertoire for the future!

Harry the preacher

Life was enjoyable at Knox, but sermon classes were a truly frightening experience. Before a private congregation of one, each student would deliver his or her effort on a spiritual theme. This would not have been a problem except that his congregation consisted of none other than Principal Thomas Eakin, who had his own particular technique of torture ....

When Harry's turn arrived, he entered the wonderful chapel, with its rows of empty pews, to see the Principal enthroned in the furthermost corner seat of the building.

'Good morning, Bonsall. Are you going to edify us this morning? I do hope so.'

'So do I, sir.'

Harry walked over purposefully to the pulpit steps, then ascended, in what he hoped was a confident manner, just in case his 'ascension' would be assessed. Once he reached the top, he looked out over the huge hall and began, preaching his heart out to the empty pews. Dr. Eakin, with his head mantled by one corner of his gown, sat impassively, as a nervous Harry gave it all he had. He continued preaching to this statuesque figure until he was finished and, after a suitably dignified pause, descended the steps, as the Principal walked down the aisle towards him to pass judgement. Without delay, Dr. Eakin launched into a dispassionate enumeration of all the good points in the sermon. Then he halted and cleared his throat.

Harry knew the turning point had come. By the time ten minutes of 'constructive criticism' had passed, Harry almost wished he had never begun.

However, all this practice was very useful at the weekends when the students were sent out to preach in country areas within a 150-mile radius. Students got half-price reductions on the railroad, so this was the logical mode of transport. On winter weekends, Harry would be met at the railway station by a man with a horse-drawn sleigh. Once he was seated beside him the man would fling a buffalo robe over Harry's knees, and off they would go like the wind. A horse that has waited in sub-zero temperatures for ten minutes is ready to race! At the rear of each church would be a shelter for the horses, with a back and a roof, but no sides or front. Directly the service was over and the sleigh was hitched up, they would all sail off again at tremendous speed, sleigh-bells ringing merrily. It was a thrilling experience!

Harry had only been at Knox for a few weeks, when a fine group of keen Christians, many of them in the Arts Faculty, got together to pray and study each week. News had already reached them that a 'rep' from the University Christian Fellowship in England had been sent out to help Canadian university students come out into the open, stand up for what they believed and form a Christian Union.

In fact, Harry and friends knew exactly what this meant, having done the same thing in the University of British Columbia only three years before – and the new 'rep', Dr. Howard Guinness, wanted to meet them. Harry very quickly recognised him as a man of tremendous faith and courage, who was full of fun but not afraid to come straight to the point.

'Victoria, Wycliffe, Trinity and other Colleges all have their own private groups. Why don't we take a united stand?' he challenged.

So they did! One Thursday evening soon after, about thirty of them met in a classroom at Wycliffe College to pray about their future – and from this meeting the Toronto Inter-Collegiate Christian Union, or the T.I.C.C.U. was formed. Harry's friend, Jim Duncan, who had led the first Fundamentalist Society in the University of British Columbia in 1925, was its first President and Harry its Treasurer. The Declaration of Membership stated simply: '*In joining this Union I wish to declare my faith in the Lord Jesus Christ as my Saviour and my God*', and the front page of 'Varsity' January 17th 1929, read:

> *New Christian Union formed at Varsity*
> President: James D. Duncan, B.A., McMaster
> Vice President: Miss Muriel David, Victoria
> Secretary: A. Hart-Davies, Wycliffe
> Treasurer: H. Bonsall, M.A., Knox

The next year it was Harry's turn to be President – and again the 'Varsity' '29 newspaper reported:

> *Christian Union Elects President*
> *New Union Rapidly Gaining Followers ...*
> Mr. Harry Bonsall of III Knox was unanimously elected President and Mr. Arnold Hart-Davies, III Wycliffe, secretary for the Inter-Varsity Fellowship of the Unions of Canada. First reception to be held at Wymilwood next Tuesday night when Mr. Noel Palmer and Mrs. Noel Palmer, grand-daughter of General Booth, are to be the chief guests. All new students are heartily invited.

From this time on, Wymilwood, the fine girl's hostel, became the centre of student outreach each Sunday afternoon. Refreshments were excellent, easy chairs luxurious and company entertaining. The enthusiastic students would invite a friend to hear some celebrity speaker like Christabel Pankhurst (daughter of the famous suffragette leader, Emmeline). Then, as the guests had begun to relax, the speaker would stand up with a short, inspiring message. Later, these keen Christian students would take their friends along to the local church and on to someone's home afterwards for refreshments and a 'sing-song' round the piano. Often students were lonely and very happy for the friendship. Many a discussion began and many a decision for Christ was made on the way home.

The Knox students really meant business where faith was concerned – and Harry thrived in that atmosphere. Every week he and a handful of others would faithfully meet up at the home of his friend Dr. Rowland Bingham (youthful founder of the Sudan Interior Mission), to pray for the new Christian union and beyond. Then every Tuesday morning he would join his friends Judson Merritt (University of Toronto) and Russell Gordon (Knox), just up the road at the headquarters of the China Inland Mission, to pray for China. On one of these occasions, Geraldine Taylor, Hudson Taylor's daughter-in-law and prolific authoress for the CIM, autographed one of her books and gave it to Harry, much to his delight.

Meanwhile, Harry was enjoying his studies, although still trying to come to grips with the theological and doctrinal positions of the College, particularly regarding the verbal inspiration of Scripture. He would discuss and debate vigorously with other students, both Christians and non-Christians, over points such as these. Even up to the time when he had finished his course at Knox, he was hearing so many different viewpoints from so many different people that it wasn't hard to become somewhat confused. However, he kept on seeking God and praying that the Lord would guide him as he tried to put his faith into practice. Harry was well aware that while doctrinal issues were important, above all he *had* to keep his eyes on Jesus.

Howard Guinness continued to move from university to university. In the thirteen months of his extended Canadian tour, he travelled from the Atlantic to the Pacific twice, like a flame of fire: wherever he touched down, there came life. By the end of his year, Manitoba, Western, McGill and the University of British Columbia all had their own Christian Unions in operation. It was an exciting time for the young students, now brimming with enthusiasm. In 1929, Kenneth Hooker took over from Howard Guinness as second delegate to Canada from Britain's Inter-Varsity (1929-30), closely followed one year later by a third delegate, Noel 'Tiny' Palmer. Noel rapidly became known on the campus as a fascinating and dynamic speaker: *'a giant of a man, with a giant vision'*. His view on life was simple: '95% for Christ is a dog's life, but 100% is heaven on earth!' It was a generation of great stature – literally. Howard Guinness 6'2', Harry Bonsall of similar build, followed by Kenneth Hooker 6'5' and Tiny Palmer, a mere 6'8'!

11

SUMMER ON THE PRAIRIES (1929)

Summer had arrived and Harry was to be posted for four months to the wide-open spaces of the Prairies. His day of departure came. Little did he realise how much he would miss those friends he had taken for granted. The train journey north through 'The Sticks' (backwoods of northern Ontario) was no mountain-top experience, but 1,000 miles of impenetrable forest and endless trees; with people on the platforms as the carriages passed by, looking grim and hopeless. Harry's mission station was Dewar Lake, 2,000 miles up the line and he had to change trains twice. There were three trains up the line (Mondays, Wednesdays and Fridays) and three coming back (Tuesdays, Thursdays and Saturdays), so if a train was missed by only five minutes, it was at least two days wait for the next one! After the forest came hundreds and hundreds of miles of flat grassland that stretched out as far as the eye could see. Harry couldn't help feeling it was one of the most dreary and monotonous places he had ever seen.

At last the locomotive drew to a halt at Dewar Lake station. Harry pressed his nose up against the window, searching expectantly for the welcoming party, but not a soul was to be seen. He gathered his suitcases and struggled out of the train onto the platform, puffing as he did so. At which point it became clear that the platform *was* the station. No building of any kind. No porter. No station master. No welcoming party. In fact, no sign of life whatsoever. Harry turned on the solitary planks of wood that were the station, in time to see the train chugging away, soon to disappear into the western horizon. He had a tremendous urge to

61

run after the train, screaming that there had been a horrible mistake, but instead he sat down on an item of luggage and waited, his chin cupped in his hands.

About ten minutes later, a slight movement caught his eye. There was definitely a small, black dot on the horizon, growing larger every moment. Within seconds the sound of a car engine reached him, and soon a grizzled farmer in an old Pontiac ground to a halt in front of him.

'You the preacher?'

'I am.'

'Well,' he said gruffly, 'I'm Andy Arthur. Come and help me sweep out the church while the others sort out the mail.'

Thirteen people lived in Andy's little shack – he and his fine German wife, his old mother, their three children and some farm labourers. Harry occupied a double bed with a farmer! Only a gauze curtain separated him from the kitchen – the one meeting place for all. As the cream separator started whirring early in the morning, and heavy feet were tramping even earlier, there was certainly *not* much quiet! And, unlike the company, the food never changed. Day after day, the inevitable mashed potatoes and bacon....

Luxury, however, soon came to Harry in the shape of a new granary. A building made of 10' by 12' shiplap, with double doors at one end, two windows (one glazed) with a two-pitched roof and gable. Furniture – one bed, a chair, a table and a chest of drawers. Cows would rub themselves against the corners. Then a strong wind, lasting a week or two, would blow the whole building about a foot out of kelter. Then *another* strong wind from the opposite direction would blow it back into place again! If ever it rained, which was rare, rainwater would creep about 1.5 feet up through the shiplap joints, at which point Harry would pile his furniture into the middle of the room!

Another aspect of life at Dewar Lake that intrigued Harry was the party-line telephone system. At least thirteen farmers shared the 'supposedly confidential' line. Each farmer had his own code call, and he alone was supposed to take down the receiver when it rang, but sure enough, as each conversation ended, one could frequently hear a further dozen receivers going down simultaneously! Then, when emergency called, a general summons would rouse all farmers at their homes with the message, 'Farmer John Doe's hayrick is on fire and his house is threatened!' Immediately all the farmers would rush to the rescue. In wilder areas there was a 'country telephone' via a strand of barbed wire that carried a mild electric current from pole to pole. In such a lonely area, it was good to talk!

Before too long, Harry took courage in both hands and asked Andy Arthur for the loan of his horse and rickety buggy to go visiting. The farmer generously agreed, but one problem still remained: he hadn't a clue about horse-riding! It was clear that riding lessons were essential. However, Harry found that Canadians were all for letting you learn the hard way. They were never too explicit in their instructions, but tended to leave you to find out for yourself, one way or another – mistakes and all.

'Oh it's quite simple,' Andy said. 'Just pull the right rein to turn right, the left rein to turn left – and remember to watch the buggy when you go through a gate. The horse doesn't realise it's there, and if you don't watch out he'll catch the axle on the gate-post and carry it away with him!'

And that was all the training Harry got. So after a little preliminary circus around the yard, in which he had a vision out of the corner of his eye of various boxes of hens flying in all directions, he sallied forth into the great unknown – or at least out of the yard. Having more or less mastered the buggy, Harry would leave every morning on visiting rounds at 8 am, driving the children four miles to school as he went. But before long the rickety buggy lost its wobbly wheel, so Harry simply had to ride the horse, Beauty. Finding it difficult at first, he bumped convincingly every time Beauty put her foot to the ground. Then, some time later, after nearly getting bumped to bits, Harry learned the secret of rising in the saddle ... at which point a kindly Irish farmer friend took him in hand and gave him a lesson on safe survival.

Amazingly, Harry survived, without being thrown once, but one of Harry's predecessors was not so blessed. He thought he'd try the farmer's bronco one day, when suddenly it bolted off like an arrow with the preacher on its back, clinging on for dear life. All that could be seen was his retreating figure with full, white shirt-sleeves billowing up and down, like a bird in flight. It was three days before he came back! Needless to say, after hearing this story Harry was very happy on poor, broken-winded old Beauty, who could never do more than three miles an hour without breaking into a lather. Except once ... once, when Harry and his horse spied a lone prairie wolf silhouetted against the setting sun. Beauty did not wait for a second look, and fortunately, neither did the wolf, who sat motionless at the roadside as the two sped by!

Harry's new-found horse-power made greater distances accessible, and he soon discovered that visiting in the Prairies was a moving experience. Farms were a mile or more apart and Harry would regularly ride for miles without passing a house, or meeting a soul. Often, the farmers' families had no-one to call and were desperately lonely. So his first job on arrival was to greet the young wife, whose husband would be reaping a mile away; chat for a few minutes; then ask for the woodpile, take an axe, and do a good two or three hours of wood-splitting. When the farmer eventually returned, caked in dust and having watered the horses, they would sit down with the family and talk about old times ... his country perhaps, maybe Poland, maybe Ireland. Then they would read the Scriptures and pray together and move on. There was never time to attempt more than two or three visits like this in one day, as it wasn't a 'visit' in the Prairies unless one had stayed for a meal, but God blessed Harry as he rode on his old horse from ranch to ranch across his vast, windswept parish! Despite being there for such a short time, the church at Dewar Lake flourished, while two other churches started up in school houses. It was wonderful to see those big farmers crowding into the tiny school-desks!

The bird and the little mouse on the prairie

Days were long, and Harry often got tired – up at the crack of dawn. Having no alarm clock, he asked God one night to wake him up, so that he could keep his 'morning watch' at 5 am. The next morning, he was sleeping soundly when he heard three loud, sharp raps, and woke with a start to find that it was exactly 5 am! But what had caused the knocks? He lifted his head just in time to see a bird hurling itself once more against the glass at the opposite side, before it flew back through the unglazed window, the way it came in!

Harry was thrilled and amazed at the way God had answered his prayer. He stepped out of bed, praising God all the more as he saw the beautiful, intense green virgin grass of the Prairie peeking through the covering of dazzling white snow which had fallen unexpectedly the previous day.

Andy's farm was at least 1,000 acres of wheatland, with great grain elevators that dominated the skyline. Every day throughout that summer, Harry climbed up to the top of a nearby straw pile where he had hollowed a sort of nest for himself, at a height of around fifteen feet. There he prepared his sermons, and every day a little mouse came to keep him company.

Harry often felt quite homesick and took daily comfort from his little friend, feeding it with sandwiches. Then tragedy struck. On a given day at the end of the summer, when all the new season's wheat was harvested and next year's straw assured, the farmers all over the region applied a match to each straw pile in the windward direction. Harry watched helplessly, as in a matter of seconds his own special straw pile and furry friend were sheathed in flames. He could do nothing to save him. Good friends were few and far between in Dewar Lake and Harry never saw his small companion again.

Finally, after four months of visiting and preaching in this unique parish, the time came for Harry to leave. On his last night in Dewar Lake, he lay in bed and reflected on the previous months. It had been an incredible summer, but a very lonely one at times. Having been so far from his college friends and his mother, he knew he would always be grateful for the way Doug Wilkie, an old friend from Knox, had offered to stand in for a week so that he could visit Vancouver. Life was tough, but friends were good, and Harry was amazed at how much he had learned in that short period. In the stillness of the prairie evening, he turned over and fell fast asleep, tired but content.

12

NEXT STOP – LLOYDMINSTER

That summer at Dewar Lake was an invaluable preparation for Harry's next stop on the prairies – Lloydminster, a town which straddled the Alberta and Saskatchewan boundaries. First, however, he was to be ordained in the First Presbyterian Church at Edmonton. He was just twenty-five years old. It was an auspicious occasion, with a proud mother watching from the pews. It seemed as if at least fifty ministers laid their hands on Harry's head as he knelt for the ordination prayer, at which point the Moderator said, 'Be strong, for you will have to bear the combined weight of the Presbytery.'

The difference about Harry's Lloydminster posting was that on this occasion Gertie would come too. Together they set off, after much arduous packing, once again taking the railroad. It was an incredible journey. Through the Rockies and a violent thunderstorm, where the lightning flashed from one snowy peak to another and the thunder echoed from mountain to mountain. First to Calgary, then on to Edmonton. Finally by Canadian National Railway to Lloydminster and a wonderful welcome.

The manse was full of women from the Church, busy putting last-minute touches to a house already made quite beautiful for them. Unfortunately, the plumbing left much to be desired as there was only one foot of it connecting the kitchen sink to a pail below, just like every other house in town. They soon got used to the daily sponge-down with only a pint of water and the water pump over the road to be cranked by hand. Their luxury was to pay 10¢ three times a week for three buckets of fresh, soft, drinking water, delivered by horse-drawn cart.

Summer days were hot and cloudless in Lloydminster; night skies frequently lit up by thunderstorms or magnificent 'aurora borealis'! Then summer changed to autumn, and with it the ceremony of fixing the storm windows ready for the winter and sub-zero temperatures. Like the early settlers, Harry and Gertie had no idea just how long and severe a prairie winter could be.

There were only two snowfalls that winter, both in October, but the snow never left the ground until the end of the following March. Every winter day was freezing, yet skies were brilliant blue and the sun shone brightly on thousands of shallow lakes. People would fish through holes in the ice and stack the frozen fish on shelves in an out-house, like so much firewood.

Between 1902 and 1905, hundreds of colonists from the British Isles – mainly Lancashire – had come to settle, but were unprepared for the difficulties of carving a homestead out of unbroken Prairie. Generally speaking, they knew nothing about farming, building, or anything vital to survive on the Prairies. It was only through the intervention of another man, later to become Bishop Exton Lloyd, that they survived at all. He came to their rescue, stuck by them and saved them; and in grateful memory to him, they called the town now straddling the Alberta and Saskatchewan boundaries, Lloydminster.

Quite apart from the challenges of winter, the job of a prairie pastor was demanding, as life in general was harsh. At the end of a particularly difficult day, Harry wrote soberly in his journal:

Today I had to bury a baby in an unspeakably lonely cemetery at a bend of the Saskatchewan River, about 30 or 40 miles north of Lloydminster. The tiny coffin lay on the rear seat of the undertaker's car and as we passed, many prairie lakes were frozen over, with the cattle standing stock-still in the middle. The grave-diggers had to keep a fire burning for four days before they could dig the grave.

On another occasion, shortly afterwards, Harry and a fellow minister sat cosily by the fire swapping 'wedding stories', as Gertie listened from a nearby armchair.

'Well, my first wedding took place at midnight, with no warning,' began Harry. 'The couple had to be married on the spot to catch the 1 am train. I had never "married" anyone before, so I had to get out of bed, look up all Dr. Eakins' lecture notes on Pastoral Theology and printed marriage forms, to see how you set about it. Anyway, they were married all right and caught that train.'

The other minister chuckled and then said, 'You won't believe what happened to me last year. I'm a minister on the Saskatchewan side, and I was asked to marry a couple around sundown, only to discover that they had an Albertan licence, so couldn't take their vows. You know how Lloydminster is divided into two halves, with the main street running north to south of the town. All to the east is Saskatchewan and all to the west Alberta. As the Registry Office was closed, they had to wait until the following day before getting one from Saskatchewan. The next day they appeared again and my wife was the witness. After a long, hard look at the bride, my wife said to the groom, "Excuse me. This isn't the lady you brought in yesterday, is it?" "No, ma'am," he replied. "I think *this* one will suit me better!"'

'You're joking!' cried Harry.

'No, it really happened!' laughed the minister.

Apart from weddings and funerals, hospital visits were high on the agenda and one tough old man, T. J. Rooks, was dying of cancer. Harry was a bit of a novice with dying patients, but quietly touched the arm resting on the sheet. 'There's a Heaven and you want to go there, don't you?'

'There's no Hell!' grunted the old man.

'Never mind about Hell,' he answered. 'There *is* a Heaven.'

Then Harry thought about all the great theories he had learned at Knox, but just decided to give old T. J. Rooks Isaiah chapter 53 instead ... and he listened. How we have all gone astray; and how the Lord has taken our sin so that we can receive peace and healing. He continued to listen and Harry prayed for him.

Next morning a young woman called at the manse. 'Are you the young minister who saw my father yesterday?' she asked. 'I don't know what you said, but you certainly did him good and I want you to call again.' So he did and T. J. Rooks clearly found Christ that day. At his funeral the church was packed with burly, tough working men and Harry was able to tell them all how their old friend had found his peace with God.

Knox Presbyterian Church, Lloydminster

Harry threw himself into the life at Knox Presbyterian Church so vigorously that it wasn't long before the church had a boys' gymnasium and club; a young woman's Bible class in the afternoons; a Christian Endeavour meeting; a 30-strong junior choir in the morning and an adult choir for the evening service. But Harry's work was too much for him. Visiting the hospital every other day, as well as all his other duties, caused him to grow thinner and thinner. The altitude (nearly 3,000 feet up) was telling on both Harry and Gertie. Neuritis started in his legs and as the weeks passed, Harry could hardly stand for the services.

The Presbytery in Edmonton ordered them both back to the coast, but the faithful members of Knox were very grieved and disappointed, saying they would close the church altogether just as soon as Harry had gone. It seemed too sad for all this nine months of work to be lost – and yet the Assembly had no replacement, not even a student to send in Harry's place, while Harry himself seemed to be dying on his feet. He couldn't walk, and Gertie had to drape an orange box for him to sit on in the pulpit, which made him appear to be standing. They both prayed and prayed for someone else to fill the gap ... but no-one appeared. Eventually, Harry was confined to his bed. Then, one morning, a wire arrived from a Rev. Andrew Walker of Tisdale, Saskatchewan. Once an Irish evangelist, he was now a Presbyterian minister earning $200 more in his own church, but had been so concerned about Harry's situation that he came at the first opportunity to offer his services. Arriving on the evening of Good Friday he said, 'Isn't it strange to be here, with such a different set of circumstances!'

'Yes,' Harry said, 'It is strange. What made you come?'

'God told me to come,' he replied, 'and my wife told me not to disobey!'

Meanwhile, Harry had been visiting four people who wanted to know more about Christianity ... and Gertie was at home praying. Many prayers had gone up for them already and it was Harry's last evening. All four gave their hearts to Christ.

God *also* answered prayer for twelve junior choir girls. Mother and son had been praying for them for weeks, when they were all invited after school for tea and cakes, with a little service afterwards. Every single girl gave her heart to the Lord that evening.

It was June 1931 and, barring illness, the end of a very happy and fulfilling year for Harry as a prairie minister. He loved the people and the work, making many friends – and although the altitude and climate had affected Gertie's health too, she had brought a large and happy Bible class of women and girls together that continued to grow when they left. Everyone was sad to say goodbye and loving messages of appreciation flooded in from different directions, including a special letter from one of the elders at the church:

Lloydminster, Saskatchewan

Dear Mr. Bonsall,

On behalf of the Session, Board of Managers and the congregation of Knox Church, we desire to say to you that we deeply regret your leaving. You have been a very faithful

71

steward in all branches in the work of the Church since coming amongst us. You have faithfully visited the sick and given cheer to the faint; and your untiring efforts on behalf of the young people of our church, have surely borne fruit, as evidenced by the beautiful Communion Services of this Easter morning. The prayer meetings which you so staunchly upheld will not cease to remember you in your new field of labor.

We believe that God's hand is on our Church in answer to your prayers and efforts. We sincerely give you into God's keeping, praying and trusting that you may be speedily restored to full health and strength, in order to continue in the Master's service.

In saying farewell, we would ask you to accept this small token of our deep affection and love for you.

God bless you, and keep you and cause His face to shine upon you, and give you peace.

T. H. Halliwell, Elder
Knox Presbyterian Church, Lloydminster, Alberta.

13

FINAL PREPARATION FOR
LAUNCH OFF!

'The steps and stops of a good man are ordered by the Lord.'

The hidden years

It took Harry and Gertie ten days to reach Vancouver, but they had a great welcome and eventually found a beautiful furnished flat with a glorious view of sea and mountains. Back to sea-level and a moderate climate, Gertie's health improved and Harry grew better by the day. So much so, that he was able to take up a post as Missioner to two small churches in Kitsilano and Dunbar Heights. In this time of recovery, little did Harry realise that he was about to embark on a series of battles that would influence his entire life.

Questions and answers

Firstly, something had to be done about all those question marks scribbled down the margins of his Bible – the issues raised at Knox had not gone away. Modernism still held an intoxicating power over the minds of thinking men in those days. It threatened the verbal inspiration of the Scriptures and, as a result, the very basis of faith. For a man who would be dedicating his life to the training of others in the love and study of God's Word, this had to be of *vital* significance.

Just at that time, a veteran English missionary to Japan, Alpheus Paget Wilkes, was passing through on his way back home. In 1902, he had been co-founder of the Japan Evangelistic Band. After a brief chat with Harry, he said, 'Why don't you come over for a couple of hours. I'd be glad to take the time to talk about any difficulties you're having.'

As Harry walked over to meet Mr. Wilkes, he was struck once again by the beauty of a Vancouver summer. The smell of roses and petunias from neighbouring gardens seemed to fill the air. However, even as he walked, Harry was compiling a list of questions he needed to ask the missionary. Doubts about the accuracy of the Bible which had plagued him since his time at Knox College buzzed around his head. At last, the house came into view.

'Come in, come in. Do sit down. Would you like a cup of tea?'

Mrs. Wilkes duly made them both a cup of tea and the grilling began. The discussion deepened, Harry's brows furrowing as another problem would emerge. His tea lay untouched and cold, long forgotten. As each issue surfaced, Paget Wilkes batted them away as an expert would bat away cricket balls one after another. He didn't seem remotely worried about them.

'You know, Harry, we've been discussing these points for two hours now, and it's good that you've raised them. But I believe your problem lies somewhere else.'

'What do you mean?'

'I think this is an issue of your will. Faith is an activity of the will, not of the feelings. Your feelings aren't a true reflection of reality. I've answered your individual questions satisfactorily all afternoon, but unless you submit your will to God, they'll just crop up again sooner or later and nag at you. You simply need to *decide* to submit your will to God, even if you feel you don't know all the answers. *God* will take care of your mind.'

Harry paused for a second, then asked, 'Will you please pray for me?'

'Of course.'

The two of them knelt down together. Paget Wilkes laid his hands on Harry's head and blessed him in the name of the

Trinity, then prayed through the issue. The next morning when Harry awoke, all his difficulties with the Bible had disappeared, never to return. The issue was settled and he never looked back.

A second major battle was now to begin. They had never taken physical health for granted, but it was still a major blow when first Gertie and then Harry were laid low by injury.

Shortly after Harry's visit with Paget Wilkes, Gertie slipped and fell on the waxed hall floor, hurting her knee. Not realising that the condition erysipelas had set in, she thought nothing of it, but carried on as usual – with dire results. For nine months, she couldn't walk. It got worse and worse. They prayed and prayed for God to make her better, but nothing happened. Very late one night, Gertie was crying in her bed, unable to go to sleep, when God spoke to her about 'quietness and confidence'. She realised she had been neither quiet nor confident. She went to sleep again but was awakened by a twinge so sharp, it jerked her knee like elastic at full stretch and then let go. Was that the cartilage springing back? Sure enough, when the doctor came the next morning, God had healed it. 'Wonderful what rest will do!' he said.

Despite this miracle, further trouble was just around the corner. The blow fell on a day just like any other. Harry had been visiting a lovely family in his parish. They had enjoyed a wonderful meal together and talked happily for some time in the living room. Noticing that dusk was falling and that rain had started pouring down, Harry decided it was time to take his leave.

'Thank you so much for having me. It was a lovely meal and I really enjoyed meeting your children.'

'It was a pleasure, Rev. Bonsall. We must arrange another time.'

With smiles all round, Harry put up his umbrella and turned to open the door. He walked out on to the verandah but suddenly missed his footing and fell headlong down the verandah steps, landing heavily on both knees. The pain shot up his legs as the family rushed out to help him.

Arthritis set in, not just in one but both legs. And of course, instead of totally resting, Harry carried on as usual. After a few days his right knee began to swell. For six weeks he carried on with school and church, until he could go no further. Only then was the doctor called in. It was at this point of crisis that help came – from the best bone surgeon on the Pacific Coast, who arranged for him to be an in-patient at Ward E of the Vancouver General Hospital, on potassium iodine, Crowe serum and hot foments every two hours. The care of the nurses and staff was wonderful and the doctor didn't charge a cent! In fact, Harry owed it to this man that he could ever walk again.

Spiritual warfare
Ahead of Harry lay one of the most difficult periods of his life. Seven and a half months in hospital, and three years on his back in bed. What was God doing? How could He let Harry suffer like this? Could there possibly be a larger purpose behind it all?

Harry lay in his bed, immobilised and confused. Wasn't this simply an enormous waste of time? He had already gone halfway through his B.D. studies. At least he should be able to finish those. What else was there to do? But somehow Harry felt sure that God was telling him *not* to do this. Instead, Harry only had freedom to do two things. One was to pray ... burden of soul, day after day ... the other to explore his Bible from cover to cover. This burden, or travail, came quite regularly, and it wasn't easy to carry. It was like the travail that comes before a birth. It would get worse and worse until a crisis came, and only go away when he couldn't pray any more. At this point he had to start praising!

One particular Sunday at about 2 pm, this burden fell upon him once again. He knew it was for the Japanese and started to pray for the 94,000,000 in Japan, but he got no rest. Then he shifted to pray for the 94,000 in California, but still no relief. Then it was for 5,000 in Oregon and the 20,000 in the State of Washington, but *still* he couldn't settle. Then Harry prayed for

76

the 22,000 in British Columbia ... and at last began to get liberty, but *still* could not settle. Finally, his prayer began to focus on one particular Sunday School held by the Japanese Evangelistic Band (Western Branch, of which he was secretary), in the Celtic Cannery over twelve miles away on the banks of the Fraser River. He *had* to keep on praying until his prayers turned into praise. Then the burden lifted and Harry knew the answer was on the way. The next day, Mr. Lawrence Harry, one of the City Clerks in Vancouver who worked with Canadian-Japanese families, entered the hospital ward and came up to his bed, very excited.

'What do you think?' he blurted out. 'We were having quite an ordinary Sunday School lesson. Everything was going normally. Then, unexpectedly, I felt strongly led to ask for decisions ... and fourteen wanted to become Christians.'

'That's terrific!' said Harry. His legs may have been immobilised, but his grin certainly wasn't, as he explained to his friend what had happened the day before.

Over the next three months, sixty more followed ... and the North American Branch of the Japan Evangelistic Band was formed in his ward in the Vancouver General Hospital. Harry became Honorary Secretary.

As Harry was reaching new depths in prayer, he was eager to do the same with his Bible. Every Tuesday evening a godly young man called Bill Philip would come to the hospital ward and together they would diligently study and explore the depths of each Bible doctrine. They would continue until they truly felt they had gained a balanced biblical view on each issue. These painful months and years had not been wasted, but would be the crucial stepping stone to launch Harry out into the future.

As his mother prayed constantly at home, others would come and pray with Harry. In fact, it was said that 'No-one in all Vancouver has been more prayed for than Harry Bonsall!' Inspirational visits from the great veteran missionaries,

Jonathan Goforth and Charles H. Judd of the China Inland Mission, were tremendously encouraging for Harry. He had prayed so much for them in Toronto. So to meet and worship with men of such outstanding stature, who survived the terrible Boxer Rebellion in China, was something very special. Their lives had a quality and depth to them that was quite unique.

By October 1934, Harry was getting much better, although still convalescing – and alongside the healing process, God was providing for all their practical needs. Whenever they fell short of money, an anonymous gift would arrive through the post, and Harry and Gertie were never in doubt that God was with them. However, one more important battle had to be fought. One Thursday afternoon that month, Harry was sitting on his bed when he suddenly felt as if he were being smothered! It was a most strange, heavy sensation, and although he did not particularly understand why, he felt immediately that what he called an '*Egyptian darkness*' had settled upon him. The atmosphere was *so* thick and oppressive one could almost cut it with a knife! Harry wasn't afraid to die, but suddenly, he became afraid of living. He could almost physically feel the power of Satan confronting him and challenging him as he prayed ... and his prayers just seemed like so much chaff in the wind.

Keenly aware of sinister forces at work, intent on bringing him down, Harry remembered so vividly a lesson learnt in 1926, as he and Gertie had followed the trail of the '98 Gold Rush. Their ship had plied an amazing and dangerous journey through narrow straights, between a sunken mountain range and the Coast Range Mountains. It was a treacherous course, with twists and turns, hidden reefs and whirlpools. Dense fog could descend at a moment's notice, but in the 1920s captains hardly *ever* had an accident, although they had no radar or sonar instruments.

Harry, then twenty-one, had been fascinated as he watched Captain Donald navigate his ship. When Harry told the Captain how he admired his ability to handle his ship in the fog, he replied, 'Yes, but the *real* secret is what I do during sunny weather. When the sun shines, I blast away every few seconds, hour after hour, noting down in my log book the time it takes for the echoes to return. Those inlets are so narrow and dangerous that it is vital to practise and train while the sky is clear to prepare for the bad days, when the fog descends like a blanket without any warning.'

As the 'fog' descended around him, Harry now saw the significance of the great leason – to *train while the sky is clear*.

Suddenly, he heard a voice, 'You have not called upon Me.'

'That's strange,' Harry thought. 'Whose voice is this? It *must* be Christ.'

So he called out that name with all his strength, three times. '*Jesus! Jesus! Jesus!*' and as he called he saw Jesus in Heaven, like a priest handing his prayers to God. Immediately the darkness lifted. Harry let go of the burden and felt a great joy and relief flooding over him. From that point he realised how important it is to have faith in a Christ who is *ascended*, and not just dead, buried and risen. At His ascension, Christ was placed infinitely above Satan – and if revival was to come, it was this authority that would be so crucial. From that hour on, Harry knew that Christ had given him His authority. Satan and the darkness gave way. He was able to pray and praise God quite freely, because Christ had already prayed him through. It was a tremendously powerful experience! *It marked a turning point for Harry*, as he knew Satan had no more power over him. From this point on, he had no more relapses with his knee. He was ready for the next step!

14

THE VISION

It was January 1935 and there had just been a terrific snowfall. In Vancouver, thirty-five inches fell in a single night. Drifts were up to fifty feet, so that an entire Canadian Pacific Railway train went missing without trace for ten days!

With the snow falling outside once more, Harry lay on his back in his room, praying. 'Lord, what is your direction for me? I'm so grateful that I'm getting physically better but I need a goal to work towards. Sometimes I feel a bit like that train that got lost in the snow, all hidden away and useless.' Harry put his hands to his face and sighed. He had seen many answers to specific prayers during the previous years, but he felt strongly that he needed directional guidance at this point in his life.

Suddenly, seemingly from nowhere, words and sentences came flooding into his head. As he heard the words, pictures formed to accompany them – vivid, stark pictures that almost seemed more real than the bedroom which surrounded him. It was a vision – and a vision such as Harry had never experienced before. As it unfolded before him, the message came alive.

A most powerful revival was going to come to Great Britain – the 'Old Country'. Not a wonderful evangelistic campaign, but a personal visitation from God to the whole nation, just as it was – sinners and all. It wouldn't be just church-going people who would respond, but hardened folk who had never darkened a church door. Confronted by God, hundreds of thousands of them would be instantly converted, and scores would follow His call to go abroad to serve Him. They would come, crying out for immediate Bible College training, and Harry was to be there and ready to meet their need.

Amazed, he could only watch and listen in wonder as God continued to reveal different aspects of His plan.

To prepare Bible Colleges for this moment would take time, like the growing of an oak tree. Once God's hour had struck, the need would be immediate. Harry's call was to return to England and get ready for this moment. He was to start in 1936 and wait expectantly for the vision to be fulfilled. It would not happen for at least fifty years!

As the words and pictures faded, Harry sat up on his bed, breathless. It was still snowing. He put his head in his hands again and rubbed his eyes. He certainly hadn't expected his prayer to be answered in quite that fashion! Going as fast as his recovering legs could carry him, Harry swung himself off the bed and limped through to the living room, where he told Gertie everything that had taken place. She was just as amazed but took it in her inimitable stride.

'Well, we'd better start preparing then, hadn't we?'

The long road home

Mother and son, fairly crippled and in a sorry state, began to take steps for the big move – back to Britain and their waiting family, not seen for many a long year – weak in body, strong in faith! Tearful farewells to precious friends were commonplace in those final weeks, but Harry was keener than ever to begin the realisation of the vision God had given him.

May 24th 1935 saw Gertie and Harry on crutches, on board the Holland-America Liner, M. V. Dintel Dyk, at a wharf in Vancouver, ready to return to England. Harry was armed with references from the Presbyterian Church of Canada!

The Metropolitan Tabernacle
Vancouver, B.C.
Pastor Rev'd W. M. Robertson
10th May 1935

To whom it may concern:

I have known the bearer, Rev'd H. Brash Bonsall, for the last seven years and have intimate knowledge of his life and character. He is an able preacher of the Word of God and a man of the highest Christian character, whose life and testimony have been the means of winning many to our Lord Jesus Christ. He leaves behind him in this city of Vancouver a host of friends who love and respect him and whose prayers will follow him wherever he may go.

To any who may open for him an avenue of service we can commend him without reserve....

Will Robertson

It was a wonderful ten-week voyage, calling at Pacific ports along the way. At San Francisco work was just commencing on the Golden Gate Bridge and Al Capone was in Alcatraz Prison on one of the islands in the Bay. Thousands of ferries were crisscrossing on their way in every direction. Many were old steamers with paddle-wheels at the side or stern. Some had a single pinion arm of solid steel, about twenty-five feet long, rising majestically out of the heart of the ship into mid-air; descending to turn the paddle-wheel then rising out of nowhere. To proceed in a dense fog at night, with these ferries uttering shrill shrieks from every direction, was a remarkable experience.

On through the Panama Canal they sailed and down the coast of Costa Rica, swarming with sharks and their pilot fish. Harry and Gertie also saw many flying fish and turtles and, on the Atlantic side, the Portuguese man-of-war with its gossamer sail and poisonous tentacles.

Every day they swam luxuriously in the large canvas tank on

83

deck and though the voyage had begun on crutches, long before it was over, these had been discarded for ever!

Harry looked out over the deck railings into the vast expanse of the ocean, humming to himself:

Wide, wide as the ocean, High as the heavens above
Deep, deep as the deepest sea, is my Saviour's love.

He was excited, but also sure that many challenges would have to be faced as the race-track stretched before him. The hard training school in those hidden years of preparation had taught him two vital lessons for the future – two stones to put in his sling – the power of simple trust in God's Word, and the power of prayer. He knew there would be giants along the way!

15

THE MARATHON

*'The race is not given to the swift or the strong,
but to him that endures to the end!'*

The Christian pilgrimage was described by St. Paul as a race to be run, with definite principles for survival and success. To be a marathon runner one not only had to be an athlete, but also a fighter. For Harry, the preparation and training had begun many years before. The goal was now set ... and the race was about to begin. What rules should he follow? How would he perform? Would he survive?

Here are some open secrets from a man[1] who personally trained with the goal of an Olympic marathon in view. These track rules come with strong biblical parallels!

1. **Know your goal and stick to it!**
Preparation, training and racing for a marathon is very time-consuming, so *it is vital to have a long-term goal*. In the same way, each runner on the Christian track needs a clear conviction of his own particular calling and long-term goal. In spiritual terms, Paul's long-term goal in his spiritual marathon was to be like Jesus.

> 'That I may know Christ and the power of His resurrection ...' (Phil. 3:10) being 'changed into the same image, from glory to glory ... by the Spirit of the Lord' (2 Cor. 3:18).

---

1. Information given by Ian Hancox, brother-in-law of the author.

This is the goal he longs for, 'the prize of the high calling of God in Christ Jesus' (Phil. 3:14).

Don't be side-tracked

Whatever the set-backs along the way ... Always keep your focus on that long-term goal:

> 'to lay hold upon the hope set before us ... where Jesus (the forerunner) who went before us, has entered on our behalf' (Heb. 6:18, 20).

> 'Looking unto Jesus, the author and finisher of our faith' (Heb. 12:2).

You will have set-backs. Don't be discouraged. Take a break if you need it! Bad runs are inevitable, and somewhere along the way you will pick up injuries and illness. When you're running high-mileage with such a volume of training, weaknesses are bound to show up. Get to know your own body. Don't try to run with injuries. Your body is telling you something. You don't need to worry about missing out on training, or feel you have to run twice as hard to make up for lost time. It doesn't work. Often a few days' rest can be a very good thing!

> 'He restores my soul' (Ps. 23:3).
> 'He rested on the seventh day...' (Ex. 20:11).

One hundred percent, single-minded commitment to your goal!

> 'One thing I do; forgetting what is behind and straining towards what is ahead, I press on towards the goal to win the prize...' (Phil. 3:14).

> 'Let us lay aside every weight ... and let us run with patience the race that is set before us. Let us fix our eyes on Jesus, the author and perfector of our faith. Consider him that endured ... so that you will not grow weary and lose heart' (Heb. 12:1-3 AV/NIV).

'Do you not know that in a race all the runners run, but only one gets the prize? Run ... to get the prize. Everyone who competes in the games goes into strict training. They do it to get a crown that will not last; but we do it to get a crown that will last for ever. Therefore I do not run ... aimlessly; I do not fight like a man beating the air. No, I beat my body and make it my slave, so that after I have preached to others I myself will not be disqualified for the prize' (1 Cor. 9:24-27).

2. **Have a plan/groundbase**

You need a lot of advance practice in all kinds of conditions to build up confidence that you can do twenty-six miles in one go! You need programme structure and a routine that suits you and your body. You need to get a lot of miles in your legs; take in gradients and build up distance every time. It's like money in the bank, or your investment for the future. You can draw on it in the later stages of the marathon.

As far as the marathon runner is concerned, he has the great advantage of being able to train all year round. Dr. Martyn Lloyd Jones picks up this point in his 'Studies on the Sermon on the Mount' when he writes, '*We must discipline our lives* but we must do so *all the year round* ... not merely at stated periods.' In just the same way as the marathon runner, 'we are in training for eternity.' Exercising the soul in a 'regular spiritual workout' with 'no let-up, no quitting half way through' (Selwyn Hughes in his writings on 'The Care of the Soul').

Selwyn Hughes goes on to say:

Exercise must be regular, if it is to do the body any good. It is the same with the soul.... You may not be a disciplined or persistent person, but the Holy Spirit is. ... *The Holy Spirit's task* is to produce within you the desire and power to train yourself to be godly. *Your task* is to co-operate ... He will help you persevere ... by providing the power. All you have to do is to provide the willingness.

No age limit!

Marathon running by men and women of forty years and upwards, has signalled this group's interest in long-term fitness! Neither is old age a problem in *spiritual* terms, for 'Moses was 120 years old when he died: his eye was not dim, nor his natural force abated'! (Deut. 34:7) and the Scriptures tell us that we will 'still bear fruit in old age' (Ps. 92:14) with our youth 'renewed like the eagle's' (Ps. 103:5) .

'As thy days, so shall thy strength be' (Deut. 33:25).

The key to the running programme is to **pace yourself**, not running ahead too soon. Patience, being one of the most important qualities. The human body grows stronger and more fit when subjected to gradual increases of physical stress. Even the most accom-plished of runners have to do warm-up exercises to stretch the major leg muscles.

3. Don't avoid the steep hills and challenges!
Train for them!

4. Know your limitations
You must know your anaerobic threshold to run at your true potential. If you run too fast you will run into oxygen debt and then you will find it hard to recover or even finish the race. If you run too slowly, you will under-achieve and not do justice to your training.

Races such as a) cross-country, b) half-marathons, and c) circuit training (exercises, press-ups, sit-ups, etc.), all serve to break the routine of training and to tell you how you are doing.

'Train yourself to be godly' (1 Tim. 4:7).

5. **Write it down**
Keep a log/diary of all your training/racing (dates, distances and times recorded). Know your limitations and learn from the past. You will be greatly encouraged when you look back and see your improvements.

> 'Do *not* forget the things your eyes have seen, or let them slip from your heart as long as you live. Teach them to your children and to their children after them' (Deut. 4:9).

> '*Forget not all His benefits*' (Ps. 103:2).

6. **Right diet (very important)**
It must be *balanced, regular, stable* and *more than average*, especially just before the race. Look after yourself!

> 'Give us *this day* our daily bread' (Matt. 6:11).

> 'God is the strength of my heart and my portion for ever' (Ps. 73:26).

Race Day
Stretching ... Drinking ...

1. **Don't set off too fast**
Run at your own pace. You know what you're capable of. It's in your diary!

> 'So run, that you may obtain...' (1 Cor. 9:24).

2. **Drink regularly at every feeding station**
Fluid replacement is *very* important.

> '*Be filled with the Spirit*' (Eph. 5:18).

3. **Think positively. Don't allow negatives to get in**
Don't allow yourself the luxury of negative thinking.

'*Do not be anxious about anything*, but in everything by prayer and petition with thanksgiving present your requests to God. Finally, whatsoever things are true, whatsoever things are honest, whatsoever things are just, whatsoever things are pure, whatsoever things are lovely, whatsoever things are of good report; if there be any virtue and if there be any praise, *think on these things* ... and the God of peace shall be with you' (Phil. 4:6-9).

4. Run with other athletes when you can
This helps to discipline and pace yourself, while encouraging each other.

'Two are better than one ... for if they fall, the one will lift up his fellow' (Eccl. 4:9-10).

'Jesus Himself drew near, and went with them' (Luke 24:15).

5. Enjoy the race and ...
'The joy of the Lord is your strength.' (Neh. 8:10).

6. Finish well!
At a certain point 16-18 miles on, you will feel tired! Don't quit! Satan's mission in life is to 'trash' God's work and God's people ... to stop us finishing the race. God's great goal is to heal, to restore and to bring to completion His master plan for mankind. You *must* 'hang in there'!

'Hold fast ... that no man take thy crown.' (Rev. 3:11).

Remember, 'They that wait on the Lord shall change their strength ... They shall run and not be weary. They shall walk and not faint' (Is. 40:31).

Also remember God's promise to you that 'He who began a good work in you will carry it on to completion' (Phil. 1:6).

'Long obedience in the same direction' (Friedrich Nietzsche) is all important in the race of life. *'It's not how you start, but how you finish'* that matters.

Harry was about to face the biggest challenges of his life. Would his years of hard training pay off? Time would tell!

16

BRITAIN 1935 – HOME AT LAST AND RARING TO GO!

The arrival in Liverpool was exhilarating, as friends and relations who had not seen Gertie or Harry for twenty-two years watched the great liner steam into the harbour. Special times of reminiscing and catching up followed in Lancaster, but Harry couldn't wait to get started, to head down to London and pursue the vision God had given him. So, on New Year's Day, 1936, he left Gertie and her family in Lancaster to find work in the capital city.

Within a very short time, however, Harry found himself in Sidcup, Kent, struck down by a sudden severe illness and on his back once more. The frustration was enormous! It was a huge trial of Harry's faith, and he also realised it must have been a huge trial of everyone else's faith in *him*! Fortunately, wherever Harry went, friends appeared to come to the rescue. In this case, it was a wonderful couple who nursed him for the whole of that year. But that year, as he lay on his back, he was again tortured by thoughts of student days – of Juliet and of what might have been. Eleven years had passed since that time, but no other girl had come even close in comparison. At that moment, he realised what a huge mistake he had made. A case of mother fixation! He thought to himself, 'What a fool I've been! I must write to her immediately and pray that I'm not too late.' He rushed for the last post. Every day Harry looked out anxiously for the postman. Maybe she had moved? Maybe, like him, she had not forgotten? Then it came. January 1st 1937.

Her reply was devastating. Harry could hardly believe it. Juliet had married only three months earlier! With the awful realisation that he had not only failed Juliet, but that he had also failed God, Harry was crushed by the news. He was doing much better physically, but emotionally, it pushed him to the very brink of a breakdown. The only way he could find peace and sanity of mind was out in the open fields – walking, walking, walking, nineteen, twenty miles a day. Surely he had missed God's best. Harry knew how much he needed the right girl. Would he be given another chance? Day after day he walked and prayed in an agony of mind until the crisis was over at last.

It happened quite out of the blue as Harry was sitting alone in the Junior Section of Sidcup Public Library. The time and date were indelibly impressed on his mind. 10 o'clock, January 7th 1937. He wrote it in his diary that night.

This morning I personally encountered the Lord Jesus. He was right there. I asked Him directly about my wife and children to come. Was there someone else? At that moment, I claimed them all in faith ... and He promised me then, that there was one special girl lined up for me. His last words were 'This shall be as if it had not been. Is anything too hard for the Lord?'

From this moment on, Harry went to work with a will, a new spring in his step, full of faith for the future. Other friends supplied him with all kinds of physical and manual jobs to build up his strength ... one in a garage, one in maintenance and repair work, another on a farm picking apples and pears thirteen hours a day. Harry loved it all, but *when* would he get started? He couldn't wait! Here he was, where he knew God wanted him to be, and nothing was happening. Even though he was having very special times of prayer and fellowship with good friends he had made, particularly the Rev. Edward Joshua Poole-Connor, he felt somehow that time was being wasted.

One evening, after praying together, E. J. asked: 'Harry, you told me you had prepared a course in Systematic Theology once before. You wouldn't mind letting me have a look at it some time, would you?'

'I was just flicking through it today, E. J. I've actually got it with me.'

Harry opened up the battered, old suitcase which he carried around with him, and produced the manuscript, by now somewhat dog-eared. 'I must make another copy of it,' said Harry as he passed it to his friend for perusal.

E. J. was impressed with Harry's work; so much so, that, without a word to Harry, he proceeded to write about him to All Nations Bible College in London. Some days later, Harry himself wrote to All Nations Bible College, applying for an interview. The Principal's reply was brief and to the point:

'Come to tea; address the students; have the interview; spend the night.'

17

ALL NATIONS

It was now February 1938. Harry walked slowly up to the steps of the impressive building in Upper Norwood which was All Nations Bible College. He looked around him for a moment, watching students on a pre-dinner stroll in the lovely, open lawns surrounding the building. Turning round, he found he was not alone.

'Mr. Bonsall? You must be Mr. Bonsall. Welcome, welcome, welcome. My name is Dr. Henry Simpson-Curr. Principal. Do come in, do come in.'

Harry followed the impressive, jovial Principal, the history of the College being explained to him as they went.

'The College was founded in 1923, Mr. Bonsall. 1923. Rev. Dr. F. B. Meyer was its first Principal. This College operated under a Society called the All Nations Missionary Union, founded in 1896. Around 1916 Mount Hermon Bible College for women began, followed by All Nations Bible College for men in 1923. The Missionary Training College and Spurgeon's College are within a mile of here and the Worldwide Evangelization Crusade Headquarters and Radio Worldwide HQ not much further. Tea, Mr. Bonsall?'

'Thank you very much.'

Mealtimes were highly dignified occasions, and Harry was impressed by the smooth efficiency of the whole operation. He sat next to a young student who was directly opposite Dr. Simpson-Curr. Throughout the meal the student was the target of a rapid fire of brilliant and skilfully worded questions in broad Scottish brogue, about his work and travels, past life, opinions and anything else of interest, much to the enjoyment of everyone else in the room! Each sentence was delivered at great speed, the words telescoped. If he became particularly excited about a point, he would repeat it several times at great velocity. No man could be a dormouse in the Principal's presence!

After they had finished eating, the Principal, or 'Prinny' as he was known, invited Harry to his office. The room was beautifully furnished and they sat down on either side of an old oak desk.

'May I have a look at your C.V. and references, Mr. Bonsall.'

'Of course.' Harry opened his old suitcase and handed them over. Prinny took in the contents quickly, then laid the papers down on the desk and said, 'We'll have you, Mr. Bonsall, we'll have you.'

There and then, Harry was temporarily taken on to start work at once. Only afterwards did he discover that one of the tutors had suddenly fallen ill on the very afternoon that E. J.'s letter had arrived. Although he had nearly recovered three weeks later, Harry was kept on. In fact, there had been no thought of a second lecturer before the tutor's illness.

Harry threw himself into his work and it was in that Spring Term that all his discipline of Bible study in the hospital ward with his young friend Bill Philip came into its own. He didn't use any of the complex theological theories of his early training. He simply used all his own study notes, and God blessed them. These students were just as intellectually alert as any 'Varsity' students, many already mature through experience in the world of business, and he felt a great responsibility for them, as the next step for many would be the mission field. How would those unreached thousands ever know if he failed them at Bible College?

Harry saw the tremendous potential in each student. As he stood on the podium teaching, he would often think: 'In ten years time, each ten men will have reached a potential 100,000 who have never heard.' It was as if those 100,000 were an unseen audience at every lecture, as the men would inevitably pass so much of it on.

As Harry lectured on 'Prayer' one day, he could almost *see* their waiting faces all around him, like a sea in place of the bookshelves that surrounded his writing students. Suddenly aware of his immense responsibility, he went on: 'Prayer has many facets, and I'm talking about practical, effective prayer here, as in James 5:16 – 'The fervent, effectual prayer of a righteous man availeth much.' But in my own experience, I have discovered three stages in almost every prayer, and there are strong Biblical parallels.

'**The first stage**: Simply waiting on God until we discover the exact territory He wants to give us. He did this for Moses when He defined the *exact* borders of the Promised Land. The prospector does this when he fixes the exact location of his claim, and if there are two boundaries revealed, a nearer and a farther one, we take the latter with the *largest* boundary!

'**The second stage**: Waiting on God for a definite assurance of the promise and not getting off our knees until we've got it in faith ... just like the miner who locates his claim, but won't dig a spadeful until his claim has gone through at the Registry Office, in case he is dispossessed! Personally, at that point I believe the promise granted actually *exists* in the spiritual realm.

'**The third stage**: Never asking again, but simply thanking God every day for it in faith as an existing fact. We may feel the urge to keep praying for it, but we mustn't! We just have to stand on the promise that has been given. Otherwise we end up dishonouring God and praying ourselves out of faith! Faith is substance – and time and again we have seen impossible things coming to pass, as we hung on to the promise in faith and praised God for it.'

Harry and the students got on tremendously well. Most days an average of three or four men would come to him with all sorts of problems – usually at their own request. They would draw their chairs around the fire, and talk ... then pray over it. They really seemed to trust and love Harry, as he did them.

On one occasion, he had been lecturing on Ephesians 5:18 – 'Be filled with the Holy Spirit,' explaining that at conversion, you may open your home to the Holy Spirit, but only as a guest to two or three rooms. The 'infilling' is when every room in the whole house (from cellar to attic) is thrown open to Him to enter and control for ever. That night, after supper, three men (including a senior student) came up to Harry's room. 'Mr. Bonsall,' they said, 'Tell us more about this.'

At once, as four learners, they all just got down on their knees. They knew God had something for them. They knew it was God's will for them to be filled with the Spirit. So they followed the first two steps of prayer. First, quietly claiming this fullness in faith – then waiting for the assurance of it. As they believed, so the assurance came; in Harry's case, after an hour of prayer; for another, an hour later; then for the other two, the next day. Shortly afterwards they discovered that all over the college men privately, or in groups of twos and threes, were doing the same thing on their own. No-one organised anything. It was entirely spontaneous. No emotionalism of any kind, but a great sense of joy and peace. Then things started to happen.

That summer of 1938 something like revival broke out in the College. Every Sunday the men would go out to preach. The first Sunday two people became Christians. The next Sunday fourteen. The next eighteen ... no fuss ... no pressure. The students were often more surprised than anyone. By the end of that term, one hundred had turned to Christ. That summer on trek about seventy more ... and so it went on. Every Saturday night, God led the students to preach to the crowds at Hyde Park Corner.

One bystander was a Countess who hadn't walked through Hyde Park for years, but felt she had been led to do so. She sent her card to one of the young students and asked him to visit her. 'You all have a joy I haven't got. What's your secret?'

The clouds of war

God was undoubtedly at work, but another dark cloud was looming on the horizon. War was coming....

Harry addressed the students at tea on Sunday in September 1938. 'Gentlemen, should war come, there will be many consequences for us:

1. Closing down the College, probably turning it into a hospital
2. Conscription of all the men into some form of war service
3. Paralysis of all missionary effort
4. Untold suffering for God's children and others
5. The condition of Europe made unsuitable for revival
6. Many evil moral after-effects
7. Many souls lost
8. God's children on both sides forced to kill one another.'

They started to pray. Fifteen of the men came to Harry's room. Firstly their prayers began to focus on a deep worldwide revival with its full, moral, social, psychological and spiritual results ... in time to save Europe ... possibly the world (just as the Wesleyan revival saved Britain at its lowest moral decline, from a revolution-type disaster). Secondly for restraining power on the spirit-forces behind any European war-seeking governments, just long enough for this revival to take place. In prayer they claimed the first and held back the second. They firmly believed that if revival came in time, war could be postponed indefinitely; but if not, utter destruction was inevitable. All that week, lectures were given over to prayer as the war planes droned constantly over their heads.

Hope flared at times when peace seemed to become a possibility, but was diminishing again by the summer of 1939 as the shadow of the approaching World War II grew blacker every day. All hope for peace was finally rudely shattered by the outbreak of war in September 1939. 'Oh Lord, what will happen now?' Harry prayed, as the students and staff listened in grave silence to Britain's declaration of war.

All that Harry had predicted, should the war start, came about. Everyone, staff and students alike, had to leave, and it was with a heavy heart that Harry went back to All Nations to collect his things. It was changed, almost beyond recognition. The place had been sold to the Croydon Corporation. Already taken over for the Red Cross as an Air-Raid Precaution Post, it was full of soldiers, and Harry was challenged at rifle-point as if he were an enemy spy. He didn't tell them he had a front-door key in his pocket!

The old College was in a terrible state. In the Hall where they used to stand with Prinny, all was noise and confusion: small tables everywhere, notes being taken and commands issued. Women in blue flannel trousers and men in tin hats swarmed everywhere in its sacred precincts and there were no College staff to be seen. Fortunately, the beloved Principal was in Edinburgh. Sad at heart, Harry went up the staircase to the first floor to pack his belongings and there outside in the corridors were boots – rows and rows of army boots. He sat on his bed in his room, now labelled 'AMBULANCE' ... and prayed. The bottom had fallen out of his happy world.

18

THE DAY OF SMALL THINGS

Once again, when Harry was in real need, God provided the people and the resources for his survival. This time, it was Edwin and Dora Dodgson who came to the rescue. Edwin had been the carpentry instructor at the College, and he was in charge of the removal. Edwin invited Harry to help him pack up the College things ... so he stayed on. Each morning he stored College books and property in return for food, plus afternoons and evenings free to do his own thing. God also knew Harry needed shelter and so it was arranged for him to sleep in the College hostel, as the Red Cross found they didn't need it after all. Fuel was an added bonus, the College having ordered a couple of tons of coke too much! God even provided a job as a caretaker for the Croydon Corporation and the opportunity to give Bible teaching to one student. It was also clear that Harry needed company, as the house was very lonely and desperately eerie with thumpings and rat-scratchings and wild wailing moans on windy nights! And so he was given Angel Igoff, a stranded Bulgarian All Nations student, who was a much-needed friend for that time.

However, not everything went smoothly at first. His Bulgarian friend, who lived at the other end of the lone corridor, strode up to Harry one evening and announced: 'Brother, God has told me we are not to pray together.' He was deadly serious.

'Why?' Harry asked, somewhat bemused.

'I'm really not quite sure,' he replied.

'Okay. If that's what you feel.'

Life was lonely enough without that! Harry returned to his room and asked God what was wrong. Within seconds, he had been shown something very simple. Igoff's mushrooms! He had said they were good and Harry thought they were poisonous. Without delay, Harry went down the corridor and knocked on his door, inviting himself to 'mushrooms for tea'. Angel's face lit up. Harry ate Angel's mushrooms and Angel ate Harry's cake. Within minutes, they had started a flowing discourse about Angel's family and Harry offered to help him with his English. They parted amicably. Then, ten minutes after he had said goodnight, there was a knock at Harry's door.

'Brother, the Lord has told me it's time to pray together!'

The pattern for the next nine months was soon set. In the morning, Harry packed up the College things and the rest of the day went about trying to start his *own* Bible College, which was to be called The London Bible Institute. Harry's new college was always uppermost in his mind. Every afternoon and evening was spent getting referees. First, he systematically approached each member of the All Nations Council, one of the first of these being Norman Grubb, son-in-law of C. T. Studd and founder of WEC.

This was to be the start of a life-long friendship and partnership in vision. As they met, they were both aware of a wonderful sense of God's presence. Norman enthused about Harry's plans, especially as Harry was eagerly pushing forward when so many Christian organisations seemed to be closing down! 'Lord, *when* can I start?' Harry prayed one afternoon in Norman's living room. 'Surely something big must happen soon.' As they prayed, Harry knew he was being given an answer: 'Who has despised the day of small things? Though the vision tarry, wait for it.'

Harry lived 'by faith' in these days – and every week enough money came in, not only for himself, but also for a small weekly supply to Gertie. In the spring of 1940, however, there were changes afoot when a letter arrived from the Principal of the Word of Life Training College. This was run by the Friends' Evangelistic Band in Kelvedon, Essex.

Would Harry join the College team as Vice-Principal? Harry

so much wanted to follow his *own* vision and start his *own* college, so he said 'No'. His reasoning went, 'If I plant a seed in someone else's flower pot, it belongs to them. I am here to plant my own seed, a Bible college – in my own name.'

The result was immediate. All answers to prayer stopped from that moment on. All Harry's wonderful weekly supply of money dried up. He was desperate. He did not know what to do, but remembered hearing that George Muller had once said: '*When God withholds supplies, He has something to say*!' Shortly afterwards, Harry received a letter from his dear friend, E. J. Poole-Connor. Once again, God quite clearly spoke to Harry. 'Open that letter in your pocket.' The letter went straight to the point: '*Harry, were you right to turn that offer down? Don't you know that God uses steps to promote His plans*?'

'Is that the problem?' thought Harry. 'Why on earth would God want me at Kelvedon? What has that got to do with the vision?' But deep down, he knew that this wasn't the point. If God said 'Go!', he must go. As soon as he did what he was told and wrote for an interview, the amazing happened. His weekly supplies started to come in again just as they had before, and Harry started preparing for another move.

So, in May 1940, the sad day came for Harry to leave the old College behind him. He slammed the doors shut for the last time and walked slowly down the rear garden path to the heavy six-foot gate that led to the track through the beech woods, only to find that it wouldn't open. Climbing the embankment of the garden side of the fence, he flung his two suitcases over it, and jumped after them to see why he couldn't open the gate. As he bent over, he saw two bricks propped up against it, one over the other ... and nestling beneath them was a baby thrush. Had there been no bricks, Harry would have flung the gate open from the other side and crushed the little bird. Instantly God spoke to Harry – as clearly as an audible voice: '*You see how I have taken care of that little bird? Can't I take care of you*?'

19

'DOSIE'

WORD OF LIFE TRAINING COLLEGE, KELVEDON
(September 1940 – July 1941)

Kelvedon village was forty miles from London and only three minutes walk from Spurgeon's birth-place! Faithfully, Harry threw himself into the work with typical energy and dynamism, lecturing on a wide range of topics from Church History and Modern Cults, English, Phonetics and Elocution, to Modern Missionary Principles and Methods, alongside Practical Missionary Knowledge (camping, cooking, tropical hygiene, translation, map-making, etc!)

Closely linked to the Word of Life Training College was the Friends' Evangelistic Band, which travelled around the villages preaching the gospel. Harry joined students and staff each weekend as they went out to preach. Often it involved children's work and Bible classes in the home. At the end of one particularly remarkable week, Harry wrote in his journal:

'A few days ago, the entire Bible class of eleven gave their hearts to Christ in one night. Miracles are a daily happening. We are marching forward on the stepping stones of the impossible, by a simple daily trust in God and His promises – working under the direction of the Holy Spirit.'

God was obviously working, but how did this fit in with the vision? Was this small College yet another link in the long training process? Harry, still desperate to get started, didn't know. All he knew was that *you don't question God, you do what you are told!* He knows best, and Harry had always been aware that he needed help along the road. The vision was so great and he was so often incapacitated in one way or another, that he had no illusions of grandeur. He had arrived in Britain, pale and thin, after three years of debilitating illness in Vancouver, with hardly a penny to his name, and he knew that God's call to him could mean years of hard times, low funds and all-out spiritual warfare. If any part of God's plan were to become reality, he knew absolute obedience would be necessary. So Harry continued with his teaching, and soon Gertie had moved house to join him as Matron.

One afternoon, Harry was in a prayer meeting with the students, when he was distracted by the sight of a young woman sitting in a corner seat. He continued praying, but his eyes kept glancing in that direction. Feeling somewhat guilty that he wasn't keeping his mind on the Lord, Harry persevered with his prayer but it became harder and harder to concentrate. Eventually, he stopped praying and took a good look at her. Tall, with a lovely, open face, brown hair and blue-grey eyes, he was immediately attracted to her. She seemed a very serene person, with simple clothes and a very calm expression.

'She's the one.' Startled, Harry knew this was the Lord speaking

'How can she be the one? I haven't even met her.'

'She's the one.'

Harry gulped slightly and bowed his head quickly, hoping no-one had been looking at him. Finally, when the meeting was over, he plucked up the courage to walk over and introduce himself. He soon discovered that her name was Doris Ashby, and within minutes they were chatting freely, as Harry found out that she was very interested in healing. For some unaccountable reason, she had felt the urge to leave her happy situation in Watford to experience something of the life of faith. As she spoke, Harry felt that he was already falling in love with her, and before he could stop to think, he found himself blurting out what God had told him.

'You're the one I'm going to marry.'

Miss Ashby, who had been on the verge of saying something else, stood there for a few seconds with her mouth wide open, absolutely dumbstruck. 'I ... I ....' She paused briefly in an attempt to regain her composure. Harry stood there nervously, not daring to open his mouth again. Just as she was about to make some sort of comprehensible response, Gertie came rushing up to them. 'Lord, lead them!' she said, rushing away again as quickly as she had arrived. By this time, all the young woman could say was, 'I'll need to think about it. Do excuse me.' And she left in a hurry.

Doris, (or 'Dosie' to nearest and dearest), was at a loss for words, and didn't know what to think. She strongly believed in obedience to God as a priority for happiness and her approach to Christian marriage was simple. God had a special role for her and if God said she should marry a butcher, then her role must be that of a butcher's wife. If, on the other hand, He chose a baker for her, then her ministry would be totally different – in the line of buns and cakes! She said nothing to anyone, but retired to her room in a great state of agitation. While she was quietly praying about it, she heard a knock ... shortly followed by a whole sheaf of papers shoved under the door. Harry's testimonials!

Dosie simply did not know what to make of the situation, nor her Vice-Principal, this highly-charged and almost eccentric young man. Looking out of her window, she saw that he was now standing out in the garden mowing the lawn, so pale and thin, with a funny hat on and wearing his tight brown trousers, brown shirt and black spindly lace-up boots. However she also knew that he prayed a lot for different people and had a remarkable calling upon him. She had been taken aback, to say the least, by his statement, but in her inexperience, it never occurred to Dosie that anyone would *dare* to say anything like that unless it were true.

Time passed as both Harry and Dosie prayed and waited. On Friday July 12th, Harry was walking from Kelvedon to Colchester, when he felt God telling him to look up. The road lay parallel with the London and North-Eastern Railway Line and the first train was a Norwich-bound freighter. '*Not this one,*' said God. Next came a London-bound passenger train, roaring away at a good forty miles an hour. Then God spoke again, '*Do you see those people in that train?*'

'Yes,' Harry replied. Now some were reading in it; some were asleep; some were sauntering up the corridor. '*Don't you see that these people are resting and at the same time being carried quickly and safely to their destination? Can't I do the same with you, your circumstances, and your marriage?*' That was it. He rushed back to Kelvedon, and asked if he could go for a walk with Dosie.

As they strolled along the narrow country lane, Harry stopped and turned. 'Miss Ashby,' he said, still refusing to call her by her first name, 'Not long ago, I spoke out fairly bluntly. This time I want to ask you – will you marry me?'

Dosie stood there looking at him for a moment, then replied, 'It's a good thing you asked me today and not yesterday. My "Daily Light" verses this evening were Genesis 2:18 – *"The Lord God said, 'It is not good for man to be alone'"* and Ecclesiastes 4:9-10: *"Two are better than one, for if they fall, the one will lift up his fellow."* God made up my mind for me earlier this evening. Yes, Harry Bonsall, I will marry you.'

Harry was enormously relieved and tremendously happy. The next day they set out to buy an engagement ring, costing £3. 17s. 6d. – just under half of Harry's total wealth. Soon afterwards, Dosie suggested that Harry come and visit her family. So a fortnight later, he arrived at their farm, looking very self-conscious, with his big Bible under his arm! Every day they went for walks and sat under various hayricks, trying to catch up on the years before they had met.

'Tell me more about the last few years,' he would say as they sat beneath one such haystack. During these times, he discovered that Dosie came from an old farming family, believed to be of Huguenot and Scottish origins.... It was a close-knit family circle – brought up on strict Victorian principles, yet full of enterprise and strong resilient characters!

Dosie was born on August 30th, 1914 and was some nine years younger than Harry. Her irrepressible sense of fun sometimes got her into hot water at boarding school, but her zest for living and generous spirit were always endearing qualities. She was very creative and wonderful with children, so a Norland's training near London seemed an obvious choice. Norland nannies aparently 'smacked the behinds of kings' claimed a national paper (without ruffling a royal hair!) They were much in demand. Standards were high, but Dosie's flair for producing delightful doggerel at the drop of a hat, or life-like 'sculptures' from a bucket of clay under the bed, kept her charges highly amused!

Dosie was a natural 'seeker' – always longing for new spiritual horizons. Her keen interest in healing had led her to the brink of Christian Science, but then she heard the gospel for the first time and embraced the truth with open arms. She was twenty-three. An 'all-or-nothing' girl, the change had been immediate. She shared her new faith courageously with everyone – even on a 'soap-box' at Hyde Park Corner! Within four months she was training at Ridgelands Bible College in Wimbledon. 'What's more,' said Dosie, 'I had no money and didn't want to ask for help from home, but my faith was such that I was convinced God would supply the money if He wanted me to train ... and supply He did, for they gave me a bursary to cover the whole two years.'

'Welcome House'

When war was announced, Dosie had moved to Watford for eighteen months as housemother to a host of German refugee children, under the warm guardianship of a Mrs. Freeman, or 'Mummiefree' as they called her. Mrs. Freeman came from a Jewish family and had freely opened her beautiful home and gardens at Nascot Wood House, or 'Welcome House' to her 'adopted' children ... Walter and Gertraud, Franci and Peter, Heinz, Rotraud, Karl, Marian, Ernst ... and many more. They were incredible times, trying to give those children a secure and happy home in the midst of all the traumas of war. All came from non-Aryan Christian families across Europe, who were persecuted by Hitler. All were separated from their parents, some of whom never got out and were exterminated in the death camps. It was a serious situation, but they managed to have enormous amounts of fun.

As she was recounting tales of Welcome House, Dosie suddenly started to laugh.

'What?' cried Harry.

'Oh, I just remembered one April Fool's Day. It was a few days before the first of April when I was aware that there was a lot of whispering going on amongst the children. Every time I approached, the whispering would stop. I knew they were up to something, so I decided to play my own game. Early on April Fool's Day, I painted my face a very flushed, unhealthy hue and hid a flask of hot water by my bedside. I managed to play a very convincing act, saying how absolutely dreadful I felt ... far too ill to come down to breakfast. In fact I was sure I had a fever!

'Any thought of jokes stopped abruptly when the thermometer registered 103 degrees Fahrenheit! All eyes were on me, their beloved Matron, as they tried to cool me down with damp cloths, brought me breakfast in bed and tiptoed around with hushed voices as they went downstairs to the dining room. They'd forgotten all about April Fool's.

'Halfway through their breakfast, I washed my face and suddenly appeared at the door with a cheeky April Fool!" The children were so taken in that it took them several minutes to recover their composure. Then one of them went out to the kitchen and came back a few minutes later with a plate of steaming hot porridge for me. When I ate the first spoonful, my mouth was suddenly burning with the taste of hot mustard, and I could see a thick, yellow layer of the stuff just under the surface. It wasn't too easy, but I managed to eat the whole lot without a word!'

They both laughed, and then were quiet again. Dosie looked at Harry with a quizzical expression, as if something strange had just occurred to her. 'When was it you said you had prayed for a wife?'

'January 7th, 1937,' Harry replied.

At once Dosie produced a turquoise-green leather prayer-book. She opened it carefully and there, written on the inside, were the words: *'Marking the day of decision, January 7th, 1937.'* Dosie had been converted on *the very day* Harry had received his strong assurance in faith four years before ... and yet all that time he never even knew she existed. They sat there under that haystack for some time, amazed at the way God works.

Wedding bells

The date was set for September 18th, 1941 at St. Mary's Church, Watford, with the reception to be held at Welcome House. The bride looked very lovely in her wedding outfit and the refugee children sang at the wedding with songs composed for them by Mummiefree. The only problem was, the bridegroom was nowhere to be found. Just in time the best man, Ken Adams, discovered Harry down on his knees leading a man to the Lord in the allotment!

From that point on, the wedding went smoothly, and within days Harry was finding out that his new bride was exactly the

110

kind of wife he had thought she would be: a practical, no-nonsense, unflappable and 'gutsy' kind of girl, with real vision, and an infectious sense of humour. One in complete control of things, but with the faith and flair to give him scope and space to be entirely himself. Together they were a perfect match ... but it was wartime and money was so short, that in the end they never did have a honeymoon. Instead they started out on the track together with hardly a pause for breath!

20

COLCHESTER 1941-45

Colchester, ancient capital of pre-Roman Britain and England's oldest recorded town, was to be the next stop for Harry and his young bride. Full of troops training for war in the 1940s, it was bursting at the seams with army barracks and thousands of young soldiers getting ready for action. They bravely marched down North Hill to the station; usually their farewell to England.

Home for the young newlyweds was 49 Constantine Road. It was not a mansion – small and rather spartan, but home! Poor Dosie hadn't set eyes on No. 49 until after the wedding, and didn't know what to expect, as that Saturday afternoon all trains and buildings were blacked out. Being near the sea, there was constant threat of invasion. Nor was there much furniture to be had, but in those days furniture was cheap as so many folk had 'upped and left' for safer waters! All Dosie could see were endless books, bookshelves and boxes of stored furniture, lent by a kind old friend who had left it in wraps while the war was on.

Harry had been asked to take over the pastorship of Stockwell Congregational Church, which was one of the oldest Congregational churches in the world, dating back to 1662. It was huge, with a seating capacity of 2,000 and well located in the old Dutch quarter – only two minutes walk from Red Lion Square. Here, at the hub of Colchester itself, crowds of people, many of them soldiers, would gather on a Sunday evening. The vast church hall was also taken over by the National Young Life Campaign (NYLC) and served as a canteen for the Armed Forces, which was a real ministry during these difficult war years. Harry plunged into his new job with tremendous energy and drive, never for one minute losing sight of his long-term goal. As far as he was concerned, whatever he achieved en route was in preparation for that goal. Like a Land-Rover in 4-wheel drive, whatever the terrain he just seemed to keep on going, but now, of course, he didn't have to worry about minutiae. Dosie looked after everything. Immensely capable, she just quietly got on with life as it came. She shared his vision and his great love and concern for people, so 49 Constantine Road was an ever-open door. Wherever they went in their married life from this time on, their home was a constant buzz of people... people in need, people in ministry, people on the move!

It was at the end of one typically busy day of visiting that Dosie asked Harry if she could have 'a word' with him. He walked into the living room and sat down opposite his young wife. He could see something major was coming, and braced himself as she came straight to the point.

'Harry, I do believe we're going to become a threesome.'

'What? What do you mean?'

'I'm expecting our first child, Harry.'

'Oh!'

'Oh, indeed!'

'Well, what should I do? Do you need any help now? You must lie down.'

'Oh, sit down and stop fussing, Harry. I'm fine. The baby isn't due for months yet. Of course, it'll make things a bit more complicated for a while, but I'm sure we can cope with that.'

'I wonder who it will be.'

'Don't worry. I'm sure if it's a boy, he'll be just like you!'

The months passed, and right on time in November 1942, Charles Henry Brash Bonsall was born. Life became more hectic than it had ever been before, and Harry, though as proud as any father could be, decided there and then that this was definitely Dosie's domain. 'Don't leave the baby with me!' he'd call out cheerfully from the nether regions of his study.

Colchester Bible Institute

He was still working, and church business took up increasing time, but Harry could not forget his vision and the need of training for Christians. He began to put up posters around town, inviting people to come for evening courses. Soldiers were particularly interested. The brochure was inviting.

Lectures *free* and *open to all*

Christian work needs proper training ... (many) cannot leave homes and business to enter a Bible College for two or three years.

The solution is in *Evening Classes*....

Don't you owe it to Christ and to others to do the best you can for Him?

True, Evening Classes are not able to give all that two or three years residence in a Bible College would. The discipline and charm of Christian community life, for one thing are lacking. But who throws away the part, just because he cannot get the whole?

God often tests His children by offering a very little. To those who neglect it, He gives no more. To those who jealously take and guard their opportunities, He opens the door to something much bigger!

How Evening Classes overcome difficulties.

Lack of education, slowness to learn, feeling too young or too old, lack of money, time – none of these need hinder you if you are really in earnest.

Each lecture is *so clear*, each point so carefully explained and all questions so readily answered, *that all can understand.*

There are *no fees,* and the *classes are open to everyone*, for the work is carried on in dependence upon God....

And the students came ... never large numbers (up to twenty a night) but of those, at least 30% went out into full-time work later on. This was the beginnings of Colchester Bible Institute. For Harry, this was all a part of preparing Bible Colleges for the great revival he had seen in the vision.

At the same time, Harry became secretary of the *Colchester Evangelical Fellowship*, a group of keen Christians who would invite dynamic and prominent speakers to Colchester. Churches and ministers of all denominations grouped together all around the Essex area to pray for a country at war, ably accompanied by the Salvation Army Band and well-reported in the Essex County Telegraph. At the end of each invitation were the words: '*Prayer Changes Things.*' Harry, as one of the founding members, seemed to have a huge capacity for production, for work and for bringing people together to work towards one goal. All these outstanding men and women became links in a chain, forming a strong band of inspired Christian leaders. Harry and Dosie were always on the move as the work went into full swing, and Colchester became a hot-bed of thriving Christian work.

Within two and a half years, Ruth Nicola Brash Bonsall was added to the family circle and Gertie had moved to Colchester to be with her son's family and to help in the armed forces' canteen. The canteen livened up considerably when her attempt to boil a can of baked beans ended up in a very messy explosion!

Otherwise life was going smoothly – until a controversial issue in his church caused Harry to move on to the next phase of the journey.

One of the pillars of the church council at that time was involved in a thriving brewery business. Harry, who felt strongly about the drink industry, felt he had to challenge him on responsibilities as a leader in the church. He even took the bold step of preaching on the subject one Sunday! The man refused to step down and Harry felt he had no choice but to resign. Very sadly, after all those years of ministry, Stockwell eventually had

115

to close. Harry had been very happy there and still left special friends behind, who kept in touch.

It was difficult to know what he should do now, with very little income and a young family to support. Ruth was newly born and little Charlie was just getting to the lively stage. It was not an easy time, but in order to earn some income, Harry bought a Jardine platen printing press with some fonts of type from a friend, who taught him how to print. Then he started taking modest orders for printing jobs in his spare time, alongside a basic salary from the Colchester Evangelical Fellowship that was still going strong. He operated his printing press from the dining room, sometimes working through the night to get orders done in time for the next morning. Then he preached all over East Anglia ... and the gifts kept coming in.

21

ALL NATIONS BIBLE COLLEGE
– A NEW CHAPTER!

From Finchley to Taplow.
September 1st 1945 to March 31st 1952

'Dosie, that was E. J. Poole-Connor on the phone. He's Principal at All Nations Bible College now, and he's asked me to come as a part-time tutor. I've a strong feeling that it's the right thing. What do you think?'

'I think we need to pray about it. Is it part of the vision, Harry?'

'Well, I should think so. The Lord wants me to establish Bible Colleges to prepare for revival. Surely that doesn't mean I can't help *others* establish Bible Colleges.'

'We have to think about Charles and Ruth, too, but of course, if we're in the Lord's will I'm sure there won't be a problem there. Still, I want to be sure.'

'So do I.'

So they prayed ... and they went.

All Nations Bible College now consisted of half of the historic Kensit Memorial College in Finchley. With a staff of four, All Nations was up and running as the first post-war student, Leslie de Smidt, a gold-mining engineer from Johannesburg, arrived and set the stage for a new era! Over the next year, the numbers increased from one to three to five to seven. Harry was the only staff member from the pre-war College days and he made it his great aim to reproduce its

117

wonderful ideologies for the young men who began to flood in.

They had to expand. British forces were being demobilized everywhere and streaming homeward. By the summer of 1946, staff and students were confidently expecting the purchase of a property in Newport Pagnell. But then came another phone call from E. J. Poole-Connor.

'Harry, please come to London at once to sort out an emergency. The deal has fallen through. We've already accepted many new candidates and Kensit College just isn't big enough. We've had to tell some of them they can't come and we've already had angry letters from a few.'

Harry was on his way. When he arrived and met the Principal, he found the situation was worse than he had thought. College records had been sketchily kept. The former bursar had just left for Canada and couldn't be traced. Harry picked up a list of names which the bursar had left and he scanned the pages, puzzled. 'What are all these ticks next to some of the names?'

'I've no idea, Harry,' replied the Principal. 'People are heading towards the College from different parts of the globe and most are actually in transit, so we can't contact them. We don't know who or how many have been promised places, and if there are too many of them, we're in trouble.'

'Lord, you know the situation,' prayed Harry suddenly. 'Thank you that matters are in hand. Amen.'

There were not too many new students. The seven who had been there the previous year simply welcomed them at the door as they arrived and got them settled in. No-one had any idea there had been a problem and operations were far smoother from that moment on.

By the end of the year, new staff had come in to strengthen the forces, and the College had made the acquisition of a glorious mansion, 200 years old, set in a beautiful five-acre estate with its own view of Windsor Castle.

Taplow Hill House in Buckinghamshire had become a rest

and rehabilitation centre for Dutch merchant seamen during the war. The Dutch had courageously sailed to England to continue the war on the Allied side, with their exiled monarch, Queen Wilhelmina residing at Stubbings, Maidenhead Thicket, and the Dutch High Command headquarters close by. Now, after the war, in 1945, when the Dutch returned to the Netherlands, Taplow Hill House had become All Nations Bible College. It was a beautiful building, situated in one of the oldest, richest and most scenic villages in England, only a few yards away from one of the most historic sites of primitive Christianity. Once associated with paganism and the seat of Anglo-Saxon kings, it had later become the centre where St. Berineas baptised his converts in 634AD.

The new 'All Nations' at Taplow was like a self-contained village, with its own spacious grounds full of ancient cedar trees and wildlife. There were seven buildings in all, the main one with forty rooms, housing at least seven married couples and fifty-four students from every walk of life. The Red Cottage, which was acquired later, gave each room a biblical name like Tarsus or Nineveh, while the bathrooms were labelled 'Mediterranean I' and 'Mediterranean II'!

There was something else unique about the College at this time. All the students were ex-servicemen. They came from the Army, Navy and Air Force. Some had found Christ during the traumas of war, and one, a keen, brave young Christian from Germany, had been one-time member of the Jungvolk, Hitler's youth movement. These young men may have been away from academic studies for six years of war, but they were all highly disciplined and extra keen to learn. For them this would be a valuable time of recovery and development.

Admission requirements were based on three things: (a) general character; (b) exam results and (c) duration of National Service – and a special two-year, post-war transitionary Diploma was compiled (in view of the age of many students who had had to postpone their university and professional studies due to war service). For most, it was demanding.

Some students were de-mobbed and came straight to All Nations with very little to their name. Another hoped 'that little things that savoured of militarism and tended to remind the students of their service experiences, might not be allowed to obscure the essential major principles of discipline!'

Lectures were enjoyable, but hard work. Each day, Harry strode into the classroom, his black gown billowing out behind him as he pressed on for the teaching platform with a pile of books tucked under his chin.

'Good morning, gentlemen. Today we will look at the sinlessness of Christ. I have seven points to make:

1. The Father said, "... I am well pleased."
2. The Lord never prayed for His own forgiveness.
3. Satan under the Lord. Satan, the accuser of the brethren, never accused Him.
4. ...'

'Sir! Mr. Bonsall,' a voice interrupted.

'Yes, Mr. Collinson.'

'Would you mind slowing down just a little bit, please, sir. It's hard to keep up.'

'I'll try to slow down a little. But we do have a lot to get through.

4. Demons said, "Thou art the Holy One of God."
5. Judas confessed he had betrayed innocent blood.
6. Acts 3:14. Peter calls Him the Holy One and the Just.
7. Hebrews 2:10. He was made perfect through suffering (as a human being, he grew to maturity).'

One might have thought that Harry would have remembered his difficulties with note-taking at Knox College! The students

120

loved his lectures – they were so full of Biblical content and bursting with rich and apt illustrations – but note-taking was next to impossible. Often students would simply put down their pens and listen. One day two lectures had been crammed into one, but only later did the students realise. They just couldn't tell where one subject ended and the next began! As a result, a student delegation was despatched to plead with Harry to *slow down*!! He listened patiently, but the students weren't sure if he really saw their problem. However, the next time Harry delivered two lectures in one session, he paused, placed his hands flat on the desk and announced with a smile – 'Next subject!'

Shortly afterwards, midway through another lecture, Harry suddenly stopped speaking. Completely out of the blue, he thundered: '*Awake, thou that sleepest!*' At that split moment someone's alarm clock (bought in town that day) inadvertently went off. Pandemonium broke out in the classroom.

Students delighted in practical jokes, particularly at the Harry's expense – adding spice to the liveliness of his lectures. One day someone planted kippers under his reading desk. He came in as usual, standing tall with his black gown and curly hair, ready to commence his lecture. It took some time for the kippers to reach his nostrils ... then he began to sniff and twitch and look puzzled ... until he finally tumbled to the source of the smell and threw open the windows with a winsome smile, as the offending kippers were whisked away.

Harry had a habit of striding across the room while teaching – looking out of the window, first on one side, then another. On one occasion he looked out and suddenly found himself eye to eye with an enormous spider, moulded in brilliantly coloured cardboard. At the crucial moment of eye contact, the spider leapt up into the air, as one of the students diligently taking notes suddenly jerked a long piece of string inside his desk. Harry was visibly moved for one split second, then relaxed into a broad smile of enjoyment. Lectures were anything but dull!

Extra-curricular activity also played a large part in college life. New measures were introduced at the College, involving 'voluntary student labour'. A maintenance party was formed, consisting of all the 'specialist' students (i.e., three electricians, one carpenter, builder, plumber and any others who could be called on if necessary). Those with particular training and expertise were commissioned to train others, not just to relieve the College needs, but also to train them for emergencies overseas!

Each student gave 8½ hours per week in service for 'the common good' – and there was no undue interference in students' studies, or in their enjoyment of life. This enabled the College to do without a full-time maintenance man and made a growing contribution to the reduction of expenditure. Most activities were catered for, including a College Printing and Book-binding Department and a Woodworking/Building team. Shoemaking, plumbing, electrical maintenance, gardening and photography all followed.

Harry was very happy, and poured his phenomenal energy into giving his best for the men in all aspects of College life; academically, practically and spiritually. Dosie was one hundred percent behind her husband, but being one of the minority of ladies around, worked increasingly behind the scenes, with all the help and back-up from a smooth-running team. Meanwhile Dosie, strictly brought up in the Anglican church, was exploring new freedom in her spiritual pilgrimage. The command 'Be filled with the Spirit' was a new dimension that she had not yet discovered, so she fasted and prayed, waiting on God to experience more of the Holy Spirit in her life. She started going to a small Pentecostal church in Maidenhead and whenever a charismatic speaker happened to be in the area, she was there.

They both became friendly with Mr. Tubby, a quietly dynamic Beefeater guarding the Tower of London. He invited them to a large convention in Slough and later asked them both searching questions about the depth of their personal experience of the Holy Spirit. He then invited them to stay overnight in the Tower of London to discuss what the Bible had to say about these things! For Dosie, this was a turning point. She longed to be filled with the Holy Spirit, and be led by Him as the early Christians were. As she waited on God, she began to experience a powerful anointing in her life ... but the standard evangelical view at that time was much more cautious and conservative. One did *not* discuss these matters!

Keenly aware of this, Harry held back. On the one hand he believed and taught whole-heartedly that 'you must *be* filled with the Spirit and *stay* filled with the Spirit'. On the other, he was very conscious of the implications of 'going overboard'! Dosie called it 'cagey', although he had always talked of a special spiritual anointing in Canada at the age of twelve, later followed by the gift of prophecy. He and his mother had both shared some similar experience, but Gertie became so afraid that anything out of the ordinary might damage her son's ministry that she later went back on this. It became like a 'lost experience' to her. One Pentecostal missionary friend had already warned them, 'If you accept the "baptism of the Spirit" experience, you'll lose your job. The devil hates it!'

Undeterred, Dosie thought, 'What's the good of keeping a job if it means disobeying the Lord!' For Harry on the other hand, the temptation was strong to 'play it safe' ... to go along with the 'establishment', rather than going out on a limb in obedience to God with ears open to the wind of the Spirit.

More than meets the eye

College numbers were now in the fifties and God was moving, inside and out of the College. The work grew and prospered in every respect. A new baby boy, Thomas James Brash Bonsall, had been added to the Bonsall family, and wonderful speakers came to visit: Gladys Aylward, Leonard Pearson, Dr. Sangster,

Edwin Orr, Montague Goodman, Norman Grubb and Duncan Campbell, to name a few. Harry himself went out to preach regularly at churches, hospitals, schools of music, and universities – once sharing the platform for a week of lectures with Dr. Martin Lloyd-Jones at London Bible College for the London Inter-Faculty Christian Union. His subject, 'The Authority of the Bible.' In the summer of 1947, different evangelistic treks went out around the country. Over 200 came to faith in Christ.

By 1949, E. J. Poole-Connor had retired, and Harry had taken over as Principal. The College, with 'H.B.B.' as editor, produced an excellent 24-page magazine with a wide circulation. As Taplow was a near neighbour to Clivedon, home of Viscount and Viscountess Astor, Harry and Dosie were invited to the annual garden party. There they had the honour of being presented to the Queen, who asked several questions about the College and students, its course, location and work. Then Harry, never one to miss an opportunity, was graciously allowed to put Her Majesty on the College mailing list!

All was well – or so it seemed. But one student sounded a warning note: *'Satan is not barred by college walls – so pray for us!'*

Trouble in the camp

Then the unthinkable happened. It took over, and almost catapulted Harry into the next and most exciting phase of his ministry. As a Christian, he knew full well that as long as one is obedient, filled with the Spirit and living fully in the will of God, one is in full possession of the weapons for spiritual warfare and fully protected from all attacks of the enemy. He also knew that if, for any reason, there is a chink of disobedience in the armour, then there is an undefended opening and the child of God is vulnerable to attack.

Dosie was going from strength to strength at this time, in her search for the full anointing of the Holy Spirit, but she could not forget her friend's grim warning.

At Taplow, after an All Nations Council Meeting in London, Harry was questioned on the subject of his interest in going to a Pentecostal church ... after which Dosie still went, but *he* stopped going. Harry felt sure later that he had disowned a spiritual experience which he knew to be of God. To make matters worse, he had then been asked to sit on the Council of a leading missionary society, requiring him to sign a document that effectively distanced him from the work of the Holy Spirit in Pentecostal circles. Harry signed. He came home and told Dosie what he had done.

Things started to go wrong.

Harry looked out of his office window one afternoon. 'Dosie, who is that standing at the edge of the grounds?'

'Where?'

'Over there, just behind the oak tree.'

'I'm not sure. They're nothing to do with the College, but they almost look as if they're praying.'

'Something's wrong, Dosie. I don't like this one little bit. Can you feel an evil presence right now?'

'Absolutely. Let's pray immediately.'

So they held hands and prayed in the all-powerful Name of Jesus against any evil forces at work in the area. At first, they felt more peaceful and the group left almost immediately, but a battle for power in the spiritual realms had begun. This was a deliberate attack from a hostile core of spiritists in the Taplow area. In fact, that same group were openly seen more than once, setting their face against the College. Harry and Dosie were keenly aware of this 'demonic backlash', as the College was going on strongly at this very time, with many signs of revival.

Now such an attack of Satan was released – it was like a revival in reverse. Anyone working in a Bible College is in 'the front line', but the crisis that was about to hit the College and

Harry was something he had never experienced in his life. The origin of the problem was a mystery for some time. However, in 1952, certain members of staff suddenly decided that Harry must be relieved of his post. Explanations were not on the agenda.

'What *can* have happened?' Harry kept asking himself. Apart from the inevitable clashes of personality that can occur, he was keenly aware of other disturbing factors.

In those days, the Principal was not even an 'ex-officio' member of the College Council. This meant that, paradoxically, he had no direct say in decision-making at any significant level. Consequently, if there happened to be any rumblings in the camp, the Principal was in not in a position to explain or to present another point of view. For Harry, as the chief executive seeking to drive his college forwards, this was really not a satisfactory situation. In years to come, he would learn that College Councils do not always operate this way.

Dosie had a clear word of direction from God at this time: '*God is in heaven and thou upon earth, therefore let thy words be few*' (Eccl. 5:2). So, she fasted and prayed as she had never prayed before....

Harry didn't really know how it happened. Nor did most of his students, it seemed – but during that time, when four of his staff suddenly talked of resignation, there was a new arrival at the college. Frequently she could be seen, deep in intense and private conversation in different parts of the College building, with little groups of students bunched around her. It became increasingly clear that encouraging a spirit of unity was not on the agenda![1]

At that time Dosie felt the forces of evil so strongly that she

---

1. *David Morris, who was All Nations Principal 1959-1982, in correspondence refers to this period:*
'Years passed and we went to Nigeria and back. On our first furlough, I was asked to go to ANBC at Taplow to address the students. I was also to ask to see Henry Bonsall, the Principal. On arrival I was met, to my amazement, by an ex-army colleague, who said he had been asked to

would stand in the lounge with her hands on the adjoining wall, crying to God for protection, while Harry was on the other side of the wall, locked in conversation. It was during this time that Dosie suffered a miscarriage. The atmosphere was grim. Harry was virtually excluded. The special annual Whit-Monday Open Day Convention and speaker had to be cancelled. Meanwhile, Harry said little to anyone, and spent *hours* in prayer, writing almost daily to Gertie with an up-date on the situation in those critical months:

January 1952

'*Dear Mother,*

'Don't worry. Praise! Praise gets the victory.

'I am deeply conscious of Satan in the atmosphere. We three are rather like an island. Humanly speaking I am on the edge of a volcano. However we have great peace and rest in God.

'I haven't changed since last term. Have *they*?

'Our friend' is having long conversations with people and Doris and I are pretty sure she is at the bottom of most of the trouble.'

---

come down and "hold the fort".

'I had been looking forward to meeting my lecturer of Colchester days – but was told that he and other members of staff were locked in part of the College and that I should not try to find him.

'I gave my talk. I think it had the quality of a "lead balloon". The atmosphere was grim. I didn't discover then, or later, why the Colchester lecturer was cut off from his own College, but I think I felt things were terribly wrong. I had not the slightest idea that I might come back one day and spend 22 years there!

'During the years I was at All Nations, I met "Brash", as we called him, many times and gained much from his relationship with God. We stayed at Pakenham Road (Birmingham Bible Institute) and I was allowed to speak to the students in very different circumstances from that awful time at Taplow.'

February 1952

'*Dear Mother,*

'Propaganda continues...

'It's plain she is lobbying with them. Last night I heard her talking with a whole lot of them at the foot of the students' staircase (more like a closely-knit sister, guide, philosopher and friend).

'I don't think I can see *any* more students, or exercise a spiritual ministry as long as this atmosphere continues. They may close the College for a term. I think a firm line is needed. Please keep praying!'

March 1952

'*Dear Mother,*

A great spirit of prayer and divine power is upon me. *I feel God has a new work for me to do.* It is so inexplicable, unreasonable, unfair – and yet so clear-cut, that it can only be a divine hand fulfilling a loving and wise divine purpose ... by Satan's power. At the same time, I have a mighty sense of God's favour and presence ... of *the imminence of a divine anointing for some special service.*

God is cutting me adrift from this work to free me for some other ... and using the 'unkindest' of processes to develop qualities hitherto immature in me.

I feel it is indeed a finger of the cross of Christ that Doris and I are called to bear – and so I exalt! (I have spent a *lot* of time in prayer.)

I have tendered my resignation. It is absolutely settled. I am going ... They were very nice – and I shook hands ... and now my dear Mother, we, who have gone through so much together, will see what gracious provision God has for us.

With love, Harry.'

Countdown

March 27th, 1952

'Dear Mother,

The old students are writing to the College for an explanation – and also sending a letter of loyalty to me....

Yesterday, I worked in the garden and planted spinach and lettuce. I intend to work it normally, to hand over a tidy, up-to-date garden....

Doris is well but does too much and won't be told!

Dearest love, ever.'

Harry wrote to praying friends, June 17th, 1952:

'It is significant that of the four members of staff united to have me out, three have already left, or are about to leave the College, with no explanation to myself or the students. The fourth may well leave. ('Our friend' is also going.) The present students do not know the facts and apparently have never given the Council a complaint against me. Their only complaint has been that three members of staff have resigned. The old students almost to a man want me back, and practically the whole of the College clientele are grieved that I am going.

I haven't had the least opportunity to state my case. And I think their decision is largely built upon the will and action of one man. I would state, in fairness to him, that I think he acts sincerely.'

This was all-out 'spiritual warfare' and Harry spent hours on his own in prayer, but his private memoirs were virtually silent. Just a brief mention marked this experience:

'At the highest peak of spiritual, economic and numerical prosperity, it was all taken away from me on March 31st 1952. My wife has been a tower of strength.'

129

Godly visitors, such as Norman Grubb, came to visit the College and were shocked at the situation. How could Harry and Dosie cope with what was happening? They had their own particular way of handling it.

'*Work the problem*'

Work the problem. Address it. Face it. Go through it. Don't run away. At this time Harry's friends, Duncan Campbell, Edwin Orr, Norman Grubb and many others were there to encourage him and pray through his next step. Apart from which, Dosie was a champion. She had a wonderfully *positive* approach to life and had her own ways of handling difficult situations. One of her funny little maxims to Harry was 'Don't lie down and die Nellie!' (Nellie was an old farm horse who just gave up one day. Without any obvious reason, she just lay down and died!).

Then spiritual motivation came from Philippians 4:8: 'Finally, brethren, whatsoever things are true, whatsoever things are honest, whatsoever things are just, whatsoever things are pure, whatsoever things are lovely, whatsoever things are of good report; if there be any virtue, and if there be any praise, think on these things ... and the God of peace shall be with you.'

It was a soul-destroying experience, but Harry was not deterred. He wrote in one All Nations article at the time: '*He that observeth the wind shall not sow; and he that regardeth the clouds shall not reap*' (Eccl. 11:4). The wonderful thing was, God turned it all to good.

The marathon runner must keep on going. We all have our moments, human nature being what it is ... but what matters is the end result! The marathon runner must *never* quit.

22

MARKING TIME

Harry did not know what to do. He had a wife and three young children to support and a vision still before him as clear as ever it was! At times like these it was prayer that held the key. Dosie took the children to stay in Colchester with Gertie, while Harry took time out to pray. Throughout the dark experience of the previous few months he had written of a great spirit of prayer and divine power resting upon him ... an imminent anointing, cutting him adrift for something new and special ... But what? And where? And how?

'National Bible Institute'?
It was April, 1952. Harry's mind was buzzing with ideas. One door had closed, but he was sure that God had *better* plans. He was looking into any possibilities for the way forward.

A beautiful Georgian and Queen Anne residence, Great Horkesley Park, came on to the market. It was situated near Colchester and boasted twenty-five acres of wooded parkland. Wouldn't this be an ideal site for a National Bible Institute? Although Harry had very little capital to his name, he sent a private printed letter out to faithful praying friends, giving up-to-date ideas on how such a place could be used!

'*THE AIM* is to give an all-round practical training for the mission field.

Five acres are arable and the rest grass or parkland, with a very large walled garden full of fruit trees and bushes which could be used as a self-supporting community farm for market gardening, pigs, and poultry farming ... also a few cows for milking. The farm could be run by the students, as well as technical programmes.

Huts could be erected to give sleeping accommodation for another 50 students, while all lecture and library facilities would be in the main building.'

Staff, projects, administration and curriculum, were all carefully worked out to link up with Harry's previous venture, the Colchester Bible Institute, which was now ten years old and still going strong. It would be called the National Bible Institute. ('National,' as Harry's eventual plan was to have a branch in every city, before spreading further afield ... and 'Institute' not 'College', to indicate a wider ministry with 'availability to all,' though careful not to compete with the newly founded London Bible College.) This was a great venture indeed, but God had other plans. As suddenly as it had become available, the deal fell through.

Harry wrote:

'I am staying on at Taplow until September and spending the weekends on preaching engagements, but my heart is not searching for a mere job. I am waiting for God's commission. In my search, I am spending weeks alone in Taplow Woods some three miles from the College, where I walk literally hundreds of miles each week, back and forth, back and forth, in an agony of prayer. The same old travailing spirit I knew in Vancouver in the 1930s has come upon me once more.'

Suddenly, in August, Harry reached a crisis point. He couldn't pray any more. The praying spirit turned to praise. He just *had* to praise, sometimes literally leaping around with the joy of victory! Hours and hours of praise because he knew that God had heard and answered. 'Am I insane?' he thought to

132

himself. There was nothing in his outward circumstances to be joyful about. He wrote again:

'No, I am not insane! My faith is surging forward and claiming something that is more real than what I can see or hear. I now know that God has heard me and will fulfil His purpose in bringing me from Canada.'

As he wrote, Harry was suddenly aware of a clear mental picture of a large house that he had never seen before, the details of which were vividly imprinted on his mind.

23

BIRMINGHAM – THE NEXT LAP

'I am alone and missing Dosie and the family. But the vision is pressing on and I am also very excited. God has directed me in spirit to call on H. J. Peacock, Headmaster of Eversfield Preparatory School in Solihull, close to Birmingham. Should I apply for a teaching post? I feel Birmingham is somehow significant.'

It was the first fortnight of August, 1952. Harry was on his way to speak at a youth conference in Bangor, North Wales, and had only four hours to spare en route ... enough time to visit Mr. Peacock. Harry knocked at the door.

'Just coming,' came a voice from inside the house. A few seconds later, the door was opened and after introductions, Mr. Peacock invited Harry in. 'Do come through and take a seat in my office, Mr. Bonsall.' Harry turned into the pleasant, airy office and admired the piano which stood at one end.

'Do you play, Mr. Bonsall?'

'Yes, a bit. I'm sure if I'd practised more, I might have been quite....' He broke off suddenly, staring at a photo sitting on the piano. He looked closer. There was no doubt about it. It was a portrait of friends he had last seen in Vancouver in 1934!

'I know these ladies!' he exclaimed. 'They were my intercessors.'

'Well, those are my aunts!' replied Mr. Peacock.

Within a short space of time, Harry had been hired as Junior Master at Eversfield – the seal on Birmingham as a centre for the new college.

That visit to Birmingham and the following fortnight in Bangor led to life-long friendships with leaders and young people. Wherever Harry travelled and preached he brought in students – and he preached up and down the land. Students for correspondence courses; students for evening classes; and prospective full-time students for the new college! Names were added to an already extensive mailing list, with correspondence immediately and untiringly followed up, often by hand.

Teaching seven-year-olds was interesting! 'And how does "Sir" with his brilliant academics take to teaching noisy little boys with minds of their own?' one fellow-teacher enquired.

'Oh, I just tell them lots of stories and give it all I've got,' Harry replied, with a laugh. Every evening he would retire to a tiny bedroom after the busy days of teaching, supervising meals and play-breaks – and all the time his mind was firing on all cylinders, exploring how to bring about God's plan. One evening, he walked in to supper and sat down at the table.

'Joyce,' he said quietly, but joyfully, to a Christian colleague, 'one of the boarders has just come to know the Lord!' Later, twenty-two out of twenty-four boarders made a profession of faith.

Meanwhile, Dosie was bravely holding the fort with Gertie and the three children at 49 Constantine Road, Colchester. Letters flew backwards and forwards with each new development. Then suddenly, things began to move....

The Headmistress

It was the October Bangor Camp Reunion – when a small, extremely dignified, elderly lady introduced herself to Harry.

'Mr. Bonsall, my name is Florence Walker. I wonder if I might have a moment of your time.'

'Of course, Miss Walker.'

'Well, Mr. Bonsall, I heard you speak at a Teachers' Prayer Bond conference seven years ago,' she said. Out of the blue, she added, 'I have a large house in Birmingham, 4 Oxford Road, Moseley, with one empty room in it for rent. The house is up for sale, but if you want it to start your new Bible College there, you can make it your Headquarters! If you don't choose to use it now, I will help you in other ways. Do you think you might be interested?'

Harry *was* interested! The conversation deepened and he discovered that this remarkable retired Headmistress had taken a leading part in starting two other Bible Colleges in Birmingham, which had sadly failed.

The WEC family – and that house again!

As soon as Harry got back to Birmingham, the first thing he did was to cycle over to Oxford Road. As he pumped away at the pedals, he prayed all the way for guidance. Was this the right place? The last thing he wanted to do was depart from God's plan. Turning a corner, he saw the house almost immediately. He gasped and his right foot slipped off the pedal as he lost control of the bike for a split second. Braking rather too quickly, he stopped with a jolt, but he didn't care. Looking again, he was in no doubt. This was the very house he had seen in his vision as he prayed in Taplow Woods!

So Harry rented the room, cycling six miles every day to Solihull and his teaching post. The whole of the top floor of the house was now virtually empty. Norman Grubb, Harry's dynamic friend from student days had become director of the Worldwide Evangelization Crusade (WEC) and was very keen to rent the rest of the floor for his 'Young Warrior' team or 'Midland Gypsies,' as he called them. Would Harry put in a word for him to Miss Walker?!

Of course, Miss Walker agreed to the solution and that was the start of many years of happy fellowship between the WEC team and Harry. Once a week, twenty or so would meet at 4 Oxford Road to pray.

Then, on January 1st, 1953, as Harry and his WEC friends were anticipating the year ahead in their Oxford Road premises, the shock came that they had least expected. Miss Walker sold the house. She herself did not know why she felt she should do this. WEC were stunned and so was Harry. 'Surely God can't be in this,' he thought. 'I must do nothing and wait to see how the matter will fall.' It was at times like this that he really missed Dosie ... but he would not have to wait long for new developments.

Early days and the founding of BBI

Harry was excited. The selling of the Oxford Road house had been a major blow, but on the very same day, he had managed to secure three lecture rooms in old University buildings at Edmund Street and Easy Row. God also gave him the first two members of his College Council – Dr. Julian Hoyte (ex-missionary from Rhodesia) and Edwin Lewis. Excited by the vision, they also longed to see God working powerfully in their day.

Now, on January 9th 1953, a group of like-minded Christians sat around a table for the first ever Council Meeting of the new College. It was an historic occasion. Harry looked round at each face: Dr. Julian Hoyte, Edwin Lewis, Dan Kerr, Florence Walker, Rev. F. Hines, Rev. Jonathan Finch, Rev. Hugh Butt, Rev. Gordon Booth, Peter Naish, Bill Pethybridge, Norman Trickett, John Tupper and Dosie, who had come up especially for the meeting ... soon to be joined by Rev. David Smith. Himself included, that made fifteen in all. First, they discussed the name.

'How about the National Bible Institute?' Harry suggested.

'I don't think so,' replied one of the group. 'That's a bit too flamboyant, too big. Just call it the Birmingham Bible Institute, then it can be placed squarely on the map at the hub of things in Britain's second city.' Murmurs of agreement greeted this suggestion. Thus, the Birmingham Bible Institute was born.

'I think that we should clarify the exact purpose of the College before we do anything else,' said Harry, clearly animated by all that was happening. 'In keeping with the vision God has given me, our aim is to be an evangelical college providing an academic training that would be available to all, with or without qualifications. Alongside this theological training would be the development of life skills and leadership skills – with missionary pioneering in view. And of course, we need to be ready and waiting for revival. I personally would like to start as soon as possible with full-time tuition, but maybe we should begin more cautiously.'

'I think we would agree with that. Let's not rush ahead too soon. Students could be let down. Let's wait for God's seal of blessing upon it and then move ahead.'

Dosie, unhappily, had to go back to Colchester almost immediately, but after that, without further delay, a course of evening classes was started at the University – nine per week in three lecture rooms. Five lecturers shared the work between them, giving three 50-minute lectures from 6:00 to 9:00 pm on Mondays, Tuesdays and Wednesdays. At least 300 attended those evening classes in the first three years (roughly 56 a week), many of whom went on to full-time service. It was not until April 1955 that the trust deed was approved, giving the BBI College and Council legal and charity status, so no full-time students were accepted until this milestone had been reached.

From the first, the story of BBI was a unique 'faith venture' run by a man and woman of vision and a remarkably dedicated team. Together they were ready to take great risks with God against all odds, in order to obey His call. Already two colleges had folded up right there in the city, but Harry still saw the vision as clearly as the day he had received it and the team pressed on with it.

Harry gave up teaching and started on his faith venture with a pittance in his pocket. With no more than £150 and no idea what he would do or where he would go, he was quite determined to do what was right, regardless, leaving the consequences to

138

God. Only a few days after leaving his job at Eversfield School, Miss Walker came up to Harry and said without warning:

'Mr. Bonsall, I am too old to get a mortgage. You buy a house and let me live in it and I will lend you £1,000 without interest for 10 years.'

The very next day Kay Duddridge of the WEC Youth Team came up to him in a similar manner, saying:

'I've inherited some money from my father, but not enough to buy a house, and WEC rules don't allow me to take out a mortgage. If you buy a house and let our Young Warrior team live in it, you can have £500 without interest for 10 years!'

So, suddenly Harry had £1,500 to play with, and there was so much to be done!

Dr. Pardhy and the first house 1953

A few days later, Harry was just about to set out for a brisk walk, when he noticed a man across the street. He knew he recognised the face. Then it came to him. It was an Indian doctor, whom he had met five years before. The memory of their last meeting became very clear. Harry had been a guest at a large medical function in London – feeling very much like a fish out of water, or the proverbial wallflower. When he looked around, he discovered that at least half the assembled company were *also* wallflowers – of two distinct camps; old ladies and Hindu doctors! Harry approached the latter and struck up a friendship with Dr. E. Krishna Pardhy. One-time friend of Mahatma Gandhi, he owned a beautiful Victorian house in leafy Edgbaston, with 19 spacious rooms (several over 24' by 14'), three garages and an enormous garden. The address (28 Elvetham Road) was only a mile or so from the Edgbaston Cricket Ground and ideally situated at the peak end of the Calthorpe Estate, with its lovely lawns, owls, cuckoos and foxes – and only five minutes' drive from the centre of Birmingham. Harry vividly remembered discussing that house.

Crossing over the road, the two men shook hands warmly. 'Mr. Bonsall, I've been meaning to get in touch with you for some time,' said the doctor, in virtually flawless English. 'I well remember our conversation that night in London.'

'So do I,' replied Harry.

'We talked much about my home in Edgbaston. Well, as it happens, I'm wanting to move on now. I was wondering....'

'Yes?' said Harry, trying hard not to be presumptuous about where this was leading.

'Might you be wanting to buy it?'

It was settled, there and then. Dr. Pardhy chose to offer his house to Harry for the College on a seventeen-year lease, for £1,300. So, for that precious £1,500, they had the house, with a bonus of £200 left over for decoration.

In March 1953, the occupants of 4 Oxford Road all moved over to their new home in Edgbaston. The three groups became more like a big family. Every Monday at 10.00 am they had a committee meeting to decide what was needed for maintenance – and they all paid it – WEC one third (or four twelfths), Miss Walker one quarter (or three twelfths) and the Bonsalls five twelfths. The next move was to decide what rooms everyone wanted. The WEC chose five rooms (the whole of the top floor flat – i.e., a third) with one large room, dubbed 'The Nunnery' for the girls. Miss Walker chose a flat in the middle floor with her elderly companion, and the Bonsall family had the rest for themselves and the BBI!

After No. 28 Elvetham Road's first prayer meeting, one friend, having quietly surveyed the scene, said 'This place needs decorating. Would you like our local church to come and help?' The result was that sixteen men and women came that Easter holiday and redecorated the whole house, while Harry tried to stand in for Dosie and feed the workers. The place was in such a state that the ladies, armed with brooms, mops and buckets, set to and cleaned it from top to bottom. During this time the ridiculous became the norm. Dr. Pardhy had left all kinds of curios in that house, old bones in the garden and war-relics. One day, several live cartridges were found. Miss Walker blanched at the thought of such things in the building. 'Very dangerous,' she muttered to herself, as she swept them into a small bag. Seeing that the others had started a bonfire for burning rubbish, Miss Walker strode purposefully out into the garden and threw the bag onto the fire, exclaiming, 'We must never allow that sort of thing here!' Panic reigned and people fled as the cartridges suddenly exploded in all directions!

The great day that Harry had been anticipating for months finally arrived. After lonely, but exciting, times, Dosie arrived in Birmingham to take over the running of the house, with the three children, Charles, Ruth and Tom, shortly followed by Gertie. From day one, Dosie was quite remarkable. She learned to live on a shoestring budget, whilst throwing her home open to all with generous hospitality and very little thought for her own convenience. Like Harry, she was totally committed to this new venture. She strongly believed in the power of prayer, particularly where healing was concerned – and could well remember, not so long ago, when her faith had been dramatically tested"…

Once in Colchester, when Charles, aged three, had developed a tuberculous spot on his knee. He was due to go into hospital for an operation, followed by long-term treatment. Family and friends got together the night before, anointing him with oil while he was asleep and claiming his complete healing. Just before the operation, he was X-rayed. No trace of bovine TB could be found. He was cleared, sent straight home and never had another sympton.

Again in Taplow, when blond blue-eyed Tom, aged two, toddled into the kitchen and clambered up to the high china sink for a glass of attractive-looking liquid. It was neat Jeyes fluid – deadly poison. As his mouth started to burn, he began to scream

141

at the top of his voice. Dosie came running and, with her usual presence of mind, immediately turned him upside down and quoted scripture over him in the name of Jesus. James, a most practical book, was one of her favourites. '*The prayer of faith shall save the sick and the Lord shall raise him up,*' said James 5, followed by the words of Jesus from Mark 16: '*If they drink any deadly thing it shall not hurt them*; they shall lay hands on the sick and they shall recover.' Dosie believed it in faith and took Tom straight to the doctor who examined him and said, 'I can't believe this. The poison appears to have got no further than his mouth. He doesn't seem to have swallowed it. In normal circumstances it should have caused burns and destruction to the internal organs on its way through the body.' By that evening Tom was smiling happily and drinking hot cocoa, as though nothing had happened!

Living the Life of Faith
On the financial side of things, Harry watched his small £150 go down to £100 and then to £1. But Bill Pethybridge, WEC leader and Council member, with sunny personality, down-to-earth endurance and unclouded faith life, kept Harry afloat. He seemed to make living 'by faith' fun.

'Harry,' said Bill, as they were decorating the hall one day, with paint dripping down their faces, 'God has shown me that if you're not prepared to live the faith life *now*, your work will end in failure.'

'But Bill, I've only got £1 left!'

'Don't worry, Harry. You've got to touch rock bottom first!'

Sure enough, a £20 bill would come in one post, followed by a £20 gift in the next ... and it stayed that way each day for about four years! Harry took no salary for years, but was still able to fund a part-time secretary out of what God gave him then. Instead of showing him a text book on Faith Life Theology, God pushed him under the same joyous roof as the 'WECers' who *lived* it day by day. To live 'by faith' was a decision, and Harry, witnessing the WEC lifestyle, wanted to make that decision for himself and the College.

24

'FAREWELL, DEAR MOTHER!'

January 1955: Gertie, at the age of 82, passed away peacefully after a battle with cancer. Faithful, praying Gertie spent the last precious years of her life amongst the family, lovingly cared for at No. 28. Comforted by the fact of Gertie's happiness at the end of her life, Harry was able to cope with her loss in the sure knowledge that she was even happier now. He wrote to friends shortly after her passing:

> 'Business address: this world
> Home address: 'in Christ'

She was truly happy ... In the last two years of her life she had her own things about her and was my 'private' secretary, mailing thousands of letters and prospectuses with her own hands and sharing our life here with keenest zest. For all my life I don't think we ever had a quarrel ... and whenever absent I have written her a letter every day. I reckoned a million pounds wouldn't get a letter to her later, so why not do it here for a trifling 2½d! I don't regret it for a moment!

For you, who loved my mother ... who prayed for us, laughed and talked with us in bygone days, in Mother's name I thank you all, and I send you, as she has asked me to do, her love. May God bless you! My mother often wished that Tennyson's prayer might be fulfilled for her and it truly was.

Sunset and evening star,
And one clear call for me!
And may there be no moaning of the bar,
When I put out to sea...

Twilight and evening bell,
And after that the dark!
And may there be no sadness of farewell,
When I embark;

For tho' from out our bourne of Time and Place
The flood may bear me far,
I hope to see my Pilot face to face
When I have crost the bar.

                    With all my love, Harry'.

25

THE VISION TAKES SHAPE

April 1955

BBI began, with its first four students in the summer of 1955 and by the following summer term had grown to fourteen ... all men. The eminent Dr. W. Graham Scroggie, previously President of the All Nations Missionary Union and Bible College, encouraged Harry to press ahead ... which was never a problem for the Principal! Graham Scroggie then became BBI's first President. The original programme of Evening Classes and Correspondence Courses became incorporated into the new curriculum alongside the regular three-year BBI Diploma. Later these full-time studies led on to the London University Certificate of Religious Knowledge, Dip.Theol. and B.D.

All the early students were men. Then, through quite an unusual set of circumstances, God brought in the first female student. Pat Ireland worked in an orphanage. One evening after work, she was in two minds whether to go home or attend her church prayer meeting. 'I'll wait for the first bus to decide,' she thought. 'If it's the home bus, I'll go home.' She arrived just in time to see the home bus sailing by! The next bus to arrive took her to the prayer meeting, where the church pianist suddenly turned to her and said, 'I've saved enough money to go to Bible College, but now I'm not in a position to go. If you want to go instead of me, you can have the money!' So Pat became the first woman student.

Later, married couples were added ... and still later those with children. Where would they live? How could they be accommodated? Housing was high on the agenda – and funds were small, but Harry believed God would provide. One day he strode into the lecture hall in his customary style and stepped onto the platform, turning to face the students. As he turned, he said, 'A word of prayer,' and launched into thanksgiving to God for all He had done and would do for the College. After the 'Amen', he began his talk:

'You all know our situation, the houses we need and the funds we don't have. How do we approach it? Well, my thinking goes like this – there were twelve men sent to spy out the Promised Land and God gave them a promise, but only two took it in faith. The rest looked at impossible circumstances and jettisoned faith – went down the drain. Faith is sticking your neck out ... regardless of human obstacles, believing in the impossible and acting upon it. That's what faith is – not belief, not feeling happy, not presumption – but *acting on the promises of God*. That's what, in the last analysis, distinguished all the Bible triumphs from Bible tragedies ... Isaac from Ishmael, Jacob from Esau, David from Saul. *One with God is a majority*. The sort of life Israel had to lead, is the same sort of life *we* have to lead – not in relation to its conditions but its working principles – and that is why the story of Exodus is up-to-date for us today. Exodus is our rule-book. We must be opportunists for God. God might want us to have every house on Elvetham Road, Pakenham Road, Carpenter Road, Charlotte Road, Wheeleys Road and the land in between! If I know He wants that, I'll believe we'll get it. God is God. Is anything too hard for Him?'

Harry encouraged the College Council to follow his direction, and as the houses became vacant, more students filled them. Harry was aware that this must have been a rather frightening experience for more conventional members of the Council, who were keen believers and willing helpers, but trained in the *usual* handling of finance!

Faith for finances ... **Running with God**

As the work grew, so God released the property. Harry believed God would work miracles, but even he was amazed at the way different houses simply became 'available' as the months and years slipped by, almost unnoticed. It was quite remarkable! First No. 7 Pakenham Road became available in 1954, almost directly opposite No. 28 Elvetham Road at the junction point of a small triangle. Ex-C.I.M missionaries, William Clark and his wife, bought the house and loaned it to the College as a hostel for the men, becoming its own 'live-in' tutor family, first class warden, cook and lecturer. Some time later this lovely house was bought for the College.

Next door to No. 7 was No. 6 Pakenham Road, another large eighteen-roomed house, with some thirty tenants and their Indian landlord. Harry with his expanding vision, had an eye on that house, but the Council had no money and decided not to venture out in faith when it came on to the market. As a result, when BBI finally bought that house in 1958 it was at a much higher price and requiring a mortgage. No. 6 was to be the first BBI-owned building.

Just before that purchase, WEC's 'Midland Gypsies' were given the faith to believe for new premises. They had no money, but God told them it would happen. Within two weeks of their announcement of moving from 28 Elvetham Road, £1,500 came in, and the new Midland headquarters for WEC was theirs. Great rejoicing followed, as one of the team danced around the kitchen with delight! At the moment of their removal, a little blue Morris van with a baby carriage on top was waiting in the road to drive in. It was the arrival of BBI's first student family!

No. 6 was in a pretty bad state of repair after multi-occupation, but thanks to hours of painstaking work on cleaning and repairing by students and a summer dedicated to decorating, No. 6 became the administrative centre of the College. Out of this house they carved a lecture room (with seats for at least 120 students), a library, a study room and several offices. With its first resident tutor, Mr. Gordon Croft BD (lecturer '57-'58), No. 6 was proudly opened by Sir Alfred Owen CBE, now a long-term member of the College Council, who later followed in Graham Scroggie's footsteps – as BBI's second President. In fact, it had been through Graham Scroggie's ministry 'on campus', many years earlier, that the young Alfred Owen had come to faith in Christ!

The administrative department at this time was beginning to need help to cover the masses of paperwork building up, but it took a particular kind of bursar to work with someone like Harry. People had a hard job keeping up with him! One day a sun-tanned Australian appeared at the College looking for the Principal. Just back from fourteen years of missionary service in Nigeria with his wife and daughter, Elijah Bingham ('Lije') had taken a temporary job at the Gardening Department of Lewis's Ltd., but was looking for greater challenges!

'We must pray together, Mr. Bingham,' said Harry. 'I think the Lord may well want you here.' So they prayed. Then Harry suggested, 'Let's ask God for a gift of £150 as a sign that you should join us at BBI.' Within three days two students had made a gift of £150 and Lije Bingham was hired. Harry arrived in the Gardening Department waving the cheque and they had a spontaneous praise meeting on the spot!

So it was that Lije Bingham appeared on the doorstep to relieve Harry of the burden of general office administration. Lije was entertaining and capable, setting up a general office in No. 6 as full-time secretary and bursar-tutor. He also became editor of the College magazine, 'Gateway'. By this time, most of the faculty were housed 'on site', acting as wardens and available to the students at most times for pastoral and academic consultation ... receiving very little material return and sacrificing a great deal in their calling. Others gave their time and skills generously; gifted men like architect Dara Variava, who worked closely with

149

Harry, drawing up exciting plans for a new College development, and Rev. Harry Sutton, who joined the College Council and became a trusted adviser.

Until this time, Dosie had done a remarkable job in the kitchen, catering for up to forty students, almost single-handed. However, the College was bursting at the seams and as yet there were no official dining rooms. The arrival of a baby daughter, Rachel Mary Brash Bonsall, in 1957, was greeted with delight, and completed the Bonsall family. At the same time Dosie's workload increased, making her daily catering feats all the more remarkable.

By the close of 1959, there was *still* an accommodation problem. Harry spent hours on his knees, fearing that the Council might pull the curtains down on further student intake. Students were steadily applying and the Council had a hard decision to make.

'Do we turn them away or ask God for more buildings?'

'I heard one of the students refer to "Pack-'em-in Road" this morning!'

'That's the truth!'

'Well, no-one said that we'd avoid difficulties if we operate by faith. If we just coasted along, avoiding nitty-gritty, real-life problems, we'd soon stop depending on the Lord.'

'That's true, but it doesn't mean we shouldn't be cautious.'

The discussions went on for some time. Different opinions were aired and countered. Time for prayer was set aside. More discussion. A decision was reached – 'The College will accept any approved student while there is even the possibility of accommodation for them.' The solution to the problem was to come more rapidly than they expected.

On 1st February 1960, Harry was called to see the owner of the house next door. He had often prayed about 27 Elvetham Road. The owner came straight to the point.

'Would you like it?' he asked. Harry also came straight to the point.

'How much?' he questioned.

'One thousand, eight hundred pounds furnished,' came the reply, 'with several years to go on the lease.'

'How long do we have to decide?'

'Till the end of the month,' he said.

'Oh well,' thought Harry, 'At least we have an extra day for leap year!'

At that point the College treasurer, who had had just about enough of the houses and their financial problems, solemnly declared, 'Mr. Bonsall, the day you talk about another house is the day I cease to be a trustee of this College.'

In doleful mood the Council met that February, when the news of the offer was given by the Principal! Rev. Ronald Evans (later Principal of Belfast Bible College) suggested, 'We've asked God for accommodation and here it is. A fine big house, fully furnished, with 25 rooms and hardly sixpence to spare. Let's get on our knees and pray.' So they did.

Sure enough, next morning a letter arrived by first-class post. It was to be the start of a chain of letters, in which Professor E. K. Simpson (an authority on Hellenistic Greek) gave £1,800 for the house and BBI became proud owners of No. 27! At last the College had a dining room, with facilities for up to 100 staff and students. Needless to say, the treasurer did *not* resign! ... So it went on. God added house after house and each was connected with a miracle. At various stages Harry and the Council together owned up to 26 houses – mostly on lease, for varying periods, to Calthorpe Estate.

26

ON THE FUNNY SIDE

While the continuing saga of faith and houses carried on, lectures were in full swing. Students listened intently to Harry as he shared the truths of the Bible with energy and conviction. Doctrines came alive, enhanced by colourful illustrations and anecdotes. Sometimes, Harry would get so caught up in what he was doing that the unexpected would occur. One night, he was lecturing with a will, as he remembered the first time he had discovered these same lessons back on Ward E in Vancouver Hospital. He scribbled on the blackboard as he spoke, his mind so full of the lesson that his hand and talk couldn't keep up with his brain. He just kept on going ... over the edge of the blackboard and continuing on the wall until he fell off the platform!

One day, Harry had arranged to give the students a lecture on youth work. It was the 1960s and Teddy Boys were 'in'. The students decided then and there to dress up as a gang ... drainpipe jeans, luminous socks, winkle-picker shoes, long dangly ear-rings, make-up thickly piled on, and cigarettes hanging out! Unsuspecting, Harry walked into to start the lecture, took one look, and nearly lost control. He just managed to compose himself in time to say:

'And there *you* go ... but for the grace of God!'

On another occasion, some of the first years started putting fictitious names on the lecture register ... names like Polycarp of Smyrna, Sidlow Baxter and others. Someone put Charles Wesley on the register, but didn't initial it for some weeks. Shortly afterwards, Harry was hot on the trail of any slackers. Looking out over his students, with no hesitation at all, he asked, 'Is Charles Wesley here this morning? If he isn't here, he will *not* get his diploma!'

Heating in the lecture hall was always a struggle and there was a pot-bellied, coke-burning stove at the end of the lecture room immediately in front of the blackboard. One morning, 'H.B.B.' almost burst into flames in a Systematic Theology lecture! He was standing with his back to it whilst lecturing – dictating notes to the student body with his usual pre-occupied enthusiasm, each time passing close to the pot-bellied stove. All heads were studiously bent, feverishly taking notes, when one lad, seeing smoke, raised his hand. Harry kept saying, 'In a minute,' as this student was rather keen on raising a hand in lectures. 'But, please sir, you're on fire!' Another quick-witted student sprang up, peeled off the burning gown from a startled and seemingly oblivious lecturer, doused it with water and stamped out the flames. Harry, now fully aware of the problem, mumbled, 'Had the gown for forty years,' turned back to the blackboard, and wrote down the next heading. The interruption took all of twenty seconds. The student body was in hysterics!

It was becoming clear that Harry was developing his own unique characteristics, if not eccentricities at times. He had always been aware that his was a 'different' kind of personality. On the one hand, he was totally consistent – on the other, one never quite knew what would happen next. He was well aware that he had strengths and also weaknesses, and that in some ways they were linked. In 1939, Henry Simpson-Curr ('Prinny') had written a reference for him:

'Mr. Bonsall is one of the most methodical and painstaking men I have ever met. Nothing is too much trouble for him. He is both helped and handicapped by his temperament, which is unusually highly strung. This makes it needful for him to exercise a certain amount of care with regard to his health. These conditions compensate themselves by his enthusiasm and energy, his strength of will and purpose.

His indefatigable industry, undoubted ability and above

all his deep piety, have made a permanent and profound impression on all the students with whom he has come into contact and endeared him to the governing body, his colleagues and myself. As a man of God he stands pre-eminent.'

All Harry knew was that he had submitted his life and his will to the Lord's work. Now he simply wanted to pass on that message to the students under his leadership. Realising that training in many disciplines was necessary, based on submission of the will to God, Harry installed courses for all sorts of subjects: academic, manual (carpentry and gardening) and character-building activities. In one course, elocution was an important component, with a Guildhall examiner coming in to test the students. They had three passages to read, one from the Bible, one from Shakespeare and a poem. On one occasion the poem was a rendering of Tennyson's 'The Charge of the Light Brigade'. In the lecture hall of No. 6 Pakenham Road one morning, a student was throwing himself into 'the valley of Death with the six hundred', when there were noises heard from the hallway. Just as the lines ...

> Cannon to right of them,
> Cannon to left of them....
> Into the mouth of Hell
> Rode the six hundred....

were reached, a shrill bugle call was heard, followed by a rapid report of fire crackers making the most tremendous noise. Did the senior student know the source of this disturbance, the students asked themselves – the sound effects rigged up in the cellar and the smell of smoke in the hall? Vice-Principal David Smith and his wife upstairs thought the end had come! As the students sat in stunned silence, however, Harry burst into uncontrollable laughter till the tears flowed down his cheeks. So the students had a glimpse of their usually disciplined Principal, hair dishevelled more than usual, gown hanging off his shoulders more than usual, laughing hysterically into his handkerchief.

27

FROM THE OUTSIDE LOOKING IN

It was a fresh March day in Edgbaston and 8 Pakenham Road was empty for once, as the whole Bonsall family had gone off for a week's holiday to the farm where most of Dosie's family still lived. In the Principal's study, books were piled up in a way which made finding one particular volume almost impossible for anyone except Harry, who knew where to locate any requested item on demand. Sheets of paper were spread over the desk, most typed, some handwritten. A Bible lay open on the left-hand side of the bureau. If one looked closely enough, one could see that the book was Philippians and that four words were underlined – '*The Lord is near*'. Close by, lying over the loose papers was a local newspaper folded over to reveal one article. Moving closer, a small picture of a man becomes visible. It is Harry. The article, written by an enthusiastic reporter, Michael Fleming, gives an outsider's view of the BBI and its founder:

'The Rev. H. Brash Bonsall, MA BD, or just "Harry" to his friends, is ... well, rather in a class of his own! ... He rides his responsibilities and taxing position as Principal of the Birmingham Bible Institute with cool ease. Always busy, never too busy. Darting about with the fearless freedom of a moth on night shift, Brash Bonsall is the right kind of man to have around ... In all he does, he has the support of a wife with long experience in Christian-work and they both go hard at two things ... praying and working. In that order ...

'A man of spiritual muscle, he adapts himself almost unconsciously to his students' wavelengths and there is no 'unctuous pie' about him ... Nothing is conventional about Mr. Bonsall! A mine of energy, this man. And vision. Not a man for merry little pipe-dreams. Ask him why he started a Bible College in Birmingham and he replies, "It's the country's second largest city and it didn't have one. I felt God's call." So simple. As for the intricate difficulties – well, faith laughs at them ...

'The notice simply states "Birmingham Bible Institute". The neat gravel paths cutting through tree-girt gardens to the stark Victorian buildings, are in tone with wealthy Edgbaston, one of the city's more serene and stately suburbs... As you listen to the throated trillings of the birds fluttering about on the overhanging branches and hear the cheerful cries of children playing in a nearby day-nursery, it is hard to believe you are within 20 walking minutes of the traffic-choked centre of Britain's second city. It's so quiet, so sedate. Yet it's a miracle ...

'The students are among Britain's most exciting young people. The antithesis of slap-dash superficiality, they strike one as men and women of spiritual muscle. Some have emerged from hard, broken backgrounds. Many have remarkable testimonies. Most, but not all, are between 20 to 30 years of age. One was a farmer, another an assistant buyer, a third a telephone engineer, someone else an audit clerk and others nurses ... The full-time staff – a panel of qualified lecturers – are all men and women in their prime, with 14 or more years of ministry or missionary experience ...

'The College's first aim is to develop character and spiritual fitness: then a sound theological and missionary education and thirdly, to promote efficiency in service. Here in Britain's second city, there is plenty of opportunity to test out a man's call by his ability to produce results. A great and needy mission field is on every hand and 10 large hospitals within 30 minutes walk, so teams of young people regularly visit the sick, while others reach out to children in congested areas. Students are expected to undertake missionary efforts in slums, services in local churches, visit the sick, conduct open-air meetings and take evangelistic campaigns. The Principal himself led from the front in the Greater Birmingham Crusade, when his support and loyalty to this great effort was unswerving. The College motto is: "*More than conquerors through Him.*" It helps when your Principal so obviously embodies it!

'On the social side, the College maintains that "religious teaching, divorced from experience and practical ethics, is an anomaly". The students give one afternoon a week completely to chores!

'Character training is stressed, because it is believed that nine-tenths of troubles on the mission field occur through character defects. Students are expected to learn "by experience" in the daily routine of College life ... the power of fidelity, courage, initiative, resource, unselfishness, fellowship and co-operation – liberated and controlled by the dynamic of prayer ... Side by side with careful business planning, BBI is deeply conscious of the necessity for dependance upon God for its many needs. Time and again, God has stepped in during emergencies and proved His faithfulness.

'Increasingly, the College is being recognised as one that produces workers of character as well as ability ... in two "streams" – those for the ministry and those for the mission field. The latter class spend 20% of their time learning non-theological subjects. They attend a motor mechanics course at Oldbury College of Further Education, to learn casting, welding, and building. They have 60 lectures in medicine, including anatomy, physiology, nursing, First Aid and tropical hygiene, in addition to 30 lessons in shorthand and typing, with 40 in book-keeping and cookery, as well as printing!

158

'It is a happy place. Warm, without being sugary. The students have, in common with their breed, that same love of banter, and uproarious disagreement on minor and major matters! Many are groping for intellectual freedom and honesty – and they are helped to do so – but they have more than a vivacious "joie de vivre". For behind the laughing eyes and casual approaches, are young people with an iron determination to go through with God ... to turn their backs on the suffocating comfort and smug humbug in a stupefied Britain, and serve the Lord in overseas bases, where they can expect nothing but hardship and suffering, with possible death. They are among the country's finest products. They mean business. Big business. For God.'

28

'A PEEP BEHIND THE SCENES'

People were a 'way of life' to Harry and Dosie. Both knew how to get alongside people and communicate. Harry had worked with many ordinary folks in Canada and knew just how they ticked. He was a classless man ... always talking to people in trains or in buses or on the beach ... wherever he happened to be. This was born out of experience, and because of his interest in so many fields – becoming a bit of an expert in some – he was able to get alongside them and talk in a language they understood. Dosie was the same. People either came to her, or she went to them ... out in the one-time slums of Birmingham, hospital visiting, or in the market.

Apart from invited guests, there were many others dropping in at all times of the day and night, unexpectedly. Many in desperate need – and the Bonsalls were not ones to turn people away. Some dropped in – and ended up staying for years – adopted into the family! Certainly, no-one came by accident. Pat Reynolds was one such person.

'Consider yourself ... one of the family'
It was 1960. The Bonsalls were on holiday in Ireland, when a letter arrived from Dosie's capable assistant, who was holding the fort in the BBI kitchen:

> 'Please find someone to cook if you can. Life in the kitchen bores me to tears!'

So Dosie took the letter and asked God for an answer. 'Please Lord, send someone who likes cooking!'

Pat Ellis (later, Reynolds) had come to Birmingham to visit her mother, who was very ill. Needing accommodation, she saw a policeman on the corner at Five Ways. Walking up to him, she asked, 'Excuse me, do you know of any residential college in the area.'

'Funnily enough, I do,' he said. 'There's a Christian place quite near,' and he directed her straight to BBI at Elvetham Road. Pat knocked on the door nervously, not sure what to expect – and there was Dosie.

'Uh ... hello ...,' said Pat, not sure how to start. 'I was just wondering if you might need any help with anything.'

'My dear,' said Dosie, whisking her through the door, 'I *knew* you'd come. I was praying for you this very morning. Come on in.'

At that point, the study door opened and a man came out. Pat looked up at him and thought, 'He has the kindest eyes I've ever seen.' It was Harry.

'I don't know where you've come from,' he said, 'but God has sent you here today. Welcome to our household. There's a room upstairs and there's no need to worry about anything!' That was it. Pat was there to stay. She became a member of the family and her daughter, Chris, grew up with the Bonsall children. They shared everything, and when Chris was married in Edgbaston, Harry acted as her father and gave her away ... a very proud moment for him!

Pat and Dosie made a great team. These early days in the Catering Department were quite a revelation for the newcomer! On a Saturday morning, they would go down on their bicycles to the market. Dosie seemed to remind many people of Barbara Woodhouse, the extraordinary trainer of dogs who became a household name. As soon as she appeared in the huge Market Hall, there'd be cries of 'Walkies! Walkies!' She loved it. Having made friends with so many of the vendors, Dosie was the recipient of excellent bargains and cut-down prices. Her bicycle would be constantly laden with bags from the front to the back (with anything up to 40 lbs of groceries)... onions hanging over

161

the handlebars and a little chicken's head peeping out of a bag. Pat's bike wasn't as strong as hers and she would say, 'I don't think I'm going to make it!'

'Come along, Pat, *keep going! We'll make it*!' Dosie would cry ... and off they'd go, with passing motorists giving them the 'thumbs up' sign! At the time, Pat felt very embarrassed, wondering, 'What *do* people think I am, with all these bags?' and there they were, absolutely spent, with their feet going furiously and Dosie's face straight set for home. Every now and then she'd give Pat a 'thumbs up' too, which just meant '*Keep going*!'

Back at No. 28 hungry students waited. Lunch. Grace, sung or said. And the meals would come out of the hatch. By the clock. One o'clock start. One thirty finish. Perhaps the greatest miracle of all was that over the years with Pat, not once was the food late coming out of the hatch. It was a miracle that the kitchen and its occupants didn't go up in smoke, as they so often returned from their pedalling campaign to the market by 12.15 on a Saturday morning, to cook fish and chips for a multitude. They had about eight frying pans on the old stove ... Dosie putting in the batter ... Pat whipping it out and on to the plate. Fast-food had never been so fast. Sometimes Pat would think, 'Pat, what *planet* are you on?' because really, if she stopped to think about it, this lifestyle just *didn't* make sense! Many a time they would be rushing off to church on a Sunday morning and Pat would say to Dosie, 'Mrs. Bonsall, we're going to be late.'

'No, my dear Pat, we *won't* be late,' and she'd put her foot down on that Middle Way.

'For goodness sake,' Pat would say, 'We're passing the police station. We'll be arrested,' and *her* response would be, '*Praise the Lord, Pat*!'

When Pat's own mother died, Dosie said to her, 'Pat, I'll be a mother to you,' and that's what she became, never failing to encourage. 'Keep going! Don't give up! Don't look back!' 'Don't worry, Pat ... Whatever the crisis ... Let's just trust the Lord, it'll be alright ...' and Pat was amazed to see that it always was!

Shortly after Pat's arrival came Maureen Carswell (later, Moor). She was desperate. 'God, if you're there, prove yourself!' she cried. As an orphan who felt rejected, it was a stab in the dark, but a sincere and desperate prayer. Within 24 hours she was on the steps of BBI. She rang the doorbell, and Dosie was there to welcome her in. For nearly three years she was like one of the Bonsall family – and she never felt an outsider.

There was much laughter and a few tears during that time. In the summer, they would sit in the garden shelling peas or bottling fruit, with the wasps flying round getting lost in the juice ... and in the winter they would sit round the fire talking about the Lord – toasting muffins. Then the doorbell would ring and there would be a vagrant, or some poor destitute person and Dosie would bring them in and give them hot soup and a sandwich *and* the gospel!

All in all, there were five regular 'tramps' who felt at home and dropped in on the Bonsall house regularly ... three of them by the name of Charlie! One was in and out of prison. Another Charlie was a bit of a comic – in fact an expert at making animal shadows on the wall with his hands and mimicking farmyard noises! But apart from these interludes there was a constant stream of rather colourful and often unorthodox helpers in the overflowing kitchen.

Like her 'Market Ministry,' with its far-reaching distribution of fruit and vegetables to friends and neighbours, Dosie saw '*The '10p's Ministry*' as a special service to all and sundry in need. It was just like Oxfam. Literally hundreds of bulging black bin bags were to come in over the years, donated by churches, youth groups and friends – packed with multitudinous clothes and items of all varieties and descriptions, washed and packed and handed in to the fold at No.8. Every so often, there would be a huge sale, with every item priced at 10p – to go towards BBI expenses. Coats and dresses would be lined up on hangers. Shoes of all sizes arranged in a row ... The problem was ... this was a spreading ministry. It was all too easy for the ministry to take over the dining room and the kitchen table ... and extend even further! For Dosie, it was just one of many ways to serve, so inconvenience never came into it.

Friends from far or near always knew there would be a warm welcome at BBI, and visitors would be treated to a large mug of tea every morning by Harry. A helping hand was also available if it was ever needed. Pastor John Morrison was an ex-boxer who had driven down from Glasgow to Birmingham with a youth team in his van. But the van had grave internal problems. It was 30 m.p.h. all the way ... stopping every few miles, as it chugged to a halt when a pipe clogged up and had to be 'sucked out' before they took off for the next phase of the journey.

When the van eventually arrived in Birmingham, John made an expedition into town with Harry. But the van refused to budge. They had to get out and shove 17 times! The next day Dosie joined them on the way to town, and *this* time they had to get out 10 times. The following day they were due to return to Glasgow. John turned to Harry in desperation and said, 'Please pray!' At which Harry turned round, laid both hands on the van in true Biblical fashion and prayed, 'Lord, please give this car a boost! It needs *more* than a miracle. Help it to reach Glasgow safely. Amen.'

John had never seen anything like it. He didn't know what to expect on the journey, but he need not have worried. The van raced up the motorway – at 70 m.p.h. It kept on going until it reached his house, where it promptly came to a grinding halt and wouldn't budge. From this point on, it was a 'write-off', with the engine all seized up, over-charged and overheated! But Harry's prayer was answered and the van was probably better off the road!

The family continued to grow in different directions as 'Ma and Pa' were adopted in one way or another. Extra Mothers' and

Fathers' Day cards would appear. Phone calls on Christmas Day, some from far afield ....students from Singapore, a family from Portugal, a doctor and his wife from Brazil. Others from Nagaland and Japan. Harry and Dosie knew what it was to be lonely and homesick.

For the children, life was highly entertaining and by and large they took each person as they came ... enjoying the students and lodgers that lived with them like family and all the thrilling stories that came with their wonderful visitors. The down side was that there was hardly any privacy or predictability in their house from one moment to the next, and they all strongly objected to the white 'Opalware' unbreakable college crockery which was their lot, not to mention the constant chips and breakages to the only decent set of 'Indian Tree' china! Charles once did an 'Opalware demonstration' on the lovely mosaic hall floor for a visiting guest who had just returned from a Japanese prisoner of war camp. Needless to say, the 'unbreakable' broke into myriad pieces with a loud smash. The children enjoyed that more than their guest, who had a headache at the time!

Nevertheless, breaks were a 'vital norm' for the four Bonsall children in the midst of the constant stream of visitors to BBI, and they would eagerly anticipate visits to Dosie's family on 'The Farm'. Train journeys in the old steam trains were always exciting, apart from the children's embarrassment at Harry running up and down the platform at each station, homburg-hatted, black coat flying, checking on their old wicker trunk in the luggage van! While Dosie's parents were still alive, the family spent every holiday, three times a year, down at the farm with grandparents, aunts, uncles and cousins, living off the fat of the land – riding horses whenever possible and getting into all kinds of mischief.

Harry insisted that if Ruth were to be allowed on the roads alone, she must cycle at least 100 miles on the road with him! So, Harry and Ruth set out on a series of wonderful excursions together (usually 10 to 12 miles at a time) along the canals and waterways of Bedfordshire ... armed with rucksacks and picnics. Conversations were always inspiring. This was Harry's recreation, as much of the rest of the time he'd be working at the farm, pounding away on his typewriter upstairs, surrounded by piles of books and papers for the following term. For the kids, they were magical days, given the full range of the farm with their three cousins, Michael, Penny and James, under the ever-watchful eye of the adults. In more refined moments, they had great fun entertaining their much-loved grandparents to lively concerts in the drawing room, after hours of rehearsal in the 'School Room' upstairs. Once they even managed an Operetta composed by Charles.

The secretariat!

When the time came to return, disappointment at leaving mingled with curiosity as to what the next few weeks at BBI would hold. One never quite knew what was coming next!

Having said this, one also knew that College matters were in safe hands while the Bonsalls were away. Daily early morning phone calls and a constant flow of letters from a succession of excellent secretaries meant that one was always kept up to date with the latest 'crisis' or development.

Harry was blessed with a loyal team of outstanding secretaries who worked with commendable 'cool' amidst his often hectic and overflowing office. Several of his team had first been students at BBI, who understood the way he operated – and he never underestimated their importance.

'Your personal secretary is a most important person,' he wrote, 'and the nerve-centre of every work. Secretaries miss nothing and forget nothing, so the simplest answer is to have one you can absolutely trust and no-one else. Put her on her honour, and she will never let you down!'

29

NOTTINGHAM BIBLE INSTITUTE ...
Branching Out

By the early 1960s, Harry was a regular preacher at different conventions and conferences, when the course of his ministry took him to Nottingham – one-time home of the legendary Robin Hood.

At this time, evangelist Dr. Eric Hutchings was leading a Christian Challenge Crusade at the Nottingham Ice Stadium, backed by a keen group of ministers and Christian businessmen.

It was a huge venture and, at first, the Crusade had ground to a halt. No-one wanted to take on the responsibility of being treasurer in case of financial embarrassment! When Scottish businessman, Jim Stevenson-Berry, heard the news that he was hot favourite for the job, he laughed over the phone. But later on, discovering that without him the Crusade would not take place at all, he changed his tune, in spite of little experience in the field. Somehow, as Crusade treasurer, God taught him how to handle the books – and so successfully, that both Crusade and 'follow-up' steamed ahead, producing a fine new team, the 'Nottingham Evangelical Alliance'. This in turn became affiliated to the 'London Evangelical Alliance'.

Enter Harry! It was at the *October 1962* meeting of the NEA Committee, when Rev. Tom Jones announced, 'A series of October lectures is to be given by Henry Brash Bonsall, Principal of the Birmingham Bible Institute. All present are invited to attend.'

It didn't take long for Harry to gauge the potential there in

Nottingham. Gathering the NEA Committee and a company of interested Christians, he shared his vision of *Bible Institutes ... to prepare for the revival to come* and announced, 'I am convinced that Nottingham should have a Bible Institute.'

The response was heart-warming. Ministers, businessmen and qualified lecturers picked up the vision for Nottingham and Jim Berry was chosen to select the lecturing team.

An executive council of 12 was formed (at least nine of whom were ministers) under Harry as Director of Studies, with a treasurer, and Jim Berry as chairman. Under his directorship, this inter-denominational Institute grew and diversified, running courses four evenings a week (usually from 6-9 pm.) and at different venues. There were more academic courses, held in a local school and College of Further Education for those who wanted qualifications (to prepare for the London University CRK and Dip.Theol.), but also devotional and general non-examination courses for the public, held at St. Nicholas Church Hall, Maid Marion Way. It was a challenging study course for Christians, covering every book in the Bible and more general topics, during 60 Friday evenings over two years (in three academic sessions – Autumn, Spring and Summer).

General Bible knowledge was the main aim, clearly expressed in their motto:

'Know your Bible: Live by it's Teaching'

Fees were minimal, with no charge at all for public meetings on Tuesdays and all expenses supplied from gifts and free-will offerings!

Lecturers and speakers came from all walks of life and were a wonderful cross-section of highly qualified men of God. There were church leaders, missionary statesmen, a comprehensive school headmaster, an engineer, an architect, an ex-communist, two former College Principals, and many more....

Forging the links

It was an exciting time. The Nottingham 'track' would link in to BBI for many years to come, with several lecturers and students taking part in both College programmes. They would often start at Nottingham before moving on to BBI. Harry valued the importance of BBI's staff, students and Council, and often used to say that members of each group would, at times, cross over to minister in another group.

Harry's investment in the Nottingham Bible Institute paid off. Several N.B.I. students went on to become full-time students at BBI ... and one qualified accountant, John Fee, came back to the Nottingham Bible Institute as treasurer and chairman some years later, with a BBI-based degree!

How did it all begin? Apparently, just after becoming a Christian in April of 1963, John attended a rally in Nottingham. It didn't take long to catch the vision. Harry was one of the two main speakers ... and what he said attracted John to attend the Nottingham Bible Institute from October 1963 onwards.

Eventually the whole family moved to BBI with John's wife, Evelyn and two small children, where they both took college courses. When they finally returned to Nottingham, John had acquired a BD and was able to give his old college invaluable help on the staff as treasurer, lecturer and chairman. After eight years as pastor of his own church, with 14 years of accountancy experience behind him, John went on to become treasurer to the Assemblies of God in Great Britain and Ireland Incorporated (based at Nottingham since May 1994). Later, their son, David came back to BBI as a student, where he met and married a Dutch student, Inneka. So one link leads on to another in God's plan ... and history moves on!

The story of the Nottingham Bible Institute would span a period of twenty years, from January 8th 1963 to December 2nd 1983, with many hundreds of lectures and many runners on the track. Jim Berry gave faithful service to the Institute for sixteen years alongside the team and at the same time came on to the BBI Council in 1962 as a strong and vibrant long-standing member. However, after the founding of NBI, a time was coming when Harry's leadership would be challenged yet again. It was hardly surprising in his strategic line of ministry. It had happened before....

30

IN THE LINE OF FIRE!

At the best of times, BBI was a 'spiritual hothouse'. Spiritual warfare was never far away. So it was, that in the mid-'60s, the Principal suffered a head-on attack from within. For Harry to be as open and 'all-embracing' as he was, also meant that he was extremely vulnerable and exposed to a wide cross-section of people, many with their own deep needs and problems.

In *this* case, one leading colleague felt that he was better qualified for Harry's role himself and eventually left, taking three other colleagues with him, along with a substantial number of BBI students. He set up a similar Bible College in the Midlands close by! It was amazing to see faces and attitudes change. Painful memories of All Nations resurfaced. Those involved with the new college found that their new venture did not run as smoothly as they might have hoped. Within a few years, it was to close.

Like Harry's previous experience in Taplow, it was a hurtful body-blow, but he and Dosie learned much of the faithfulness of God and the wonderful loyalty of praying friends during those months of severe trial. They spent hours and sometimes days in prayer alone with God ... hanging on, keeping their own counsel and saying little. To Dosie, the same verse from Ecclesiastes 5:2 was a guiding factor once more, as it had been in 1952.

'God is in heaven and thou upon earth, therefore let thy words be few.'

A letter was sent to Harry, written by one of the students:

171

'Just to let you know that we are praying much for you at this time. We sense that you are carrying a great burden of sorrow and heaviness and we just want you to know that we are concerned for you and your situation. Although we don't know the details of your burden, we hope we can lighten the load by praying for you. We realise that we are only young, rather pathetic students ... so young and weak in the faith and our prayers inadequate and feeble, so that we can't take the place of all the old prayer warriors that have so recently gone home before us, but I am sure God will listen to the cries of His awkward little babies in the nursery of faith. Please be assured that we love and respect you very much and we feel very grateful to God for what He has taught us through your lectures and your life.'

Loyalty, for both Harry and Dosie, was a priority and out of that trauma came a wonderful loyal band of staff and students with the blessing of the Lord upon them. Harry never talked of this afterwards. It was put behind him.

Later, when the crisis had passed, the Vice-Principal, David Smith, wrote:

'In the face of adverse criticism, Mr. Bonsall kept quiet and committed the matter to the Lord.... We saw H.B.B. at his finest – not answering back, but trusting the Lord to bring him and the College through the storm.'

Harry and Dosie wrote to thank their friends not long after this traumatic experience:

'Prayer to us is like a supporting naval barrage, without which we could not advance, much less board the enemy ships. We have been so conscious of your help to us as prayer warriors, with broad-side after broad-side of prayer going up for us, silencing the enemy guns, covering us as we went into battle, breaking down all alien opposition and heartening us by divine help.'

Harry and Dosie began to realise more than ever the significance of praying friends and the support they so much needed. One particular letter meant a great deal.

'Dosie,' said Harry. 'Look at this wonderful letter we've just been sent.'

'You read it to me.'

Harry adjusted his reading glasses on the end of his nose, and began:

'Dear Mr. Bonsall,
Some time ago the Lord wished me to write a letter of thankfulness on behalf of every student who has passed through BBI, but I delayed to write at that time. Please forgive me.

We do appreciate all that has been done for us. Some of us have come out of lives of sin into the love of Christ, without much education, often without a great deal of money. Yet you have taken us in because of the call of God upon our lives. We have received training in the lectures, also through the Spirit of God. The training has included chores, which have been of great benefit in training our thoughts to do the job and not to look to others.

Having God's call upon your own lives in obedience to Him, you opened this College and have given everything in answer to that call. To your delight you have seen students shaped, fitted out and sent forth to serve the Master in different spheres and capacity, seeing them rise to the top in the place where God has called them ... and their works do follow them.

Who am I? I am every single girl student – every single boy student – every married student – every child that has

173

come to BBI and every child born here.

We are, dear Sir, the family of BBI. The College name has given us entrance into churches and homes all over the world, because of you and your wife's delight in obeying the will of the Father.

Please receive all our heartfelt thanks and appreciation for having given us the chance to be trained, then sent out to serve our Lord Jesus Christ.

May God bless, prosper and strengthen you for each day's task.

Signed,
Every Student.'

31

TO PRAYER!

'He lives in the heartland of prayer'

Thus said Andrew MacBeath, the saintly Principal of the Bible Training Institute in Glasgow, when describing Harry to one prospective BBI student.

With his amazing memory for names and details and numerous prayer diaries, or inner circle letters to praying friends, Harry knew what his priorities were. For him, *'To prayer*!' was like a charge to war. Finishing one such letter, Harry wrote:

'Well, this has been a long letter has it not? Yet no matter how far apart we may be, remember, we can always meet at the throne. I have not changed one iota. Do let me know all you can, so that I can pray for you intelligently. As I know, so I pray. I go over each name systematically, never leaving it until I know I have "prayed through" for it, according to the light I have. However impossible the need, write to me. I shall count it God's gift to me to "pray through" for you. I shall confidently expect to see the same mighty hand moving in your life, that is now working in mine. *Don't count me too busy. I always have time for prayer.*'

Many times one could peer out of the back windows of No. 28 to find Harry down at the bottom of the garden – going back and forth, back and forth, praying ... sometimes with head bowed, intent ... sometimes with arms pounding, as if making his point and request to God.

As certain students were leaving at the end of the College year, the Principal's prayers would become more direct and specific, and ears would prick up. He would start off, praying for one particular student (perhaps, after that student's farewell sermon in Chapel prayers). Then he'd go on to pray in great detail. He'd start to pray for their wife or husband whether they had one or not (i.e., present or future!), and often one would feel he was moving into the prophetic realm. So they all looked forward to that particular prayer, just in case they found out anything new about their future life!

One sunny Thursday in the summer of 1964, a student, Geoff Birch, discovered the Principal on some steps painting a picture rail. 'I have some good news, Brash,' he exclaimed. 'Marilyn is expecting our first baby.' Harry, standing halfway up the ladder, stopped painting – with the paintbrush in one hand and paint-pot in the other – and cried out, 'Praise the Lord, brother. Let's pray!' He prayed, as he always did, specifically and eloquently, tracing the child's life from birth to demise – for health and safety, for conversion and, in particular, a perfect marriage partner for the unborn infant! The couple closed their eyes, but as the prayer went on, for some unknown reason Geoff opened his. There was Harry praying fervently, still on the ladder, holding paint and brush, but swaying backwards and forwards. The more fervently he prayed, the more he swayed! Quickly Geoff clasped the steps with one hand and held the other at the ready an inch or two from the Principal's back. At length, Harry happily opened his eyes, smiled ... and continued painting, oblivious to his close shave with disaster. Nearly 30 years later, Geoff would thank God that all Harry's prayers for their son had been been answered.

The Case of the Overhanging Cable.

On one particular occasion Norman Gidney, one of Harry's good friends and financial advisers, was going to an appointment in New Street, Birmingham. As it was raining, he locked his car and

Canada (1913 - 1935)

top: Farewell to England. The Bonsall Trio (Gertie and 'Sonnie Boy' aged 8, with Henry).
centre: Graduation day (aged 20). University of British Columbia (Arts '26).
bottom left: The young carpenter (Vancouver).
bottom right: A sermon in the making. Harry at 24.

All Nations Bible College (mid 1940's - early 1950's)

Harry lectures to young recruits - after the war.

Dressed for the Queen.
(Lady Astor's Garden Party - just down the road at Clivedon.)

All Nations Bible College, Taplow, Berkshire.

She's The One

top left: 'She's the one.'
top right: Harry (Principal of ANBC 1948 - 1952.
bottom: The Bonsall Family (Rachel, Charles, Ruth, Tom - from left) Birmingham.

Birmingham Bible Institute (Founded 1953)

top: Early days at Birmingham Bible Institute.
inset: *'How can a young man keep himself pure?*
  By living according to your word.' Psalm 119:9
bottom: Near the end of the race, but still running.... Faith laughs at the impossible!

made a dash for the building across the road. In his haste, he bumped into a man who was walking briskly in the pouring rain, wearing a grey overcoat and a black homburg hat. Norman immediately apologised – at which point the two men recognised each other.

'Brash, how lovely to see you,' he said. Harry, the taller of the two, put his arm around Norman's shoulders and promptly said, 'Let's have a brief word of prayer.'

Norman was understandably a little *embarrassed* standing in the middle of New Street in Birmingham in the pouring rain, with Harry's arm around his shoulders, about to be prayed for! But as Norman loved him and had such tremendous respect for him, there was no way he could resist his request, so Harry began to pray. At which point Harry, being slightly taller, bent his head forward and the water that had accumulated in the upturned brim of his black homburg poured down Norman's neck – an experience of water baptism which he took without a murmur, though still embarrassed about what was taking place!

Harry's prayer was very short and ended with the phrase '... *and Lord, will you please protect Norman from high voltage cables. Amen.*' The two men gave each other a hug and Norman ran into the building, extremely uncomfortable and very wet!

When he went home that night, Norman relayed the story to his wife. She was highly amused. 'Brash is finally losing his marbles,' said Norman. 'He prayed that I should be protected from high voltage cables!' However, the following Saturday morning a Sunday School party came to spend the day at Norman's farm in Warwickshire. In order to get their bus through the gates of the farm courtyard, Norman had to take a broom and climb on to an iron gate to lift a sagging telephone cable. That cable ran right across the gate, so he lifted it up with the broom for the coach to come in. He was wearing a large straw hat, which he hardly ever wore, when something knocked the hat off his head as he stood there on the iron gate. Norman looked up with horror and went cold with the recollection of Harry's prayer, as it was a high voltage cable that had knocked off his hat. Wearing that hat had saved his life, as the iron gate on which he was standing would have been a most powerful earthing of a very high current. It took Norman a long time to get over the shock and miracle of the experience.

On another occasion, Harry was praying earnestly for one of his students out in Africa, as missionaries were being expelled from that particular country at the time. (His method was to take one student each morning, keeping a record of the date and name, and to focus in prayer on whoever it might be). Some time later, this student came to see Harry and Dosie. She told an amazing story. 'I was about to be shot. Guns were lined up, when all at once, for no apparent reason, my attackers dropped their guns and fled.' It was with great excitement that they discovered that the date and time of her escape coincided *exactly* with Harry's personal prayer time for her!

Harry seemed to be able to find a prayer appropriate for every occasion. He looked back once again to what had seemed the lowest point of his life – those three years of immobilisation in Vancouver – as the training ground for his prayer life. Now, in the heat of his ministry, no-one quite knew when or how a prayer would be delivered. A student might be walking down Pakenham Road towards No. 6 for a lecture, completely lost in thought about some essay or other they had to write, oblivious to all around, navigating by instinct, when all of a sudden he'd be there in front of them. Without a moment's hesitation, head bowed, he'd launch into some sort of mumbled blessing. It would all be over in a few seconds and he'd carry on his way, leaving the student standing there sort of 'prayer-shocked' for a moment or two, then they would recover and continue on their way. The amazing thing was, so often the Principal would hit the target and they would find themselves really 'blessed' ... some trouble suddenly lighter to bear, a problem starting to make sense, a sadness lifted.

One student, Peter Studd, had just come straight from the Royal Navy to BBI, so when Harry prayed for him and his fiancée, Mary, he started using various nautical terms! He began to pray that they would be 'guided by His light' as they 'set sail on this new voyage of life'. There may be 'storms and waves that could overcome them' but he prayed that they would 'stay on course' and not be 'overwhelmed by the events around them'. Halfway through this particular prayer, the phone started to ring. 'Hold on, Lord, just one moment,' said Harry, as he went to answer it. When he came back, he started to pray again as if nothing had happened.

Other examples of the power of prayer were numerous. At one time, Harry was taking a teaching mission in farming country in the north of England. A farmer's cow was very sick and Harry offered to pray for it. To the vet's astonishment, the cow recovered. Some time later, another farmer had a sick cow and it couldn't stand. He remembered Mr. Bonsall praying for that cow and decided to lay hands on *his* cow and pray. So he did ... and the cow got up in the best of health!

Another time, H.B.B. was conducting an interview for a prospective student. Her mother had accompanied her and was invited in for coffee. Somehow she never left the room. The interviewing committee began to question the student, but in the process, a question was addressed directly to the mother as to her spiritual standing. She was at a loss to answer, and Harry – never one to lose an opportunity – spent the next hour counselling her and eventually leading her to the Lord. The student's own interview was totally forgotten and she was asked to return the following week!

It was into this rather extraordinary atmosphere that Rev. Bob Dunnett and his wife Di came to join the staff of the BBI family – Bob, an Anglican minister, was a great man for prayer who, like Harry, was keenly committed to preparing for revival.

32

'HE'S MY BROTHER!'

Support and encouragement from students and staff mirrored a larger network of Christian leaders in challenging positions, who wrote and prayed for each other. As running partners on the same track, they knew what front-line battles were all about! Over the years, wonderful people visited the College and No.8 Pakenham Road; like Corrie ten Boom, F. F. Bruce, Brother Andrew, Demos Shakarian, George Verwer, Roy Hession, David Watson, Duncan Campbell, Gladys Aylward, Norman Grubb, Jean Darnall, Floyd McClung, Edwin Orr, David du Plessis, Campbell McAlpine, Dennis Clark, Arthur Wallis, Mildred Cable, Willie Burton and many others. They just fitted in quite naturally with the rich, changing tapestry at BBI, in a network of mutual inspiration and accountability.

Friends came in a constant stream from a fascinating spectrum of nationalities and walks of life. Harry and Dosie seemed to strike up friendships wherever they went: not just with Christian leaders around the globe, but on the bus, in the street and in the market place ... In spite of their hectic lives, they were both marvellous letter-writers, so there was a constant flow of letters sharing prayer concerns, asking advice, giving encouragement ... all in the great family business of world-wide evangelism. There were letters to and from college principals, scholars, evangelists, teachers and preachers, missionary statesmen and women and dynamic revival pioneers. Bible colleges such as BBI would interlink with worldwide organisations such as Operation Mobilisation, WEC and Open Doors.

Norman Grubb, Harry's true friend from early war days, and WEC pioneer, was a constant source of encouragement:

'How I remember that little board meeting we had ... and your launch out in weakness and emptiness in the founding of the BBI. Somehow we instinctively knew to stand by you – and how right we were. We saw "the Spirit man" in you and stood square by you.... There we stood, having learned just one thing – to listen to God for His way and then obey in faith.

'"Fire attracts fire" and very soon the young men and women were beginning to flow in for training – not just training in theology, but also in the working of the Holy Spirit....

'So you see why I follow on with great joy and delight when your annual report comes in with your enlargements in the ministry ... and laugh and follow ... because you have that truly liberal spirit ... not suspicious or restricting, but drawing and welcoming ... and now ... Look! Look! See what has happened! WEC. (and CLC born out of WEC) have at least 2,000 full-timers in 50 fields!

'We obeyed like Caleb, and had a taste of "wholly following", sensing you as God's man. What lessons we have learned, and by God's grace we have both wholly followed!

'I love to hear of the continued interweaving of the college with WEC. It's an honour for us, knowing of your links with all evangelical missions, that you always have a WECer on your Council...'

Living for Christ!
Norman'

This was followed by a letter from *Len Moules*, missionary statesman and General Secretary of WEC:

'Harry, you are a WECer right to the core, and although you

may not be officially appointed with our ranks, your spirit marches with us in the fellowship of Studd and many of those who are permitted to enter into his vision and principles of world-wide evangelisation. God bless you, and thank God for the privilege of having your friendship and fellowship these days. Len'

Brother Andrew van der Byl, with his world-wide 'Open Doors' ministry, was a challenge to all the staff and students of BBI over many years ... and a great encourager to the Bonsall family.

'Dear Harry and Doris,
Hallelujah! Your recent letter and magazine is bristling with vision. I love it!
God loves it. And that is more important.
Yes, we continue to prepare for the Day of Revival – even if it comes after us – makes no difference. God's kingdom will come.
Yours in this great battle,
Brother Andrew.'

Dr. J. Edwin Orr, the Irish American evangelist and his wife Carol were friends of Harry and Dosie for over 50 years. His prodigious writing on revival (35 books in 44 years) and worldwide travels, made him one of the greatest authorities on the history of religious revival in the Protestant world. In fact, he wrote one book during six months in the Bonsall home and used their printing press for the job. It was a wonderful time of fun and fellowship for Harry and Dosie, inspired by their guests' child-like simplicity and faith in the reality of the miraculous. Letters came and went frequently.

One began:

'Dear Harry and Spice, You two never change!'

In another to Harry, he wrote:

'I am retired, but busier than ever! Last year I preached to 50,000 in Nagaland where churches have doubled to 200,000 membership in five years... This year I am equally busy ... and looking forward to a vacation! Edwin'

Harry knew that there was nothing like another man of God to keep him on his toes. *Godfrey Buxton* was an old family friend, closely involved with All Nations Bible College. His letters were always full of life.

'Dear Harry,
Many happy returns of the day. In your sixties ... you are getting near 'borrowed time' but I can assure you, the Lord will not let you pack up! How rich we have been to have had your prayers for 20 years ... I pray for a fresh anointing as your many students assemble. What a privilege you have to minister the Word of God to them! There is much on your plate for prayer and hard work; and even if there is extensive dry rot in the church, may there be none in your preaching!
    Yours with joy,
    Godfrey Buxton.'

Rev. Duncan Campbell, who also loved to visit the Bonsalls, was God's man in the Lewis revival of the mid-twentieth century (1949-53) and introduced a new spiritual dimension to Harry and Dosie and their young students. He spoke powerfully to them on the power of the supernatural over influence, reputation and academic qualifications. Harry would listen with rapt attention and mounting excitement, as Duncan Campbell shared inspiring stories of revival to staff and students alike.

William Booth-Clibborn (President, *S*alvation *O*verseas *S*ervice, Portland, Oregon).

'Dear Friend, Faithful Brash-Bonsall,

'This comes early to you so I get a reply by Christmas. You must be swamped with work, for I note how your marvellous efforts have grown and expanded.

'Learn to delegate authority and responsibility to others and spare and don't kill yourself with an overload. Have read much of the publications and papers you sent me – all good and inspiring! I am praying for you.

'With love and prayers for your success in Christ's Work,'

'William Booth-Clibborn'

Ken Adams (founder of the Christian Literature Crusade, and Harry's best man, wrote from CLC Inc., Pennsylvania, USA:

'Dear Brash,

'...The CLC work world-wide continues to expand. This month we are seeing two new stores added – in Brazil and Chile. As you see from "Viewpoint", we need some workers in Venezuela urgently. Maybe you have some who would qualify!... Well, the Lord has done great things with BBI and CLC since those early war days back in Colchester, hasn't He?... All praise is His!

'Our much love to Doris and yourself.

'As ever,

'Ken and Bessie''

George Verwer (Founder and Director of Operation Mobilization). In the early days of Operation Mobilisation, when some did not understand or support George's new and pioneering methods, Harry was behind him all the way, sending students to join the OM teams in different inhospitable parts of the world! George and Harry were in the same line of business ... and as such they constantly encouraged and prayed for each other over years....

Harry knew this was what 'brotherhood' was all about!
George wrote:

'Hello Brash....

Thanks for your love and faithfulness,

Yours for Revolution, Reality and Revival,

George.'

'I am sitting here thinking about you and also praying for you ... How I praise God for the example you have been ... the way you have persevered in running the race and for pressing on in such a vital and important ministry.

Looking forward to seeing you in the not too distant future,

Yours for the uttermost parts of the Earth.'

'We are launching one of the most important initiatives in the history of our work next summer, called "Love Europe" ...'

Harry:

'Dear George,

Thank you for your prayers at this time. Only God knows how much I need them....

I am continually bearing you up in prayer....'

George:

'Your example and perseverance is a great challenge to so many.

How can I pray for you more specifically?'

Harry:

'You have always been a great blessing to us, George, and I know you will continue to pray for us.'

George:

'We praise God for various people from BBI who are labouring with us and we long for that to continue in the years to come. The battle is intense but the Lord is with us in the midst of the battle. Keep on keeping on!

In His Grace and Grip,

George.'

Harry looked up, after reading his wife this latest letter from George Verwer. 'Dosie, *this* is what Christian teamwork is all about ... training, support, loyalty and encouragement ... sharing your vision with team mates on the running track ... holding on together and praying it through to the finish! Thank God for our friends and their love, prayers and support.'

33

MORE FAITH – MORE HOUSES

Student numbers were steadily rising over the years as more and more couples with children applied. The same question reared its head. Should they be turned away? A ceiling had to be put on the numbers somewhere. At a Council meeting it was emphasised. 'Married couples can only be accepted after all single students are assured of accommodation.' But what could be done for the married couples?

Backing on to the College headquarters at No. 6 were more houses along *Gough Road*. One, *No. 97* (in a very poor state, with not even a bath in the place) was offered at a reasonable rental, on condition that £2,000 first be spent on plumbing and decorating. '*Before they call I will answer*' was the text that came to mind ... for, by the next morning, an anonymous donor left £1,000 for repairs. This was followed closely by an offer from the director of a heating and ventilation firm, who pronounced the house structurally sound and promptly offered to pay for the plumbing! So it was that this house became the first all-married students' quarters, and Mrs. Florence Cross (who spent many years of voluntary service working on BBI correspondence courses), moved in as warden.

After No. 27 Elvetham Road came *No. 29*, run as the College Nursery, prompting an article in a Birmingham paper, headed 'Babies in College'! The following year BBI branched out into a highly sought-after area of stately homes, close to the BBC (Midlands Division). *No. 8 Carpenter Road* had once been the residence of the renowned Chamberlain family. It was a most impressive Georgian house with a lovely garden sweeping down to the Birmingham/Worcester canal. *No. 8* and *No. 16* were then offered to BBI by Calthorpe Estate on a rental contract. Together they became two men's hostels, housing some 30 young men and a couple of married students. The chaplain and his wife, Bassee and Joyce Kingdon, moved into No. 8 as wardens, whilst the general secretary and his wife (Lije and Winnie Bingham) took over at No. 16 followed by Rev. Bob Dunnett (later to continue in the footsteps of David Smith as Vice-Principal) and his wife Di. *Nos. 3, 4 and 5 Pakenham Road* became available, followed by *Nos. 101 and 103 Gough Road*. Then later *four houses in nearby Wheeleys Road and six more in Charlotte Road,* just around the corner. Every one seemed to have a miracle behind it.

At that time *Nos. 1 and 2 Pakenham Road* became vacant, and on their first request to Calthorpe Estate, BBI were told, 'Not for sale, or rental!' Lije was not so easily deterred and was eventually allowed to view the premises. 'Ideal for our needs,' he thought, '30 rooms, four bathrooms, a large kitchen and very large studio ... ideal for a lecture room.' Unfortunately, vandals had beaten them to it and ransacked the place. All the lead had been stolen, as well as the hot and cold water tanks! At least £2,000 would be needed for plumbing repairs and re-decoration to up-grade the premises for immediate use, and there were only a few weeks to go before the next session!

At last Calthorpe Estate offered the lease at a very reasonable rental ... but where was that vital £2,000? The July Council decided they could not go ahead without the seal of a loan or gift to cover the cost. The deadline was *Monday morning, August 31st*. That very morning, Lije had a phone call from the College's solicitors. A client of theirs had just offered the College an interest-free loan of £2,500! Immediately plans were begun to prepare the premises for students. Water tanks and basins were ordered as time was running short.

That Sunday, Lije was preaching at a local church and

mentioned the story over lunch. Amazingly, his host just *happened* to be the foreman of the firm handling BBI's order for water tanks! 'I'll give it first priority,' he said. The water tank had to be a special size. Two days later a lorry arrived, carrying the *exact* size of storage tank required, unwanted by a previous client! Professional decorators completed the job in double-quick time and 20 girls, two married couples and wardens moved in. So it was, that the largest room became a second lecture room, with the College Chapel on the ground floor and, as if that weren't enough, the £2,500 loan became a gift!

It was 1969. The lease of the first special house, No. 28 Elvetham Road, had expired. Three years later the order came for demolition. It was a sore wrench for Harry and the family to part with that happy home where the work began, but God had other plans and gave them this promise:

'I will settle you after your *former* estates' (Ezek. 36:11).

In the end, all three lovely Victorian homes in Elvetham Road were demolished, 27, 28 and 29, but in their place came something new.

On October 21st 1969, *No. 8 Pakenham Road* (St. Luke's Vicarage) was put up for auction. BBI had nothing to offer, so didn't attend, but this house was different to most of the others owned by Calthorpe Estate. Because it was a Vicarage, it was completely *freehold*. A Georgian house, with 18 rooms, it had a magnificent two hundred foot sweep of lawn.

Out of the blue, the agents phoned up and asked Harry 'Do you want it?' 'Yes,' he replied in faith.... And then the miracle happened. Four anonymous friends between them volunteered to lend him the full price of the property at a very low rate of interest – and it was no mean sum! In this way God *did* settle them according to their former estates – and kept His word.

By the time BBI was 21 years old there were 19 houses in use with 300 rooms and 110 students in residence; not to mention families and staff members with children numbering over 50.

Harry wrote in his journal:

'Truly, "*Little is much when God is in it.*" God continues to work in amazing ways. All the houses are Victorian or neo-Georgian, with vast gardens ... and, although they are large, unheated and often in poor condition on arrival, they are proving ideal for College needs, when ready. Money is never plentiful, but the challenge of putting them all to rights, one by one – cleaning, decorating and repairing – is throwing us all together on God, both staff and students, and is definitely good practical missionary training. No central heating or luxury decor in the middle of the African bush!'

Holding the fort

The maintenance work needed was enormous. A noble team of maintenance officers laboured under hazardous and demoralizing conditions in order to up-grade the ever-expanding 'BBI and Associated Hostel' properties – all in various states of repair. Life was not much easier for College bursars and book-keepers, who showed great calibre and tenacity in coping with a host of frustrations!

Many passed through the disciplines of BBI training on College 'chore' teams, only to re-emerge later as members of staff. Don Foster was one prime example. Don was a Yorkshire farmer. He came to BBI in 1964 from Waterfield Farm near Doncaster, without academic qualifications but with a double quota of patience and determination and a warm welcome from H.B.B. Over a long eight-year period of training he jumped hurdle after hurdle until he finally achieved his goal – a BD Honours degree. He then went on to re-invest all his BBI lectures in the service of training others ... for a further 22 years! First, giving lectures in New Testament Greek, then assisting Vice-

Principal David Smith with Old Testament Studies and Doctrine for External Examinations (i.e. the highly complex field of critical analysis) and finally, giving lectures in Archaeology.

BBI was definitely a character-building experience and the warmth of fellowship and family spirit was something special. Staff, students and friends gave their time ... working with a will. Several friends from Birmingham gave regular voluntary service. One young friend, who worked in a clothing factory, came every Monday night and helped Dosie with sewing for the children. Another, foreman of a wire factory, came to help with the maintenance every Saturday for three years. This was the voluntary spirit of active service, and God never seemed to allow anyone to give this sort of help freely without Himself rewarding them. Several got much better jobs. Others were blessed in their marriage and family life ... and the general feeling was, 'We're all in it together!'

'The Associated Hostels'

These lovely old houses seemed to come in rows, or blocks of land. Harry did not play monopoly, but he knew that in this beautiful, leafy area, blocks were more valuable than the odd, dispersed house ... so he eventually decided on his own policy. He called it 'The Associated Hostels' ('Hostels' for students, 'Associated' with the College).

During one Council meeting, Harry made a suggestion: 'If there is any risk of a strategic house being lost because, quite understandably, you are hesitant, I will take it over in faith in my *own* name – thus securing it for BBI accommodation wherever necessary. When "my" houses begin to make a profit, I will stop taking a salary as BBI Principal. After all, we're not here to make a profit.'

For the first six years, Harry not only took no salary, but actually paid secretaries out of his own pocket....

By 1973 BBI was in possession of over 20 houses, now making accommodation possible for up to 200 students! With this system in operation Harry was then able to borrow money, using his own freehold house as collateral for the loan, which the College could not do because of its charitable status. He was also able to move *faster* than the College could, which he did when St. James' Vicarage came into his orbit on a strategic triangle of land between the two roads, Elvetham and Pakenham. For £20 a week he made an arrangement to take the Vicarage over, knowing that in a month or so he might have to hand it back! In fact, having re-wired and upgraded it, this beautiful period building was eventually handed on to the BBI, who were then able to buy it 'freehold'.

So Harry's vision was made good. House after house was added and where the College couldn't buy a house that was offered, Harry housed the students in his 'Associated Hostels'. Houses which he filled initially with university students under the heading of Associated Hostels, were ultimately used for BBI accommodation. He even made use of the sad demolition of those lovely old houses in Elvetham Road, by picking up marble fireplaces, chimney pots, old bricks, tiles and doors to re-install into College houses. *Nothing* went to waste!

34

THE TEAM

Harry and Dosie, because of their strength of character and consistency of life, somehow held the fort and sailed through situations that would have finished lesser mortals! In *their* race as running partners they worked together as one harmonious team, proving that 'Two are better than one....'

Neither had airs and graces – or thought much of their own needs at all. They had little, but they shared it with generosity ... and it grew! Both had a great love for people and compassion for the needy. Tolerant of failings in others and willing to look at the best in everyone, they were also ready to give opportunities to the most unlikely of people – and a second chance, if disappointed. When hurt or let down, neither criticized or held grudges. On one occasion Harry counselled a student who was hurting, '*Best to leave some things with God, Mike.*'

The gift of keeping in touch
It was this quality coupled with the ability to communicate with anyone of any variety or creed, that led to such a wide range of quality friendships. Not only did they have the gift of making and giving friendships – they also *kept* friendships around the world, for life. Because people were important, however busy they were, they would stop and listen; remember tiny personal details and keep in touch. Letters and visits mattered. There were at least 4,000 names on their mailing list ... basically an 'extended family'!

Harry wrote:

'Dear Old Students, remember you are always part of the BBI family ... all the present students know they will be old students themselves one day – and you'll be assured of a warm welcome!'

Hundreds of letters were sent to and from Harry and Dosie – personal letters of concern, advice and counsel, appreciation, thanks and encouragement. Harry's principle was to try and reply by *return* of post. His letter of thanks for a gift of £1, was as special as that for £100.

Both ran the course of life with a far-seeing eternal perspective, that seemed to keep them going, regardless of obstacles. 'Set your affection on things above' ... 'for where your treasure is, there shall your heart be also' (Col. 3:2; Luke 12:34), was one of Dosie's guidelines. Both had the same singleness of purpose and transparent integrity. What they said and what they did entirely matched up. They just taught by example ... lived the life! But in order to do this, they had to follow highly-disciplined lives, 'rather like the order of the monasteries, where discipline, work with the hands and prayer were all-important' – prayer being a vital part of life, not some kind of academic exercise.

For Harry it was simple, in spiritual as well as physical terms. 'Plan your work and work to your plan. Work when you work. Relax when you relax.' Rather like the pattern of Thomas Edison, the inventor, whose order of life seemed so natural and effortless. According to his wife, he would work long and hard, then lie down on the couch and immediately fall asleep. 'Never does he show any disunity of mind ... no impeded flow of energy. He is like a child in God's hands.' So it seemed for Harry. To bed on the stroke of 9.00 wherever possible, and up at the crack of dawn. If guests were at home, he quickly excused himself! Not so Dosie, who was frequently left 'holding the baby' – and who, like the virtuous woman of Proverbs 31, often worked until the early hours of the morning to prepare for the day ahead. She still got up to join him. 'How did you sleep?' Harry would ask next morning. 'Both eyes shut!' she'd say with a laugh. 'I just ask the Lord to double the strength and make up the hours ... and He does.' Her faith and stamina kept her going... Her problem, when she had one, was never admitting to weakness!

Harry consistently carried out an almost ascetic routine. Early morning 'watch'. Cold wash or bath. Huge pint mug of strong tea with lashings of sugar in it. Regular early morning exercises (which could be heard going on vigorously in the next room!). Prayer. Bible study. Breakfast. Lectures. More study. Main meal. Short rest. Chores, or carpentry, perhaps. Long brisk walk (up to 20 miles on occasions). High tea. Piano playing, then study (to the strains of Tchaikovsky or Beethoven). Read a novel (Dickens, perhaps). Supper. Bed.

Meanwhile, Dosie prayed with him and worked alongside him in a wide variety of activities – again without complaint and seemingly effortlessly. One could never plan the day completely because in an 'open house' the unpredictable happened every other minute – doorbells, callers, telephones. The unplanned just *slotted* in ! Because the day was already prayed over and handed over early in the morning, it didn't seem a problem! All in control.

Dosie was a very strong character, but at the same time very gentle and full of grace. She really *had* to be. It was a life of contrasts – one minute there'd be a whirlwind of activity, gown billowing up the road to a lecture; washing machine churning away; the next ... listening in rapt attention to someone with a problem. Given that Harry was such an individual, she had to get used to all kinds of little eccentricities and frustrations, but she worked around him, fitted in with his schedule, helped him to relax ... and produce, produce, produce! One day, as he was about to leave for a lecture in the midst of a hectic morning, Dosie thought he looked a trifle weary. Having only had five hours of sleep herself the night before, she quipped: 'My dear Harry. It's not the end of the world yet. Winston Churchill was in his *prime* at your age!'

Both of them, individually, had a hand in endless projects. Harry wrote so many articles and letters; prepared so many lectures; preached so many sermons; wrote books; kept scrap books (files of stories, newspaper cuttings and illustrations), family records, slides and photographs – all meticulously boxed, labelled and stored in shelves, drawers and filing cabinets. He had an incredible filing system, a large number of well-worn suitcases for storage and travel, boxes of historical records and literally hundreds of little red memo books and diaries. He lived with his pen, always taking notes.

Travelling frequently, Harry visited numerous people, churches, youth groups, Christian Unions at universities, colleges, hospitals, factories and even railways! Over the years, his small team of printers had manned the printing press and equipment with excellent results. In the end, he started his own Quernmore Publishing Company, with its own printing equipment. On the creative side, he used much of his spare time in woodwork and construction, building a beautiful garden summer house to study in, away from the crowd, and large solid shelves to house literally thousands of books on every imaginable topic from 'Punch' and 'Boys Own' annuals, to Dale Carnegie's 'How to Win Friends and Influence People.' Always soaking in new and valuable information, he particularly enjoyed Hebrew lessons with his friend Rabbi Reuben Brookes (Director of Education at the Singers Hill Congregation, Birmingham). In quieter moments he listened to and composed music. Sometimes he wrote poetry.

Dosie, on the other hand – apart from her special gift with children and role as unofficial 'Mum' – wore almost as many hats; as College matron, taking pastoral classes, sermon classes, lectures in child health and infant welfare (setting and marking exams), and preaching on many occasions in and out of College, sometimes as often as Harry (with two, three or four outside engagements a month and the occasional big rally). She sat on literally hundreds of College Council meetings ... spending her spare time wholesale buying at market and auction, or as private social worker and counsellor, chief cook and bottle-washer....

Preachers and Teachers

Chapel prayers were over one morning, and the bell announced the start of classes. Talking and laughing died down as the Principal made his way to the platform.

'Good morning, ladies and gentlemen,' he began. 'Our lecture today is entitled, *How to Make the Plaster Stick*!' Harry always loved this lecture.

'Using stories takes more than knowledge and skill; it takes a sort of unfailing instinct. You've got to know what will appeal to folks and what won't. Then, how to put it over. When you plaster a wall, you know, three ounces that stick are worth a hundredweight that doesn't! Today we are giving some suggestions on how to make the plaster stick. Lots of stories help the lessons to stick.... Fellows like and remember stories. A lesson with plenty of them is like a room with plenty of windows. Stories let the light in on a subject, but you don't want a lesson that's all stories, any more than you want a room that's all windows. Choose or reject your stories, as a boy deals with a box of toy bricks – he builds castles or houses, palaces or dock-yards with the *same* bricks, just as he wants – so it's really his own work. If you want to reach people today, you've got to be ready to sit on the edge of a wagon, or workbench and talk to them in their own lingo. Know how they feel. Know how they think, and use simple, direct language that will go right to the heart of the problem. That's the way to reach them.... *Don't preach, talk*! If you've got something to say, say it. Don't use masses of words. "Stand up! Speak up! Shut up!"

'For example, you want to tell a group of children that they've got to keep on trying, even if things seem impossible. Tell them a story.... One day two mice fell into a jar of cream.

197

One said, "It's hopeless!" sank to the bottom – and drowned. The other said, "It *looks* hopeless! but at least I'm going to do the best I can!" So ... he swam round and round and round ... until the cream turned into butter ... and out he got! A child won't forget that story easily, nor some adults for that matter.'

Harry's teaching gift meant parables and stories all the way, because for him, theology was all to do with the way God interacted with everyday life. The common and the academic flowed alongside each other quite naturally – a very unusual mixture. He did not live life in compartments, but as a whole.

Dosie's talks at Chapel Prayers were equally captivating: topical, to the point, and highly entertaining. One day, she spoke on the subject of '*Rats*'. Her verse was Romans 12:9: '*Abhor that which is evil.*' Dosie had a horror of rats, as childhood experiences on the farm had taught her that they could be very dangerous when cornered.

During her short talk, she suddenly made her point by standing on a chair, clasping her hands together in horror, exclaiming how she 'abhoooorred' rats. Her message was clear: 'Just think about the most *loathsome* thing you can possibly imagine. *That's* how you should feel about sin!'

They not only preached about what they believed, but had a great deal of moral courage to stand up against the crowd. Harry had stood out strongly against modernism at university. Dosie, as a very inexperienced, new Christian had braved a soap box at Hyde Park! She prayed intensely for Britain for years, as part of the 'Intercessors for Britain' prayer chain ... and lobbied constantly for and against important issues, like Sunday Trading. She listened to World News, reading the papers and keeping abreast of Parliamentary Bills and modern trends. In spite of her hectic life, she wrote many letters to Prime Ministers, Members of Parliament, the Archbishop of Canterbury and of course, the Royal Family – who received leather bound versions of 'Daily Light' on special occasions such as weddings, birthdays and jubilees.

35

FAMILY MATTERS!

The Bonsall home may have been way out of the ordinary, but it was fun! Each member of the family had their own strong opinions on life, and as they sat round the huge, oak dining table airing their views, the lively conversation more often than not would end up in a full-scale, ding-dong debate. Harry would then disappear, returning with a pile of books to prove a particular point! If it became too heated, Dosie would pull out the family Bible with a heartfelt sigh – and read the whole of Psalm 133. 'Brethren should dwell together in unity...!' They knew it all by heart!

Life was always exciting, as visitors came and went constantly. Some were unforgettable, like Corrie ten Boon (one-time prisoner of the Nazis), or Mildred Cable (with little adopted 'Topsy' of the Gobi Desert). Then the children would sit round the fire, spell-bound, as wonderful missionary pioneers told their real-life tales to a rapt audience. Gladys Aylward of China was quite a character, and told them once how God had saved her as she travelled on a very dangerous mission, by making her invisible! Willie Burton of the Congo, another dynamic pioneer who had witnessed the power of prayer as a man was raised from the dead, was also a family friend who would sit with little blonde Rachel making 'jumping' animals out of his handkerchief!

The whole family loved practical jokes, particularly Charles who came into his own on April Fool's Day. The others tended to be 'partners in crime,' with many highly creative and original efforts, though not all their guests appreciated salt in the sugar and glue on the door-handles! Like Harry they all loved music, being accustomed to at least *two* pianos and a piano stool that was constantly 'bagged'. Harry loved to play duets with the children. Tom, whose musical ability was outstanding, would also compose – with manuscripts scattered around the place. The Bonsall family had little in material terms, but Dosie went out of her way to locate the best piano teacher available and took all the children to music lessons, exams and competitive concerts.

All the children were encouraged on the road to free enterprise and Tom excelled in this line, starting first with a successful 'mushroom business' in the cellar, that involved spreading steaming compost over the springs of double beds! This was later followed by a 'chicken business' in the garage of No. 28 (starting with 80 small chicks, in partnership with their Portuguese lodger, Ludgero). Having been brought up on a farm herself, Dosie seemed to thrive on this kind of life, later investing in bantams of her own and even a small Welsh pony for Rachel – housed in her friend's garage up the road! They had all kinds of animals, from rabbits to cats and dogs, who usually ended up with large litters of puppies. It meant endless work, but Dosie loved it.

Bonsall birthdays were fantastic, with birthday cakes in every shape and form. One year Ruth had a whole farm on a tray – with a chocolate farmhouse, shredded wheat haystacks, blue duckpond, green jelly grass and all the animals! Dosie always managed to go that extra mile for the children, to let them know they were equally special. When Ruth was homesick at boarding school, Dosie wrote her a letter every single day for at least a year, having stuffed her school trunk with wonderful surprises.

There was always plenty to laugh about and no shortage of unusual goings-on. As the days were long and full, Harry regularly took a short nap after lunch. On one particular occasion he put on his pyjamas, woke up in a hurry and forgot to take them off! There was a Council Meeting that afternoon and as they were sitting in session, to her horror Dosie suddenly saw an expanse of blue and white striped pyjama leg appearing underneath his trousers. She didn't know what to do. It was no good giving him a nudge. He'd always say, quite clearly, 'My dear, what's the matter?' Then she hit on a plan. Going over to the kitchen hatch in the sitting room she called Tom with the message, 'Go and ring the front doorbell *immediately* and ask for Mr. Bonsall.'

It worked. As soon as the bell went, Dosie left the Council to answer it, called him out of the meeting and then said, '*For goodness sake, Harry, take your pyjamas off!*'

On the road

At the age of 50, Dosie started attempting her driving test ... touring around the crowded streets of Birmingham. One, two, three, four, five tests in all she took before she eventually passed. But she did not give in. She was determined! First of all, she was quite frightened by the Birmingham traffic, but she took to the road regardless and became the family taxi driver ... driving hundreds of miles around the countryside.

Harry never drove, but was a pretty good 'back seat' driver. He would get into the car with great aplomb and heave a deep sigh, with a heartfelt '*Lord, preserve us!*' Sitting in the co-pilot's seat with his map, he would give clear directions throughout the journey interspersed with 'U-Turn' or 'Sheep on the road!' He also constructed a large and prominent square black box to take all the numerous pieces of luggage that usually accompanied the family. This way the Bonsalls were quite easily conspicuous when taking off for any length of time!

Old, classic cars were a Bonsall trademark. Most of them were saloons, with beautiful leather seats and walnut fascia that would soon be collectors' classics. Charles would pick them up for £10 or so – and became a dab hand at taking the best bits out

201

of one old masterpiece to rejuvenate another! This made life very exciting because, whether it happened to be the Morris Traveller, the Humber Hawk, or the sporty Hillman Minx, one never *quite* knew what would happen next. One day, Charles picked Ruth up after a hard day's work at the hospital and nearly lost her completely as they sped round a fast bend. The door, still unfinished and temporarily held on with string, suddenly flew open. Fortunately, he grabbed her before she hit the road!

On otherwise quiet Sunday mornings, a rapid burst of 'revs' would break the silence, and all the flats in No. 3 Pakenham Road would suddenly be aware that Mrs. Bonsall was taking off! She was a most reliable taxi service for car-less friends in need of a lift to church.

Returning from one summer holiday, Harry and Dosie had a very remarkable deliverance. The back tyre of their Morris Traveller burst and shot them clear across the crowded A37, into the path of swiftly on-coming traffic. Harry shouted one word, '*Jesus*!' and He *instantly* took over. The car stopped dead, within six inches of a fast-moving vehicle tearing towards them in the opposite direction. A family travelling behind them had seen the bulge growing on the inside of their tyre some distance behind and couldn't seem to attract their attention in time, but kindly stopped and came to their aid. Within half an hour the tyre was replaced and they were back on the road as if nothing had happened!

36

ONE VISION

'Mr. Bonsall, when you talk about revival, what does that really entail?' asked one student. 'Well, we've got a lecture on that very topic next week, so most of your questions will be answered then. But, basically, God will sometimes choose to meet a person, community or country face to face. He moves sovereignly by the power of His Holy Spirit in the lives of human beings, bringing new life, or revival.'

'Have you actually experienced that?'

'Personally, I've known God renewing me, but I'd say my first experience of revival power was in 1923, when Charles S. Price came to the "Arena" in Vancouver. I was 18. The place was packed and at the altar call at least 300 stood up for healing in three parallel lines. As Dr. Price touched them, most dropped instantly, healed under the power of God. The whole city was shaken! Dr. Price was, in many ways, the "Finney" of the second quarter of our century. Few who attended the first of his four Vancouver campaigns in 1923, will ever forget it. It was in a great cheerless ice arena, with seats clear up to the ceiling, crammed two hours before the services.'

'Was it hyped up at all?' asked the student, troubled by the thought of men trying to 'do God's work for Him'.

'No,' replied the Principal, 'not at all. Believe me, I was worried about hype as well at the time, but there just wasn't any. The simplest shortest sermon; no frills or gimmicks; the powerful presence and awesomeness of God descending on the audiences day after day; the "mourners" benches instantly filled with people, crying to God for mercy. There was only one explanation possible. *God came down*. During the last ten days of the great Belleville Campaign, there was an average of over 1,000 conversions every day! The preachers would weep ... and the workers couldn't handle all the people at the altar. It was so jammed that they couldn't move around ... aisles filled clear to the back of the building ... kneeling figures ... tears ... prayers ... songs.... Never have I seen anything like it in all my experience!'

'Why don't we see more of that kind of thing today, though?'

'Well, God is doing a great deal in miraculous ways throughout the world. But I know what you mean. That is what I long for with all my heart, too. That's why this College exists. God will do it, you know. He's promised! But we must intercede for our country, night and day if we can. That is the key. Revival and deliverance must come soon to the church, to minister to our nation and then to the world. When it comes, Spirit-guided organisations with leadership, discipline and control will be all-important. We here in the College need to be on our knees, on our faces and on our toes, in expectation of this event!'

Because 'preparing for the revival to come' was the goal at the centre of their lives, Harry and Dosie made it their priority. They longed for it, laboured for it, fasted and prayed for it and passed on their vision to the hundreds of students who came within their orbit.

Dosie sparked off a renewed emphasis on revival during Chapel prayers, urging staff and students to seek God with prayer and fasting. 'How *much* do we want revival?' she asked, 'How *much* are we willing to sacrifice for it? It's no good singing, "Be bold, be strong, For the Lord our God is with us", if we haven't got enough backbone to get down and *pray about it*! Are you willing to stand in the gap?' After this, revival prayer meetings became a regular part of BBI life. Dosie was a great believer in prayer, often fasting on behalf of others for several days.

On one memorable visit, Duncan Campbell, God's man

during the Hebrides Revival of 1949-53, had made the comment, 'It only needs *one* committed person to bring about revival.' That was enough to prompt Dosie to fast for 30 days, with this end in view. Later she would do the same thing for Harry, earnestly asking the Lord, in her straight-forward way, to liberate him from 'the fence of his intellectual inhibitions'!

Harry had lived in the light of his 1923 student experience for years, feeling sure that he had received some kind of special anointing and prophetic gift at that time. Gertie, too had gone along to 'The Arena' and had been moved by her experience of the power of God at work, but later withdrew from it. For some time after his arrival in England, Harry was hesitant in talking about his own pilgrimage in this direction, but Dosie forged ahead for all God could give – and when she married into the Bonsall household, she brought a great fervour with her; launching out to all kinds of charismatic meetings and conventions and encouraging Harry to do the same! Gradually, Harry recognised his need to be open to God on these issues. He had not forgotten the spiritual consequences at Taplow of his decision to sign a document agreeing to have nothing to do with Pentecostals. Dosie tried again. 'Come with me to Hockley this morning, Harry. I know you'll enjoy it, and they have very sound teaching.'

'Okay, I will. But I'm going to take notes and check them up just to make sure.'

Hockley

Hockley Pentecostal Church in Birmingham was unique. Founded and led for more than 50 years by two remarkable women, Harriet Fisher and Olive Reeve, it was described in one report as '*One of the most thriving churches in the country, with a congregation of over 500 and a series of Sunday Schools – at one time, eight of them – reaching a total of 800 children....*' Both young women longed to be missionaries, so they trained as nurses. Olive had a definite call to India, but when the war intervened God brought *India* to them as Asian immigrants poured into the neighbouring district. Olive lost no time and started an Asian Sunday School in her garage! Harriet's mother had five children, four of whom were born with a terrible, crippling paralysis – but Harriet, the youngest, was different. Before her birth, her mother had experienced a dramatic anointing of the Holy Spirit, which swept through the house like a mighty wind and settled upon her. It was the time of the 'George Jeffreys' revival ... and Harriet was born soon afterwards – entirely healthy – and determined to make up for the physical limitations of her brothers and sisters. She seemed to be born with a great zest for life and springs in her shoes!

Hockley was different. It was not so much the numbers, as the tremendous joy and exuberance of its services, where the gifts of the Holy Spirit were allowed to flow freely, with healing and prophecy.

It was to this church that Dosie and Harry eventually came for fellowship and prayer, often bringing students and friends with them. It was a very deprived area, but at Hockley one never quite knew *who* was coming, or *what* would happen next! Wonderful speakers would arrive from different parts of the world ... mighty men and women of God, who had heard of Hockley and wanted to take part in their ministry.

Harry with his Presbyterian background and Dosie with her formal Anglican upbringing certainly had a change of scenery here ... but God spoke to Dosie after the shock of her first visit, pointing her to the uninhibited worship of King David, who thought nothing of dancing before the Lord. David was far more interested in pleasing God than in worrying what other people thought about him! From that time on, her doubts disappeared. She would say, with a smile, 'When you go to a football match, you don't look at the spectators, you follow the ball. So don't look around to see what everyone else is doing, just keep your eyes on the Lord!'

So it was that Hockley became a very important spiritual oasis 'and back-up station' for BBI and the Bonsall family. Harry himself had numerous pockets sewn into his jackets, lined with multi-coloured 'beeros' (as he called them), filled with little red memo books for quick reference. He then proceeded to record sermons, prophecies, and interpretations in shorthand, to check them up with Scripture after the service! Even Greek and Hebrew translations were used, if necessary! This way, he knew that all was in order and as it should be.

37

'THE REVIVAL AND THE BIBLE COLLEGE'

As promised, lectures on revival were next on the agenda. The students, always fascinated by this most exciting of topics, listened intently as Harry delivered the message on this subject so close to his heart:

THE NEED FOR REVIVAL

Revival is the mass working of the Holy Spirit in the church as a whole, or in any part of it – an extraordinary power sent for an extraordinary purpose. Christ's first aim for this age is two-fold:

(a) the gathering out of the world of a people for Himself (the church), and

(b) the bringing of that church into full likeness to Himself.

He has never promised to convert the world systems in this era. This age, like every other age, ends in judgment ... but it is quite possible that before it falls, God will ordain a lightning-like work of the Holy Spirit throughout the world, gathering in a vast number at one stroke to complete the church ... holding back the curtain of judgment in answer to believing prayer, till this is done....

While God is not aiming first at changing the world, but at forming the church, He is concerned with conditions in the world being *helpful* to its formation. He may well control and even change these to give us a short respite to work out His plan. If we take it, there will be blessing ... if we lose it, there can only be disaster! We are living in an interval of mingled opportunity and probation.

Revival is the means God waits to use, to bring His two-fold plan to pass. Christ used this means through His church at Pentecost: and has used this means ever since. Only as His way is followed will His ends be won. Revival will be sent for this purpose and this purpose alone – and will be sufficient in power and duration to *finish* the task. Like Ezekiel's river, revival may start (without tributaries), in a small *local* way only to increase in depth, volume and force; not ceasing until its complete work is done. *Christ's plan and method today is the same as at Pentecost – world-wide evangelism through world-wide revival.*

How Revival is Brought About

The coming of revival today is the church's responsibility, not God's. God *already* wills it and waits to send it, but only when certain laws are obeyed by man.... It is the church's duty to fulfil these laws. Finney truly said, '*You can have revival any time you are willing to pay the price*!'

And what is that price? According to Finney there are two laws:

1) Repentance.
2) Prevailing intercessory prayer – or, the prayer of faith.

1. Repentance

Repentance has a twofold aspect:

(a) a turning by the church from every sin, and
(b) turning to God in total surrender to His will alone.

To illustrate the point. A certain small town became paralysed because its water supply failed. There were hundreds of taps, but only a trickle of water, because a tramp had maliciously inserted a plug of rubbish at the mouth of the intake main, right by the reservoir. There was any amount of water in the reservoir all running to waste, but not until that one small plug was removed, could it become available to the villagers.

Just so, there is no lack of power with God – power to bless the whole church ... and through her, the world, but sin has blocked the cistern. It is *sin* that makes God's promises *seem* to fail. The church's first task is to search for these hindering causes and remove them, because until these are put away, there can be *no hope* of revival! Most commonly found amongst evangelicals today are the sins of....

(1) *compromise* / alliance with modernism

(2) *failure to witness* / failure to put missions first

(3) *honouring conventions,* or putting the opinions of a clique before the Holy Spirit

(4) *bitterness* / lack of common courtesy and straight-forwardness in dealing with people

(5) *uncleanness*

(6) *jealousy* / non-co-operation between evangelical leaders

(7) *show* / a desire to take all the credit

(8) *denominationalism* / exclusivism, cutting out all others from one's interest

(9) *evil-speaking* / the simple Scriptural rule that when anything is wrong you tell the person offending *first* ... and *in private*. Wesley stressed this point

(10) *touchiness: lack of moral honesty*: blaming others or bearing a grudge when rebuked, instead of admitting a fault and making it right.

2. Prevailing intercessory prayer

Intercessory prayer is prayer for interests other than one's own – and *prevailing* intercessory prayer means ... 1) prayer according to the will of God, and 2) prayer that *holds onto* and *achieves* its object. Let us study these two factors.

(a) Prayer According to the Will of God

True prayer is ignited by the Holy Spirit and so is *always* according to God's will. Prayer that is not according to God's will brings disaster.

Never think of a prayer as wrestling with God to make Him willing to do what He doesn't will to do. Any wrestling in prayer is with Satan, or sometimes with self, but *never* with God. True prayer is not the means of making God willing to do *our* will, but rather the instrument whereby our will is aligned with God's, receiving it in faith as a *finished fact*. God's will is then brought to pass in the world. This is the highest form of prayer.

Revival and prayer are inextricably linked. The Christian at prayer holds a key position in the world. In fact one Christian on earth can do more than one thousand in heaven! For Christ and the Christian hold the two key places in the universe:

a) Christ (at the throne in Heaven, the audience chamber of the King) who constantly sends down help, and,

b) the Christian, who holds the place of '*outpost*' in the world, but keeps continuous touch with his Lord.

As each Christian on earth prays in faith (itself an act of will) for God's will to be done there, something creative happens. God's power is released and His will is done on earth, just as it is in heaven.

(b) Prayer that Holds on to and Achieves its Object

All prayer according to God's will that does *not* achieve its object, not only discourages men but dishonours God. Why 'unanswered' prayer? There are many reasons in Scripture, but not one excuse. The Bible always promises '*whatsoever*'.

There are two kinds of prayers ... a) simple – just 'asking and taking', and b) obstructed – when the 'asking and taking' are opposed by all the powers of darkness.

There should be no wrestling in simple prayers (apart from wrestling with oneself). But wrestling with Satan is involved in the latter type, when the intercessor would bring in revival. The intercessor must *know* how to prevail. There are laws involved, just as there were 25 centuries ago, when the beautiful and brave Queen Esther risked her life by interceding to the Emperor of Persia for her people, the Jews. She won through and their lives were spared.

Today, the only one place where this can be done is in God's audience chamber. It is there that issues are decided – and what is transacted there in secret today, takes place openly in the world tomorrow. Two battles are now being waged – an earthly and a heavenly – and he who would win the earthly one, must first win the heavenly. Only when revival 'intact' is won in the secret place of the Almighty in prayer, can it be realised in the world. The audience chamber of the great King is the most important place in the universe. It is the *one* place Satan has his eye on. No doubt he wonders why humans do not realise its importance! ... Just like the Christians, Esther's method is intercession. Just like Haman's, Satan's method is accusation. But Esther prevails!

Every Christian, even the weakest and most sinful of us, stands like Esther endued with all these amazing privileges, at a time of strategic importance ('for such a time as this'). It is also God's will that we should *use* them, just like Esther ... and prevail.

OUR RESPONSIBILITY

There are four reasons why every Christian should practise prevailing prayer as a priority, just as the apostles did.

1. Conscience Demands It
Every Christian holds the golden key in his hands to unlock the prison-house of millions. If he does not use it, he is guilty before God:
    (a) of the good which *could* have come to pass, or,
    (b) of the evil that could have been averted.

What would have happened if Esther hadn't risked her life or used her privilege ... and what will happen if we ignore God's clear command and neglect to intercede for the immortal souls of others. Even the humblest Christian has the privilege of prayer and God will hold us responsible for our use of this to its fullest extent.

2. Love Demands It
We must pray for our neighbour as we would pray for our own loved ones. One day a young man fell off a steamer and was rescued unconscious. The ship's doctor had been applying artificial respiration for half and hour, when the captain appeared. 'It's all right, Doctor,' he said, 'Leave him now, you have done your best.' Just then someone said, 'It's your son, Captain.' With a shout, the captain sprang forward, stripped off coat and vest, brushed the doctor aside and threw himself over the prostrate form. Like a madman he worked over him, until, after four hours of steady toil, the first glimmer of consciousness returned to the young man. He would do it for his *own* son, but he would not do it for another's son. How many Christians are like that captain? How do *we* love our neighbour?

3. Expediency/Need Demands It
In war-time, we do not expect soldiers on active service to knit socks. That is something those at home can do. On the foreign field missionaries must certainly pray, but often they are exhausted, ill, overworked, lacking in privacy, or objects of direct Satanic attack. Therefore, all praying possible should be done at home!

4. Self-interest Demands It

In the ancient Roman Empire, the household often contained hundreds of servants. The steward's work was to feed them. As he faithfully did this, he himself was given his own portion of the very thing he was giving to others. It is like this with all Christian stewardships, such as prayer.

When you have prayed '*through*' for, say, China, then India, then Africa, God will suddenly say, 'Stop. Now what can *I* do for *you*?'

If your praying seems ineffective, is it because your prayers are only for yourself and your own interests? Set apart a definite time to intercede for others and God will bless your private prayers. Incidentally, nothing so adds to the power of personal evangelism, or so develops the personality (strength of will and self-respect) as the practice of prevailing intercessory prayer.

THE PRINCIPAL LAWS OF PREVAILING INTERCESSORY PRAYER

Success in prayer however, as in all else in the Christian life, depends on rigid obedience to certain laws. Religion is like science. When prayer fails, it is because certain laws are disobeyed. Find and correct the broken law and results will come again. There are quite a number of known laws of prayer, but the following are paramount.

1. Prayer Must be According to the Will of God.

'*If we ask any thing according to His will He heareth us*' (1 John 5:14). This is vital. All other prayer is *un*answered, or a curse, if answered. 'But,' you ask, 'how can I know the will of God?' The well-known story of F. B. Meyer entering Holyhead harbour by steamer one dark night, illustrates this:

'How do you know the harbour entrance?' he asked the captain. 'See those three shore lights?' the captain replied. 'When those three lights are in a straight line, I know I am heading straight for the harbour.' Our three guiding lights are The Bible, The Holy Spirit and Circumstances. When all the facts are known, these three are *always* in line.

The Bible always reveals God's will, especially in principles. This gives the ground for prevailing prayer. '*The Lord is not willing that any should perish, but that all should come to repentance*' (2 Pet. 3:9). How often saints have launched out in fear and trembling, like Hudson Taylor, with determined and implicit faith in the literal meaning of the very words of the Bible. They dared to pray for what they only dared to believe was God's will to give. As they waited on Him, their own wills were yielded to His will, and the element of daring vanished. Then they began to realise that it was not a question of His will to grant the request, but of their willingness to make the request, although they didn't know it. Often when God calls us to prayer, the vision of what He means to give us is blurred: the intercessor waits in stillness, and as he does so, the Holy Spirit shows the *exact* thing to be prayed for at that particular time.

I once heard a minister describe how he felt impelled to kneel down at his desk one morning and pray for one of his elders while he was in the middle of preparing his sermon. He prayed till he felt the burden pass, then went on with his sermon. Next time he saw that elder he asked what he was doing at that particular moment. The man hedged, but finally confessed that he was on the pier of a bridge about to commit suicide, when a strange influence came over him and impelled him to stop.

2. Pray in Faith

'*What things soever you desire, when you pray, believe that you receive them and ye shall have them*' (Mark 11:24). A. Paget Wilkes used to say, 'Let the prayer of desire pass into the prayer of faith: remember it is the prayer of faith that saves.' There are over 35 recorded miracles of Christ and in all but about three, there is a distinct mention of faith. '*According to your faith be it unto you*' (Matt. 9:29), '*If thou canst believe*' (Mark 9:23), etc. Faith is like the pulley-belt which links the machine to the central driving shaft. There may be endless power in the shaft, but if the pulley-belt is slack or broken, it is lost to the machine. Christ, omnipotent though He was, could do no mighty work in Nazareth where He had been brought up – the *one* place He would have wished to bless and heal.

Many Christians mistake counterfeits for faith. Three counterfeits are belief, feelings and presumption. If someone gives me a remedy I may believe it will cure me, but if I stop there it does me no good. If, however I *drink* the remedy, I feel better. The act of drinking is 'faith'. Many church-goers believe the creeds, but are as much lost as the heathen, because they have never *acted* on them in saving, appropriating faith. They mistake **belief** for faith.

Other Christians mistake **feelings** for faith. But feelings have no more to do with faith than the proverbial man in the moon! Oh, when will Christians get out of bondage to this fallacy?

Faith is the root; feeling the fruit – or part of it. No farmer sows a harvest. That comes after; he merely sows bare grain. Just so, when the Christian is prepared to sow *bare faith, void of feelings,* he will reap a harvest of answers ... and plenty of feelings will come with them!

Don't confuse faith with **presumption**, as many do. Presumption is acting, yes, but acting and launching out on God for things not warranted in His Word ... Get off this ground! You are on a quicksand. You are resting on your own works, not on the death of Christ on the cross.

True faith is to believe that God is true to His nature and His word ... simply holding God faithful to Himself, as shown in His promises in Scripture, or directly through His Holy Spirit. True faith is 'to hold fast to the faithfulness of God'. Micah 7:20 may help here. It is very strange. It reads, '*Thou wilt perform the truth*

to Jacob and the mercy to Abraham, which thou hast sworn.'
One would have thought that it was foxy Jacob who needed the
mercy, not upright old Abraham. The answer is this. When God
made the covenant with Abraham He was under no obligation to
do so. So that was His 'mercy'. But once that covenant was made
to him and his seed, God was bound, by all that He is, to fulfil it.
That was His 'truth'.

3. Use the Name of Christ
He said, '*If ye shall ask anything in My name, I will do it*' (John
14:14). Faith springs from using this name. In daily life, if you
ask in another's name it means you avail yourself of the other
person's resources and authority. The bride uses the
bridegroom's credit at the shop; the right to use her husband's
name, as far as he gives it! So does anyone's signature on a
cheque.

It's no longer a question of *your* resources, but the bank
account of the one whose name is on the cheque. Christ said, '*All
the Father hath is Mine*' (John 16:15). So when He said, '*Ask
anything in My name*' (John 14:14), He opened all His resources
to the poorest Christian!

Using another's name also entitles him to all that person's
authority. Just so, the clerk with power of attorney; the
policeman issuing commands in the name of the law; or, the
ambassador coming in the name of his government with all its
weight behind him, are examples of this in every day life.

Do you realise that Christ's name (for your free use) is '*above
every name*'? God has commanded that *every* knee must bow to
it, (Phil. 2:9, 10) '*of things in heaven, and things in earth*',
including Satan himself! So when we put, 'in My name' into our
prayers we can claim all God's will with holy boldness, although
fulfilment may seem impossible at the time, in the very teeth of
the full fury of Satan's opposition.

4. Mention the Blood of Christ in your Prayers

In Revelation 12:11 it is written that the saints overcame Satan '*by the blood of the Lamb*'. It is by His blood that Christ has defeated Satan. All things are *physically* possible with God, but not *morally*. How? (a) He '*cannot lie*' (Tit. 1:2), (b) '*He cannot deny Himself*' (2 Tim. 2:13) and He cannot bless where there is sin, nor forgive sin without an atonement: '*Without the shedding of blood there is no remission*' (Heb. 9:22).

Both the intercessor and the one for whom he pleads have sinned. Herein lies Satan's great power. By His blood Christ atoned for the sins of the whole world ... and where a man repents and puts his faith in that blood, that atonement becomes effective and his sins are put away. It now becomes morally possible for God to hear and bless. Through the blood of Christ there is *nothing* now that separates us from His omnipotence, ... *nothing* that He cannot or will not do in answer to prayer, to fulfil His loving purpose. So it is, that when Satanic forces press around the Christian, somehow it is the mere mention of the blood of Christ in his prayers which puts Satan to flight.

5. Use a Direct Appeal to Jesus Christ

Many good Christians are afraid to pray to Christ, but it is both scriptural and reasonable. As our Mediator and High Priest, He not only passes on our prayers to the Father, but may receive them Himself and also pray them again for us, adding His own to them. Both Paul and Stephen called on Christ directly. Can't the Bride address the Bridegroom?

Please excuse a personal reference. Some years ago I was going through a time of pain and also danger. After a clear revelation and promise of my life's work some time before, Satan laid me low for three years with one setback after another. It seemed to build up to the point where I felt I was about to be destroyed. Evil forces seemed to be everywhere. All prayer failed. I called on the Father day and night, but could not pray 'through'. I became too weak to pray and hardly dared to believe. Then, late one afternoon, a voice seemed to say, 'You haven't called upon *Me*.' This seemed strange, as I had been calling on God day and night and it certainly wasn't Satan's voice. It was Christ's. With all my strength I called out, '*Jesus*' three times. Instantly, He was there before me, standing at the right hand of God like a High Priest and I was able to tell Him everything, knowing that the Lord heard. At the same time I was filled with wonderful peace and joy and faith as the Holy Spirit filled me. My strength returned and within three hours I was able to get through direct to the Father. It was so easy and natural, as Jesus had already presented my prayers to Him.

This marked a turning point as far as Satan's opposition was concerned. From that time on, I never felt afraid of Satan and never will. Victory has always been given, in the face of Satan's opposition.

I am certain that this faith in the all-victorious Christ, was the secret of the faith and victory of the Wesleyan revival. Linked with Christ, this is how the intercessor must take the prey from between the teeth of the lion. '*Resist the devil, and he will flee from you*' (Jas. 4:7; Eph. 6:11-17). Never capitulate to Satan.

6. Follow 'The Three Steps in Prayer'

Step One
Be still before God and find out what He wants to give before you ask for anything. When God promised the Holy Land to Abraham, He defined its *exact* boundaries, 'from the river of Egypt to the great river, the River Euphrates' (Gen. 15:18). Not a foot more was his, not an inch less.

In the 'Trail of '98', when the gold-seeker came to the Klondike, he had to *exactly* locate and drive his claim between four stakes. Just so, God has a Promised Land for every one of His children – a life-plan; perhaps as a missionary; perhaps some other work. They must seek God's face, quietly waiting before Him, for the revelation of *exactly* what this is. Apparently George Müller spent as long finding out what God wanted to give him, as he did actually praying for it...

If it is a house for a new venture, find the exact number of doors and windows if you can, and – be definite! The Promised Land seemed to have two sets of boundaries – a much *smaller* set, scarcely east of Jordan (which Moses seems only to have in his mind) and an *infinitely larger* border promised to Abraham, several times bigger than the Palestine of today.

When, in prayer, two boundaries appear in your life (a smaller, immediate boundary – and a distant, much greater one) the rule is, *always take the greater*, which includes the less.... You will find this at the heart of all God's will for you.

Step Two

Wait before God until He says, 'Yes,' or until you can claim it in simple faith. After the goldminer has staked his claim, he has to register that claim at the registry office. If he started digging before his claim was registered, any other miner could put in a claim first and dispossess him. You must come before God *as soon as possible*, determined not to leave until you have obtained *all* He has revealed for you to have – 'Not a foot more, not an inch less.'

If you plan to come for half an hour a day for a few weeks, you will probably wait years before getting an answer.

If you come *determined* not to leave until He grants it, I doubt if He will keep you waiting many minutes for the answer. He has never kept me waiting more than two hours! Sometimes He will say, '*Say no more, I have heard you*'. Sometimes, though rarely, He might ask you to come back later. In other words, 'pray through.' But don't leave till you have a definite assurance, or take it in faith, that your prayer is heard. Probably, at that moment, the thing you have prayed for *actually does exist* in the spiritual sphere.

220

Step Three

As soon as this definite assurance is given, do not under any circumstances pray for that thing again. If you do, you will pray yourself out of faith. It dishonours God when He has promised something, to ask Him again. Instead, when the urge comes on you to pray for it again, praise God for it. Thank Him for it as a finished fact. As you do this, *"faith is substance"* and without any further prayer effort at all, you will find that the things you prayed for come to pass, one after the other, like buds opening.

It may take years, but it will surely come – and at the right time. What exists in the *spiritual* realm, becomes evident in the physical realm – through faith.

7. Abide in Christ

This means living and acting in His strength alone, but above all, taking Him into your confidence in *all* things. Placing all things into His hands. Acting directly under His control.

If you ever lose touch with God the Father, the reason is ... you have lost touch with Christ. *Find Christ first.* But there is more. If you only have Christ as Saviour and Lord, He may only be 'a tool', or a 'means to an end.' *Seek Christ for His own sake first,* not for His gifts or service. This will revolutionise your praying. Like this ... before you pray, fix your eyes steadfastly on Christ and fill your whole soul with what He is. Wait until you are filled to overflowing with His love before you think about your petition. At this point, prayer will become effortless ... all joy. He will seem more anxious to give, than you to ask. You will clearly see His will and *want* it too. At the Last Supper, John, leaning on Christ's breast, could have asked for the world if he wanted, scarcely lifting an eyelash or a finger.

To illustrate, a friend of mine had a small boy of three who cried at the tea table. He wanted cake, but his father wisely insisted that he have bread and butter. When he had eaten

221

enough, his father gave him cake. A young lady missionary present went upstairs to her room and burst into tears. She had been asking for something which God had withheld, because she knew He wanted her to have something else *first*. So, she put it right and gave God the first option ... then peace came. Some days later her own request was granted.

Is Jesus your first joy and possession? If not, God will hold back the answers to your prayers until He is. As Saviour we *trust* Christ, as Lord we *obey* Him, as Friend we must *love* Him. 'Trust and obey' is true, but in fact 'Love, trust and obey' is the *full* formula for a happy Christian life. If you withhold your love, you withhold yourself – and you withhold all. Only as you give Him your love in constant communion, can you know His. Only as you tell it to others, will you be sure of it yourself.

8. Obey the Holy Spirit in Prayer

Let *Him* tell you what to pray for, how and when to pray for it – and when God has heard.

9. Keep the Morning Watch

Of Christ it was written, '*He* (the Father) *wakeneth morning by morning, He wakeneth my ear to hear as the learned*' (Isa. 50:4). God's saints are frequently early risers, undistracted, fresh, unbiased. You have got your plans for the day and have committed it to God before it begins, and above all you have given Him 'the cream' of the day. My personal rule, unless otherwise engaged – early to bed and up at dawn.

If you are not already keeping it, start tomorrow. Perhaps you are worried about not waking up in time. Then go to bed that much earlier. Leave yourself the eight hours of sleep that God sees you need and He will do the rest. '*He wakeneth.*' It's astonishing how He does it in different ways. Often He does it through His Spirit. Often He uses natural wakefulness, or other ways. I remember once, dead tired, sleeping in a one-room shack in the Prairies and asking God to wake me up at 5.00 am. There were two windows in my shack (one at each end), but one of them had no glass in it. It seemed only five minutes before I was startled by three distinct raps on the glass and woken up just in time to see a bird dart out through the paneless window! It had tried to fly in one window and out of the other, striking itself three times on the opposite pane ... I glanced at my watch. It was exactly 5 am! You will always find that God is far more concerned to meet you than you are to meet Him.

10. Get all the Information you can
It was information about the ruined Jerusalem that led Nehemiah to pray, which in turn led on to his commission to rebuild it (Neh. 1:3-4). Be sure you give all the information others need to pray intelligently for you, faithfully and immediately.

11. Always Thank God for Past Answers
Nothing is so stimulating to your faith or so better prepares you for further requests (see Phil. 4:6, 7). Besides, it is only courtesy!

12. Be Sure Your Life has No Sin in it
'If I regard iniquity in my heart, the Lord will not hear me' (Ps. 66:18). Especially beware of an unforgiving spirit. In a crisis, Satan often sends temptation to stop effective praying.

13. Cultivate Instant Obedience to All God's Commands

14. Pray With Your Only Motive, the Glory of God
You may be praying for what God wants to give you, but for your own glory, not His at all. Once you put this right, it will show. Somehow it will put an entirely new pentecostal power into your prayers.

15. Be Very Definite in Prayer

Christ often asked petitioners, '*What wilt thou*?' (Luke 18:41). Vague indefinite praying is not Bible praying. Your prayers should be as clearly defined as if you were filling in an order form for a mail order house (Acts 4:29, 30) ... and as accurately fulfilled!

16. Be Still Before God

Give Him the opportunity of speaking to you *first* (Ps. 4:4). I know one Christian who could not remember being still fifteen minutes before God to hear Him speak, in all his fifteen years of earnest praying! George Müller, on the other hand, said that the best part of *his* prayer was the fifteen minutes after he had said, 'Amen.'

17. Do What You Can to Bring about the Answer

God will not give His full attention if you are not sincere in your request.

18. Fasting is Scriptural and Distinctly Helpful

Be careful, though, not to injure your health. Always eat well afterwards and do not fast too frequently. Often a slender meal instead of a full one can constitute a fast. Results are obtained from fasting that cannot be gained any other way (Matt. 17:21).

19. Pray Also with Others

There is a power in corporate prayer above that of private prayer. But corporate prayer in turn gets its power from private prayer. In fact, the best corporate prayer is often when there are only two or three, but absolutely like-minded (Matt. 18:19, 20). They should all 'agree' first before they pray, on what to pray for. Alternate praying, where each will pray several times and very briefly – often with silence in between – is most effective.

224

WHAT REVIVAL WILL DO

Revival will bring about world-wide evangelisation. It is simply God's method of doing His work. By it, the church will do, with one stroke in a single generation, what without it He could not do in a millennium. Humanly speaking, it is utterly impossible ... so was 'the feeding of the five thousand' (John 6) but when that boy gave up all he had, to be taken, broken and used by Christ ... the impossible was done. So today, shall we limit Christ and say that if, in all His church, He can find *six* lives, put into His hands like the loaves and fishes, to be broken and used by Him, this shall not be done? By faith it shall! Make no mistake, God has *no* other method. It is this or nothing.

Revival means the church, or any section of it, being used by a supernatural power to do a supernatural work. The church is like the machinery. The Holy Spirit is like the steam that drives it.... The Holy Ghost as a person, is waiting to use the church – and has been kept waiting (in greater or lesser degree) for twenty centuries, for her to let Him.

The whole problem of the mission field – of the souls of countless myriads – depends on her answer to this waiting Guest.... If the church utilises this power, it will increase in volume like Ezekiel's river (Ezek. 47:1) until the whole work of God is finished. Converts will come in incredible numbers, many of them key people in business, society, education and government – from every stratum of society – the nine tenths who never go to church no less than the one tenth who do!

In short periods these will reach a maturity and depth of Christian experience that would shame Christians today, at our present low level of spiritual power. Almost as soon as they are converted, they themselves will become ardent soul-winners. Many will receive their call to full-time service abroad at about the same time. Giant doors to service will open miraculously, as men are ready to enter them. Miracles will attend their entrance.

Money too, in undreamt-of quantities, will be liberated – just

225

exactly as it is needed. No more, no less. Being Spirit directed, it will be given just where and when it's needed, so having twenty times its present value. And the church will be divinely directed to enter the right door at the right time. She will not waste twenty years knocking on a fast-closed door in one field, when tens of thousands in the *next* field are crying for the gospel – and dying without it. Societies, led by the Spirit, will recognize the men God has chosen in each particular field and send them out – and their work will remain. Their converts will not remain in the cradle to be hand-fed, but will grow fast, leaving the missionary free to pioneer other fields.

How Revival is Brought About

May I repeat the words of Finney. 'Revival will come anywhere, anytime the church fulfils two conditions: a) repentance, and b) the prevailing prayer of faith.'

I asked James Stewart, the well-known missionary to Europe, 'What is the secret of your success ... of these multitudes of conversions?' Without hesitation he replied, '*Partnership with the Holy Ghost*. For me it's an experience too sacred to speak of.'

Fellowship is when two people share their resources and divide. If one only gives and the other only takes or vice versa, it is, in neither case, fellowship. Both must give and both take. The Holy Spirit wants *all* from me, but at the same time He wants me to take His infinite all, by faith according to my need – to share my love, my thoughts and all I have with Him. We do need that *personal* sense of the Holy Ghost as a person, equally distinct from the Father and the Son, that Finney had. Without this revival can never come.

Even rationalistic historians agree that 'The Wesleyan Revival' was a decisive factor for good, in three eighteenth century revolutions. (1) The Industrial Revolution – it went a long way to meet the social and emotional problems that developed: and (2) because of this helped to save England from a French Revolution: then (3) provided spiritual leadership after the American Revolution, when all the Anglican bishops withdrew from the USA. Basically, a charismatic experience means the immediacy of Christ's power here and now (*hic et nunc*), *not* there and then (*illic et tunc*).

WHAT REVIVAL WILL DO TO THE CHURCH

God's presence will be here in her midst – not just in Heaven – and those who deal with the church, will realise that they are dealing with God. There will be many new phenomena (God's presence being the only explanation). Power will be the key word.

To be like Christ ... to do His will ... to pray, to understand, to witness, to give, to suffer and to prevail.

The lighthouse window does not need to *produce* light. It only needs to have the light within and let it shine out through clear panes. So, the church will suddenly be like Christ – sweet, holy, glowing with love, peace and strong faith, yet at the same time sane and watchful. Age-old sins that have long stumbled unbelievers will go in a night and men will see Christ in the church and will say, 'We have seen the Lord!' This is how it will be.

With that, Harry stepped off the platform and strode out the door.

38

THE BBI TRIANGLE

'Give me this mountain....' (Josh. 14:12)

Harry picked up the *Evening Mail* in January 1973. A small article at the bottom of a page caught his eye. The paper announced that '*the 120-year old St. James's Church, Edgbaston has been declared 'redundant' by the Church of England*'. For the parishioners it seemed a tragic day, but for Harry, with the College now bursting at the seams with incoming students ... a gateway to opportunity! For this beautiful old church (designed by the celebrated architect of churches, Teulon) with its fine accompanying vicarage, was situated on a half-acre triangle of freehold pine land and directly adjacent to most of the BBI hostels. Harry had seen enough of God's work to realise what an important addition St. James' Church could be to the BBI development. That evening, as he contemplated the way forward, and prayed at his desk, he wrote excitedly in his journal:

The Birmingham Bible Institute now faces the greatest opportunity of its 22 years of history. From an initial student body of four, enrolment has reached a total of 130, with 150 expected in October 1975 ... and others applying. Most of our College houses are on short leases or rental. Here at last is our opportunity to provide a permanent headquarters for BBI.'

Pushing away a lock of silvery hair from his eyes, he read through what he had written, a little smile playing on his lips as he savoured the thought.

'The acquiring of St. James' Church, Edgbaston, situated opposite our hostels, will provide an auditorium to seat 250 people, with ancillary lecture rooms, library, lounge and offices.... Later, with more modern seating, we could accommodate as many as 400. The project not only preserves an historic landmark of architectural beauty, but will be the means to extend and perpetuate this vital ministry to a modern world.'

As he sat there at his desk, Harry, longing for that promised revival, did *not* see the giants. Like the spies on the verge of Canaan, only the fruit was obvious. The purchase of the freehold triangle with vicarage, church and its year-long conversion would involve a mere £200,000!

Things seemed to be going ahead smoothly. Once again at his desk, he picked up an article by news writer David Coomes, in his full report '**We are Thrilled with God**':

'College Principal, the Rev. H. Brash Bonsall, is more concerned with the practical benefits of the conversion, than with finding the finance, which he is sure will come in, if God is behind it!

'The new Chapel, he enthuses, will retain much of the dignity and sacredness of the chancel end of the Church, where a magnificent stained glass window will dominate. The organ will be rebuilt and used in worship.

'Quite apart from the practical delights of space and expansion, there is also a deep spiritual significance to this site. To begin with, the Rev. Philip Browne, first Vicar of St. James's, was an ardent evangelical. One of his sermons in 1852, was entitled "The Dynamic of the Holy Spirit"....

'Even more significant, *Dorothy Kerin* (who was later to found Homes of Healing) lived in the area for 18 years, was once healed during a communion service in St. James'

Church and claimed to have been told in a vision, that the day was coming when spiritual life would go out from that church to the whole world. Her words that *'Healing light will stream from this church to the ends of the world'* didn't happen in her lifetime, but Mr. Bonsall believes that it will now.'[1]

Harry's 'Church in the College' campaign took off in a big way! Churchmen rose in support. Money came flooding in from different parts of the world in large and small denominations – all given with love and commitment to the vision of revival.

The church and vicarage were to be sold separately, and so for BBI to purchase both would mean a very big step of faith. It was obvious that this triangle of land would be ideal for the new College, with the old church on its pine-clad hill as a central 'beacon'. So BBI made an offer which, by some miracle, was accepted. The cost of the church alone was £40,000 which of course BBI did not have. Thus began three and a half years of prayer and endless red tape until that £40,000 was handed over. By September 1976 *'Phase One'*, with the purchase of the Church (£45,000 with interest and legal charges), was complete!

February 13th, 1976 was a red-letter day in BBI's history, when the Archdeacon of Birmingham handed over the keys of St. James's on behalf of the Bishop, who was unable to be present because of illness. Also present was Mr. Michael Calthorpe. His grandfather, the Rt. Hon. Lord George Calthorpe,

---

1. 'The Vision of Dorothy Kerin' by Bishop Morris Maddocks (Hodder & Stoughton) describes how Dorothy Kerin touched the lives of thousands through her training ministry. She was the founder of Burrswood Christian Healing Centre in Kent, where church and medicine have a remarkable partnership. A pioneer in the church's ministry of healing, she was also a mystic. Bishop Maddocks reveals the unflagging faith which fuelled her every move that lives on in the expanding work of Burrswood today, in the Acorn Christian Healing Trust, and in a growing sense of mission inspired by her vision.

had not only given the land, but actually built the church there in 1850 – for the princely sum of £3,691!

The ultimate purchase of church, two plots of land and the vicarage took place in four stages between 1976 and 1978. £106,000 was given (in today's terms around £750,000!) Deadlines were met by a hair's breadth. God's hand was clearly in evidence. By May 1977 the Council Plot was purchased for £9,000. By September that year a further £6,000 secured the Curtilage Plot. By March 1978 '*Phase Two*' was complete, with the purchase of the vicarage plus interest and legal charges (for a further £40,000), bringing the total raised to £100,000 – all in answer to the prayer of faith. 'This has to be a remarkable miracle,' thought Harry, as he remembered his arrival in Birmingham with only £150 in his pocket!

Jubilee year for BBI!
1978 ... and 25 years on.

In order to prepare the church for Open Day, a dedication service was planned. Charles Eaves supervised the task force of some 50 students, each giving five afternoons for a whole term, to work on the church decorations. Much repair was needed to roof and windows, with the major task of installing modern services such as plumbing, heating and electricity. Repairs to the huge beams were generously gifted to the College by the Calthorpes ... and so the restoration work began.

Excitement reigned! Following the restoration work came the building of a two storey area within the north transept. The choir area was also rebuilt to provide a tiered platform to seat over 100 students for public occasions. Then the big day came when the new '*BBI Tutorial Centre*' was dedicated. Michael Calthorpe gave a stirring account of his own pilgrimage and dynamic experience with God. It was a marvellous Jubilee day of praise and expectation.

'*No matter if we look back or forward,*' Harry told the reporter, '*The theme is the same. We are thrilled with God. It is admirably* suited to being a centre for revival in Britain,' he continued, 'right in the heart of Birmingham, its central city. Within three more miles are a series of cities within a city – large areas housing immigrants of all nationalities and creeds: Chinese, Indian, Pakistani, Caribbean and African. Mosques abound. We don't *need* to cross the ocean – they are at our doors. Within a mile or two are two great universities. Within seven miles, spaghetti junction, where the motorways of England intersect. Here we are preparing to meet a future need.'

Road blocks

Then, the problems started. Harry had always known that the project was humanly impossible. But he fully expected the work to go ahead nonetheless. As the properties had been purchased, now the pressing need was funding for renovation. Projects for housing schemes on the Triangle needed grants and for the next three years *grants* were applied for, but constantly blocked for one reason or another, wasting valuable time. *Loans* could not be released from the Bank, because the Charity Commissioners would not agree to release the deeds of the property as collateral. Different *Housing Associations* were approached, but in the end, all attempts to secure support came to nothing. Different *experts* in the fields of building, architecture and fund-raising were brought in. Meanwhile, as renovation plans for the church were constantly being stalled, the structure of the building itself began to fall into disrepair.

With the need for immediate action to maintain the structure of the church, some came in with different views and ideas, who felt that the church was becoming a liability. It was a combination of these factors that seemed to limit and halt the progress on the plans for the 'New BBI'. At the same time BBI was further required by Calthorpe Estates to bring the existing BBI housing – which was also in need of constant repair and full of students – up to scratch. As a result, the emphasis shifted from the church, to renovation of College buildings.

The frustration after such a glorious beginning was enormous! Harry was adamant that the church must be protected for its original purpose under all circumstances, and tried to get people to carry on with his vision. A new board of directors came in with new ideas – a different generation of Christian businessmen, who were also concerned about the liability to the College of a deteriorating church building. Clearly, some kind of bridge was required from the old visionary faith order to the new.

What had happened? Had Harry, who was always so extremely productive and far-reaching, over-reached himself? Certainly, there were strong opposing factors; spiritual forces at work, and even clear evidence of witchcraft and occult practices in operation within the empty church as it lay open to the public before College occupation. It needed a strong unified body of prayer to counteract the evil influence left behind. Several prophecies were given about the Triangle and many days of prayer and fasting. Unity of vision was vital. 'Prepare for the revival to come,' was Harry's challenge with a clear prophecy given to BBI at that time, simply stating, '*If the College will work for revival I will prosper it ... and if not I will scatter it.*' The 'vision' and the 'blessing' were inseparable.

Sadly, Harry was not to see the fulfilment of his dream. Like Moses he only saw it from afar. But the story has to be told ... and the vicarage on the BBI Triangle that remains, is now in full use by the College. That beautiful church still stands in its needy condition, waiting for a decision on its future. Serious interest has been expressed in its purchase. It is surrounded by a large area of freehold College property with its own potential for the future....

Did the church perhaps become, for those concerned, '*A Bridge Too Far*'? Or will the vision *yet* be fulfilled?

A New Lease of Life

The day came when schooldays were through for all the Bonsall children – Rachel, by far the youngest, being the last to go. At last Harry and Dosie, having worked *so* hard, were free to enjoy some well-earned trips abroad *together*. They didn't waste much time ... and Harry's camera was always at the ready with endless rolls of film. He just loved taking photos – natural photos recording people, historic places and events – clicking away in the assumption that one in three perhaps, would be a good one! His famous phrase was, '*When you shoot, shoot quickly – and shoot from the hip*!'

Firstly, they travelled with Rachel to Afghanistan to visit Ruth. She had married Murray McGavin, a Scottish ophthalmologist, and gone out almost immediately to this beautiful country to work with the International Assistance Mission. Murray was then Medical Director of the N.O.O.R. Eye Hospital in Kabul.

Then, in 1977, the most historic trip beckoned for Harry. Canada, the land of his childhood and youth, was the destination. A huge lump formed in Harry's throat as the plane landed at the airport. He could not believe all that had taken place since he had left this wonderful place forty-two years previously. He remembered the aspirations and expectations that had accompanied him on that sea voyage to Britain – some overly idealistic, but most deeply instilled in him by the Lord. This visit, with Dosie and Rachel, evolved into a four and a half week preaching tour, visiting life-long friends from student days all along the way, and culminating in a television interview in Edmonton, on 'The Prairies – Before and After'.

Trips to Israel, the USA, Tanzania and Germany followed. On the Israeli tour in 1979, led by his old friend, evangelist Peter Scothern, Harry was so excited he outran the party, hurrying ahead to leap into the Dead Sea, then the Sea of Galilee. Wherever there was water, he was in it! His trip to America in

1981 was a special lecturing tour to Jordan College, Michigan, to help set up a student exchange programme to BBI. And so it went on.... Out of these years of teaching, preaching and writing came a new venture.

39

QUERNMORE BOOKS
(Bonsall Publishers Ltd!)

Harry firmly believed in the power of the printed word and in particular the authority and richness of Biblical text. Again and again he would emphasise to the students one of his guiding principles: *'Write it down ... Put it in print ... Pass it on.'*

From his earliest days in Britain, Harry put this principle into practice, helping to produce top quality magazines and writing numerous courses and articles, particularly for young people, in the bi-monthly British Youth for Christ magazine, 'Vista.' He wrote seven studies on 'The Authority of the Bible'; eight studies on 'The Adventure of Becoming a Christian'; and another series called 'Look in the Book', on how to study your Bible. He wrote a series of 300 articles in 'The Christian' magazine over three years, on 'The Interpretation of New Testament Words' (in Greek) ... and so it went on!

Quernmore Books was born in 1981 out of fifty years of pastoral ministry alongside forty-three years of teaching, writing and making a record of every lecture to print for future reference. It was also born out of many years of faithful, painstaking work and experience; starting with the printing press in Colchester, then at All Nations with Bill Worboys, moving on to the capable hands of dedicated men who formed the backbone of the BBI Printing Department. The productive team with its Heidelberg press, set up a training module for weekly classes on camera work, lithography, litho plate-making, and finishing, working at first with very well-worn printing and lithographic equipment. Gradually this was replaced by more advanced machinery, in order to produce quality literature.

Edward England was Publishing Director for Hodder and Stoughton, and producer of the 'Renewal' magazine – an expert in the editorial and marketing field. With his advice as publishers' consultant for the publication of 'longer run' books, and Taylor and Harper as publishers' agents, Harry set out his aims for the future:

'Quernmore Books, recently formed and privately owned is designed to prepare, print and publish sound evangelical literature (along with copies of the Scriptures) for students who will serve Christ as workers. Basically it belongs to the area of Christian education – though not exclusively.

Its aim is to publish:
1. not less than six titles per year (all A5 paperback, good clear print, 130 – 230 pages)
2. to supply by return of post
3. never to run out of print.'

Books by different authors started to roll off the press. Books such as 'What Every Young Christian Should Know', 'Things to Come', 'Avoiding the Leap' (A philosophical introduction to theology), 'Bible Manuscripts', 'Bible Geography', 'Introduction to the Bible', 'The Art of Public Speaking and Preaching', and 'Revolution: Communist or Christian?'

Harry's main work, however, was a treatise on 'The Person of Christ' in four volumes (published by the Christian Literature Crusade, with a foreword by Professor F. F. Bruce). His aim was to make theology come alive to the man in the street. The reviews were impressive:

'Most scholarly works published this century are devoid of devotional content, concentrating on bare facts, dry theories and dull explanations.... These days a book is either spiritual or scholarly and 'ne'er the twain shall meet!' ... but 'The Person of Christ' Volume 2, like its predecessor, is an exception. The Rev. H. B. Bonsall intends the books to be primers, or elementary texts on the Person of Christ, but let the young student have no fear. The hard nuggets of scholarly fact are there, made to glisten and gleam by the heart-warming illustrations and inimitable style of the author.... Buy it! You will not regret it.'

(*Stanley Jebb,* BBI Lecturer and Pastor)

'The Person of Christ' Volume 2 is 'one of the most fascinating study books I have ever read – so full of valuable information and spiritual enlightenment... a boon for pastors and students and worthy of a very wide circulation.'

(*Maynard James* – Editor: 'The Flame')

'A masterpiece in clarity of expression and deep penetration, presented in a way easy to read and understand ... I began to underline what I considered to be vital and outstanding passages, but gave up doing so, as I found that I would have had very little left not underlined!'

(*H. Jenkinson*)

'An engagingly readable and yet highly learned treatment of the relation between Jesus Christ and the Word of God; offers an astonishing wealth of historical detail and psychological insight. An unusual offering with something to interest everyone, from a versatile evangelical.'

(*'Christianity Today'*)

As former students read through the first chapters, they could almost feel themselves back in the lecture room with Harry. By committing a lifetime of experience, knowledge and intimacy with the Lord to paper, and publishing it, Harry was convinced that the Truth of Jesus could be spread long after any author had passed on. In this way, like the Olympic torch, the flame would not be allowed to go out.

40

LOOKING BACK

It was one Monday morning late in October, and a few weeks into the start of another academic year. Nights were drawing in, but days were mellow, with chill autumn sunshine, the smell of wood fires and a definite hint of winter in the air.

This day was special, set aside as a 'Quiet Day' for the BBI students, who were chatting quietly as they waited for a visiting speaker to begin. Silence fell as a large, blond Dutchman took the floor. Johan Companjen, once one of their number, certainly had many gripping stories to tell, and didn't waste a moment. He told them about the years after BBI. How, with his wife, Anneke, he had experienced life in Vietnam before the terrors of a communist takeover and eventual evacuation in 1975. How he had later joined the 'Open Doors' team with Brother Andrew, first as Director of Development in Holland, then as his Personal Assistant.

Then, the tone of his talk changed. 'You know, we Dutch people are pretty big, (as you will have noticed!) but we love BBI.... Well, I shouldn't get into the emotional thing here (or Brother Andrew will fire me as I'm meant to be speaking about Open Doors!), but BBI never goes out of your system. I warn you in advance, that's a disease that stays with you for the rest of your life – and I really mean that. I don't think there is one week that some kind of principle that Mr. Bonsall taught us here doesn't go through my mind, not one week ... and it's exactly the same for my wife ... and other students as well!'

Harry, now in his seventies, sat enveloped in his gown, head in hand, at the far corner of the platform, with Dosie by his side.

His thatch of curly hair was silvery now, but he was listening intently. At Johan's last words, he looked up with a smile. Johan changed his tack.

'Now, here you are, a new generation of students. Maybe you wonder, what am I learning here? When you leave, you'll find out! After a year or two, you'll say, "Well, I wish I had those hours once more, that I could really get dug into the Word again."'

Then came the challenge. 'When we first went to Vietnam we had difficult times there. If God has given you a call, leave the timing to the Lord, but *be faithful. Be faithful here.* I saw many students at BBI with good things, but I also saw students who were too lazy to study ... very spiritual in the way they talked about things but ... well, you won't fool God and you will feel sorry. There are *no shortcuts*. Take God seriously and then He will take you seriously too. *May God help us to be faithful.*'

Harry nodded gently to himself. 'Yes,' he thought, 'that's exactly it! He has learnt well. It's a new generation of students and that's just what they need to hear.' Harry stepped onto the platform and put his arm around Johan's broad Dutch shoulders and gave them a fatherly squeeze. He loved having these 'old students' back to share with the rest of the BBI family. How wonderful, he reflected. All those generations of students. In his mind's eye, he pictured thousands of keen, young faces that seemed to merge into one wider picture, spanning the years. Harry felt a sudden urge to be alone.

After lunch, he donned his hat and overcoat, picked up his stick and rucksack and set out on the long hill down the old University Road. His stride was still firm, but less brisk than it had once been. Harry's brow furrowed as he followed his line of thought to his destination – the lake outside the University Hall. There was an old, wooden bench there, where he sometimes sat watching the ducks and friendly squirrels. Harry rested his hat and stick on the bench and carefully eased himself down onto it.

He had become painfully aware of a certain slowing-down process of late. There was still so much he felt he needed to do, but physical limitations held him back. Was he running out of time? His thoughts sped back to student days in Vancouver and the incredible vision that followed. Suddenly, Canada seemed like yesterday. How little they had known of what would take place in the years and decades to come. Harry remembered vividly God's call on his life; the way God had so clearly told him to come to England to found a system of Bible Colleges, fanning out from London. He had envisaged Bible Colleges throughout Britain and maybe into continental Europe.

He also recalled his second goal: to promote the spreading of revival from churches in Britain, to Europe, then the world – and not just revival, but also the gospel. He so desperately longed to get the gospel to every country in the world in *his* generation – and in particular to mobilise the young. To train the most unlikely, and to make leaders out of them. His final plan had been to mobilise prayer, serving the whole Christian church in all denominations.

At the time it had seemed well nigh impossible, but Harry's faith had been stirred by that vision. And what about those youthful days in Canada and his longing to follow in the giant footsteps of those amazing missionary pioneers, Paget Wilkes, Jonathon Goforth, Charles Judd and the Taylors? Instead the Lord had laid him low – flat on his back – to make his own particular call and vision sure!

Harry took a long, hard look at himself as he sat there deep in thought on that old bench and asked himself, 'Have I been faithful to that call? How much of my vision has become reality? Have I really obeyed my Great Commission ....or have I failed? And what about Revival? It's just around the corner, I'm sure of it. But will I ever *see* it?' Still more questions came thick and fast, as Harry reflected on his life. 'Have I really done my best? Perhaps I've spent too much time focusing on BBI, when I should have worked for the larger vision to come...?'

241

Reaching for his rucksack, Harry pulled out a thick sheaf of letters, articles and prayer cards. He adjusted a pair of well-used horn-rimmed spectacles, and began to read. They had come from hundreds of former students, going back to the early days at All Nations and stretching right through the years of BBI ... and beyond. Each name that he read was not only a name to him, but also a face, and a personality. He remembered the hopes and aspirations of each one, and it amazed him to see how so many of these had been realised. Many had gone on to serve God all around the world, while numerous others were doing the same throughout the United Kingdom, in Christian ministry and in secular jobs. He began to understand just how much had been achieved in every continent through All Nations and BBI students, who had decided that 'to live is Christ'. He knew, too, that some had even discovered the truth of the other half of that verse: '... to die is gain.' Harry reflected quietly on the achievements of Leslie de Smidt, John Haywood, John Harper and others, who had given their lives in missionary service. No, he had not wasted his time and effort. The letters he regularly received from former students showed clearly that his life had produced real and tangible results. True, he had probably become too focused on the administration and development of BBI, with its regular housing shortages and financial pressures, but through it all the vision was clearly being fulfilled, at least in part.

Harry carefully slipped his papers back into his rucksack, and rose slowly from the bench. Walking home, he reflected some more on his mistakes and achievements, so that when he finally arrived at No. 8, Pakenham Road, he lost no time in heading for a typewriter and committing them to paper, with a view to sharing them with the students:

The Red Sea Route'

'Thy way is in the sea and
Thy path in the great waters, and
Thy footsteps are not known.' (Ps. 77:19)

'Looking back, I have discovered something about myself. I like the 'land route' ... committees, salary, all provided beforehand! Left to myself I would always chose it. All cut and dried, of course ... choosing only what I can do in my own strength without any help from God. But *God's Way is through the sea!* Right into the path of utter impossibility. Not around it, over it, or under it, but in it! Right into the heart of that impossible situation that can only be changed by the miraculous divine power of God. *'Thy footsteps are not known.'* The children of Israel had no idea how God could lead them ... five minutes before the waters parted, nor yet five minutes after they had returned.

'With splendid ingenuity I dodged the Red Sea Route for years, till there were no other options left but the Red Sea. All my disasters came through dodging it. Isaiah 63:13 says, "*He led them through the deep as a horse in the wilderness, that they should not stumble.*" I have since found that this is the only region of perfect safety and peace, with all the joyous liberty of the horse trotting and cantering in the wilderness – its native prairie. Now, whenever the way leads through the Red Sea route of utter impossibility – I go straight for it with open arms! It is always the quickest and most perfect route of all.

'If God has called you to work for Him, you may rest assured that sooner or later, (and probably sooner!) His path will lead you right into impossibilities. This is when you must go right forward, confidently expecting a miracle!'

41

'OUR PRINCIPAL – AN OCTOGENARIAN'

David Smith, much-loved tutor, in charge of Old Testament studies for more than 34 years, took over as Vice-Principal after the time of crisis in 1965. David's own inspiring yet scholarly lectures, personal influence and wise counsel, quite apart from his wonderful sense of humour, left a deep impression on Bible College students over the years. In 1985, to celebrate Harry's 80th birthday, he wrote the following tribute:

'During the summer vacation, our Principal and Founder, passed his Eightieth Milestone ... and on Saturday 5th October, Mr. Bonsall led us into the new session. Undoubtedly, he has become the senior Bible College Principal still on full active service, in the United Kingdom, The Americas ... and possibly the world.

'Do we realise how privileged we all are – staff and students alike, in having a share in the exploits of such a "man of God"?'

A modern Moses

'*So Moses ... did exactly as the Lord had commanded ... Moses was 80 years old*' Exodus 7:6-7a NEB (adapted).

'Throughout Old Testament history God did every major work through individual leaders: Joshua, the Judges, Samuel, David, Solomon, and Elijah ... above all God worked through the Man – Christ Jesus!

In Exodus, the Lord was about to initiate an immense piece of work – the deliverance and redemption of Israel from Egypt with their transformation from a vast number of serfs into a nation. To execute this, the Lord chose one man, Moses, with his elder brother as a mouthpiece.

To found a Bible College in the Midlands, at the heart of Britain, the Lord used one man – Henry Brash Bonsall – who like Moses, did exactly as the Lord commanded him! 'Now Moses was 80 years old.' Now Mr. Bonsall is 80 years old.

I have known and worked for Mr. Bonsall for over 32 years! How do I appreciate him?'

An Appreciation

1. *First and foremost as a TEACHER OF THE WORD*
I have a biography of Dr. J. Campbell-Morgan by his daughter, entitled 'Man of the Word'. This can be equally well applied to H. B. B. To my mind, as one nurtured in sound evangelical Bible teaching, he stands in the succession of Dr. F. B. Meyer, Dr. G. Campbell-Morgan and Dr. W. Graham Scroggie, our first BBI President.

2. *Secondly as an INSPIRATIONAL LEADER, especially anointed for this piece of work*
(a) '*The Lord's anointed*', as used of Saul and David. He has led strongly from the front – but always seeking the views and advice of those nearest to him in the work. Final decisions were with him as Principal, as he understood the Lord was leading him.

(b) H.B.B. was the '*man of vision*'.
For the rest of the early tutors, we were the privileged ones to put the vision into reality.

245

(c) *He brought out the best in his helpers.*

Some leaders try (i) to dispatch those they find difficult or, (ii) to change their aides beyond recognition. H. B. B. did not, but accepted them as they were. He always gave considerable scope to departmental heads, not breathing down people's necks or checking on them in gestapo-like methods.

(d) *Open to new ideas.*

He may have been our senior in years, but Mr. Bonsall was always ready to try out new methods; tape recording, overhead projectors, videos, new kinds of equipment and innovation.

3. *His Pastoral Heart – loving concern for all.*
   (a) He made us all feel 'at home' and most necessary ... to the latest recruit in the kitchen.
   (b) Always put people 'in the picture', keeping them informed in their own sphere.
   (c) Saw BBI as one great family, with himself as – 'brother' and later 'father.'

His loving concern for all of us was greatly aided by his phenomenal memory – more like a human computer. To mention a name would invite a wealth of detail about the person concerned. Address, telephone number, family circumstances, etc!

It even extended to pets ... giving thanks for Nimrod, a new pet at No.6 in 1963, who happened to be a Manx cat with no tail!

4. *A Man of Prayer and Resilient Faith*
   (a) Disciplined prayer life.
   (b) Prayer relevant for him in every situation.
   (c) Conversations with God in simple style.
   (d) Resilient faith in disappointment and adversity.
       (i) the troubles of 1965
       (ii) loss of Elvetham Road properties

(iii) serious accident to BBI student

(iv) the present state of St. James' Church project

5. *A Conservationalist*

(a) *in material things*

Arrived with only a suitcase in 1952, and proceeded to found a College with no material things, apart from his clothes and books! Loaned much of his library to the College, while Mrs. Bonsall used all her own domestic equipment to cook for the students.

(b) *learning materials*

'Milking' magazines and using resources that others threw away.

(c) *people*

Caring for broken people, drug addicts, drop-outs ... and those with serious marriage problems.

(d) '*Faithful in all his house*' (Heb. 3:5).

Moses was the pattern in all his wise use of material and personal things. A wise custodian of all entrusted to him – and so has been our Principal.

6. *A Man of Venture*

The BBI is here today, because Mr. Bonsall ventured his all in 1952. Nothing ventured – nothing won!

(a) His use of 'The Gateway' College magazine twice a year.

(b) His use of Christmas letter and card to possible students who have lost touch.

(c) Optimism about applicants. Seeing 'born leaders' in the most unlikely people.

(d) Ideals for students to come back as staff. Many examples. To quote a few:

> Stanley Jebb (5 years New Testament Tutor),
> Don Wootten (4 terms NT Tutor),
> Don Foster (13 years as Tutor),
> Charles Eaves (Maintenance Manager),
> Michael Button (Registrar)
> and many secretaries, amongst others.

(e) Network of Bible Colleges.

7. *A Man of Humility, Grace and Forgiveness.*

It was said of Moses that he was '*the meekest of men*' but my experience of Principals, Head Teachers and Co. has been the opposite. They keep their distance from their subordinates – and are not noted for their humility and grace. Not so Mr. Bonsall.

In the face of adverse criticism in 1965 from certain members of staff and students, when they judged him by superficial matters from the shallowness of their own experience ... Mr. Bonsall kept quiet. He was at his finest, committing the whole matter to the Lord, just as Moses did. Subsequently, he has been the epitome of grace and forgiveness to those that wronged him and I personally regret that I did not show the same grace to those who gave me plenty of flack because I stood firmly with him. '*We deeply appreciate our leader and Mrs. Bonsall – who has been the complement of himself – a team of two!*'

One dear Black Country brother said, 'We haven't had a visit from *King Harry* for a while!' Yes, that is how we feel, who labour with the Bonsalls. Moses went on to do yet greater work after he was 80. He lived to be 120. H. B. B. is the 'Lord's Anointed'. Long may he reign!

It was later in the early 80s that Bob Dunnett took over from David Smith as BBI Vice-Principal. In January 1986, following the huge impact of 'Mission England' (15,000 people in Birmingham's National Exhibition Centre), the whole College took time out for three days of prayer and fasting, and Bob

Dunnett began to take a leading role in a major prayer front in the city. The 'Prayer for Birmingham' team focused on the aim of 'revival in the nation', bringing Christian ministers and leaders together throughout the country for a national call to 'Prayer for Revival'.

42

GOING FOR GOLD!

'...trailing clouds of glory do we come, from God who is our home.' Wordsworth: 'Intimations of Immortality'

Harry was 83 years old. The extended family was enjoying their customary summer holiday in Bude, Cornwall. Despite being on holiday, he was still desperately keen to preach. So it was that on that Sunday morning in August 1989, H. Brash Bonsall was announced as the speaker at Chilsworthy Methodist Chapel, Devon. Harry rose slowly to his feet and moved gradually towards the pulpit steps, with one leg dragging somewhat. The steps were managed with great difficulty, and many in the congregation, including some of his closest relatives, held their breath, wondering if he would ever make it to the top.

At first glance, he might have seemed to be a man who was weak and fading, with little left to give to others. When he finally reached his destination, some thought he would have to rest for some time before being able to commence. Not so. No sooner had Harry gripped the pulpit, than he turned to face the congregation, announcing with authority, 'Word of prayer,' and launching into an impassioned plea for real change in the lives of those present. With a voice strong and vibrant like that of a young man, he preached with power. Half way through his sermon, quite suddenly, Harry's voice boomed out dramatically in a solo rendering of the old hymn:

'Will your anchor hold in the storms of life?
When the clouds unfold their wings of strife

When the strong tides lift and the cables strain
Will your anchor drift or firm remain?

We have an anchor that keeps the soul
Steadfast and sure, while the billows roll;
Fastened to the Rock which cannot move,
Grounded firm and deep in the Saviour's love.'

No sign of weakness there! Those in the congregation that day just *knew* that here was God's man.

Harry once said, 'I don't think I could ever retire.' Nor did he! Physical faculties may have slowed him down on the racetrack, but mentally and spiritually he was as sharp and on the mark as ever – fighting keen to push forward, with the promised revival in view. Like Moses, he stood breathless on the brink of the 'Promised Land', with all the signs of God 'on the move' around him.

At 70, Harry had developed late-onset diabetes – perhaps triggered off by the inordinate amounts of sugar he piled into his pint mug of tea early in the morning! It was diagnosed whilst in the pulpit one Sunday, by a young doctor in the congregation, who noticed his extraordinary thirst. Glass after glass of water!

In his 80s he started to lose control of his right hand, then the left. Regardless of this, he continued to preach, lecture, write, produce and publish. As his hands began to lose their strength, Dosie helped him in every way she could. 'It doesn't matter that he can't use his hands,' she confided in a friend. '*I* can be his hands and do everything for him.'

Harry still tried to go for walks, but an infected foot made this increasingly difficult. This man who had done everything with such keenness, was forced by physical difficulties to slow down to a snail's pace. One day, as Harry was about to head out for a short walk and some fresh air, Dosie went up to him and fixed his hat. Then she stepped back, smiling. ' Stand up, Harry – and you *will* look handsome!' Harry made a valiant attempt to lift himself straighter, and looked down at his wife with a slight twinkle in his eye.

He became increasingly helpless, but as Dosie could do everything for him, he wasn't too frustrated. He had no pain and felt quite well, and they *enjoyed* the time together. One evening, Harry said, as he had often said before, 'When I go, I hope I go quickly!' Then he added, 'Don't you pray me back!' He knew Dosie's praying power all too well. Without a moment's hesitation, she laughingly quipped, '*How mean*! What about *me*?!'

Life was still hectic in these last days. Plans to be made, lectures to be given, problems to be solved. Not too busy, though, for an interview with Birmingham's 'Evening Mail', and a radio programme in 1989, with Pebble Mill. In typical style, his parting shot over the air was, 'I haven't seen the revival yet – and I *sure* would love to see it!'

It was true that retirement had never been a word in Harry's vocabulary, but when Dr. Richard Massey, Director of the Deo Gloria Trust felt led to take up the baton and step into Harry's shoes, the moment came to 'hand over'. The 'Mail' recorded the moment:

'Aged 85, after 37 years in charge of the Birmingham Bible Institute, the Rev. Henry Brash Bonsall, renowned for his academic ability and all round training for his students, has decided to "call it a day" and retire....'

So often, following dinner notices or Chapel prayers' announcements, Harry would hand over his 'mike' to the Vice-Principal with, 'Over to you, Bob!' Now, it was, 'Over to you, Richard!'

At the finishing line

The final valedictory service was a wonderful night, as staff and students from around the globe (Nagaland, Seychelles, Holland, Belgium, Canada, America, New Zealand, Finland and the Home Countries) stood up to cheer him on. Two months later on September 8th, it was followed by an even more moving tribute from crowds of old BBI students stretching way back over the years.... Their stories were hilarious ... and the timing was perfect! Harry just sat back and enjoyed every minute. It was a grand finale! Dosie leaned over to someone else on the platform, commenting wryly, 'I've often said, "It's a pity that so many *nice* things are said about you when you're not there to hear it." Well, *he's hearing it all!*'

A Heavenly Choir

Only two days after his special Thanksgiving Service, Harry reached 85. The Bonsalls were celebrating with a family party at No.8, when unexpected guests arrived. 'Who can that be?' thought Dosie, as the doorbell rang.

It was their old friend John Morrison! John, with his van (a different one!) and a small team of singers, had been driving along the motorway heading for Glasgow, when they distinctly felt 'a call' to turn off their route and make for the Bonsall household in Birmingham. Not knowing why, they arrived with their instruments, to discover that there was a party going on. One quickly produced a tie from nowhere and presented it to Harry, who proudly put it on. Before long, they turned to face him and burst into song with a special birthday message ... 'We Love You with the Love of Jesus...' and somehow as they sang, a powerful anointing seemed to come down upon them. Charles felt that he had never heard anything like it. It was as if the most beautiful angelic choir and instrumental backing had been specially commissioned for the occasion, like a royal 'send-off.' In fact it sounded like heaven ... and all of a sudden, he wanted to be there.

A week later, Harry was quietly sitting in his chair, eating lunch. Dosie slipped out to the kitchen for a moment. Walking back, she turned towards Harry. There he sat with his arms by his side ... his eyes closed. 'Harry?' But he was gone.

Dosie, in a dream, went to find their friends in the College nearby and they all came back with her, sitting around with him so peaceful in his chair, as if it were the most natural thing in the world.

The odd thing was, a day or two later his friend, Professor F. F. Bruce had joined him in the ranks of heaven, closely followed by another dear friend from student days, Kenneth Hooker. Three old soldiers, no doubt praising the Lord and having a great theological debate! Someone must have had a lot of pleasure arranging *that* one!

Other tributes rolled in:

'I almost heard all the trumpets!' (*Geoff Percival*)

'What a mighty man of God he has been.' (*Colin Whittaker*)

'A glorious man, full of faith and prayer. Wonderful in his life and witness; in touch with God and caring for his fellow men. A man of letters, but at the same time a man of action ... a teacher and a missionary.' (*Richard Dugdale*)

'I loved him and thought him one of the 'choice saints'' of this century.' (*David Morris*, former Principal of All Nations Christian College)

'A most lovable ... inspiring man of God.' (*Colin Peckham*, Principal of The Faith Mission Bible College, Edinburgh.) 'Unique in his personality and ministry.' (*Mary Peckham*)

'I was shocked today, to see that my friend went to be with the Lord. A gem in human flesh, a memory that never fades. He seemed so invincible – always active and creative.

He was not afraid to think and write the unconventional ... and certainly part of his greatness lies in those thoughts and writings. He committed his life to the eternal and eternity will record his contribution to the world. It was great. I miss him.' (*DeWayne Coxon*, President Jordan College, Michigan, USA)

Padre Jim Duncan, with Harry at the founding of two Inter-Varsities in Vancouver and Toronto, when reminiscing on the past, could only say with amazement:

'In those early student days of the "Fundamentalist Society" I would never have thought my friend Harry, that quiet and highly-strung young man, could possibly have achieved all he has in his lifetime ... but the truth of the matter is, he has outstripped us all!'

43

RUNNING FOR REVIVAL

Rev Bob Dunnett, former Vice-Principal of BBI;
later Honorary Vice-Principal

Looking back after 20 years of working with Brash, it is very difficult to accept the fact that when I first joined the BBI staff, having just turned 40, he was well over 60! Great energy *poured* out of him, physical and mental. A prodigious memory for facts, a prodigious output of correspondence (all completed by 8.30am), an avid appetite for reading, an endless capacity for committee meetings and an *alarming* speed of movement on 'chore' days, all sustained by an omnivorous appetite, a Churchillian post-lunch nap and walks of several miles at a time to keep any incipient arthritis at bay!

For the first ten years at least, it was mostly a case of hanging on to this man's tails and seeking to keep his feet on the ground, particularly when the winds of vision began to blow strongly. I still wonder what he was like in his 30s and 40s!

He was still moving powerfully as he reached seventy and only as his eightieth year began to loom, did serious signs of flagging appear. The last four years, however, saw this immense physique crumble, the tall erect figure begin to stoop and the eyes close sleepily over the agenda papers. As we all expected, he died with his boots on ... at the age of 85!

All this *seemingly tireless energy* was *devoted to a single-minded vision*. The first *impression* of his vision was, that he lived utterly for the College. There was, however, something deeper than that – *there was a purpose behind the College*. The bottom line was a vision of revival, and the College was there to serve that vision.

I am not aware of when he felt the first stirrings of such a vision for revival. But I am aware, however, that he was old enough to have been personally involved with the likes of Jonathan Goforth, and he must have been deeply aware of the extraordinary happenings in China that were part and parcel of that veteran missionary's ministry. Goforth's home base was in Canada, and particularly at Knox College, Toronto, where Brash Bonsall spent his formative years. Brash's avid reading habit would have undoubtedly collected all the information going on revival in China. Interestingly enough, one of the last things he became involved in shortly before his death, was the dissemination of a reprint of Rosalind Goforth's biography of her husband – a classic document on revival.

Brash Bonsall's vision of revival, however, came from a deeper quarry than the testimony of others, crucial though this might have been at first. *His* vision was of the nature of a *prophetic* revelation. It appears to have come to him in the 1930s at a time when for many long months he lay on his back incapacitated and unable to walk. They must have been months of immense frustration for so active a person. He endeavoured to turn them to good account by studying for a further degree, but found that the concentration was missing. All he found liberty to do was to pray and intercede. He frequently described how a travail of prayer came on him during that time.

This all came to a climax that was to be of strategic importance to his life and ministry. God spoke very clearly to him that He was going to send a revival of very great significance ... and that this revival would impact Britain, with very large numbers of people from all walks of life finding their way to Jesus. It was here that Brash found the direction for his life. It was clear to him that he was to go back to Britain, starting a Bible college against that day of revival. *This was a prophetic vision on a very high level. He was obedient to it ... and the fifty years that were to follow fully vindicated its validity.*

He could not possibly have foreseen the appalling events of the Second World War, or the manner in which the decades which were to follow it would see such devastating obliteration of the major moral landmarks that he and his generation took as foundational for their society. He was yet to appreciate the fact that this was to be a *revival in the midst of a scorching moral wilderness* and that God was speaking a most important word over this nation. Neither could he foresee precisely how the College would relate to this outpouring whilst he was still alive.

However, in obedience to the vision, and with so much yet to become clear, he was back in England before the Second World War and on the staff of All Nations Bible College. The war interrupted progress, however, and it was not until the early 1950s, that he was able to move out in obedience to the call to start a new College. He came to Birmingham and from that moment all his energies were devoted to the development of the Birmingham Bible Institute. So much so, that perhaps at times the vision of the College might have obscured the vision of its purpose.

One thing was certain. Faith and prayer were to be the essential foundations of BBI as it developed. The impartation of an intercessory heart, which Brash experienced in the '30s, left an indelible mark upon him. He was *always* a man of prayer. There was nothing he would not pray over. He would pray with anybody, anywhere, at any time and about any thing. It could be embarrassing, it could be amusing, but it was always challenging. He was no stranger to early morning intercessions, and no stranger to nights of prayer. If prayer is the essential stuff of a revival spirit, Brash undoubtedly had such a spirit. *He left the prayer mark on BBI.*

Arriving in Birmingham, he had nothing but a rented middle floor of a large Victorian house. The future College with its buildings and staff lay in the hands of God. There was no other source ... and so faith in the call to start a College and the promises that surrounded that call, were the basic ingredients of what was to develop. Faith and prayer became the prevailing categories of the College.

'A College against the day of Revival' – that was the task. Brash saw this task as one which would equip future leaders with a thorough grounding in Biblical truth and principles. He drew up and exercised his ministry in those earlier decades of the 20th century, when the battle of liberalism was fierce and when so many of the training establishments were succumbing to the destructive criticism of the primary authority of the Scriptures. He was determined that any who went through the new College would have *no* doubts about the value of the Word of God and would base their life and ministry upon it. He often voiced the belief that he was called to College work, called simply to provide teaching and training of a kind which had virtually disappeared in many denominational structures.

The success of that determination was due not simply to Brash's vision. It was due in the main, to those whom God put alongside him in the work – and of paramount importance was his wife. *Doris Bonsall* was unquestionably God's gift for Harry Bonsall. Their engagement and marriage was unique, and she *was totally in the vision with him.* Utterly loyal and devoted to Brash, she was never afraid to disagree with him. A great woman of prayer and fasting, she prayed over everything, especially the family ... for she was a great family woman with a great love for her family. *In a real sense the College was an extension of her family* and she sought to take a real concern and interest in all the families that joined BBI. She also had a great burden of prayer for the well-being of the nation, and made no secret of her opinions on what was wrong with it! Just like Harry, she had immense energy and was prepared to use it whenever it was needed – whether in cooking, cleaning or speaking ... and she was an *excellent* speaker.

Brash was a visionary, and a visionary in a hurry. Others kept his feet on the ground, and made things work. This was nowhere more clear than in the production of the nitty gritty of a working and effective Biblical syllabus. Without any question, I think, David Smith, his Vice-Principal for many years and himself a man of remarkable gifts and very considerable output, made the teaching programme actually work for a College that in my time, grew to a peak of about 150 students. He made it work well. He shared absolutely his Principal's concern for the Word of God that stemmed from good Brethren and Baptist roots. Along with Brash he was a great hoarder. Between them, apart from other things, they had *vast* quantities of books. That of course was to be crucial to the development of the Library. And of course, both had remarkable eccentricities that were to make the College quite unlike any similar institution! Riots of laughter and riots of protest frequently followed each other in this convulsive society!

For many years the greatest lack was someone who would put the rapidly acquired properties into the same excellent shape as the syllabus. Brash accumulated rented properties at an alarming rate, and though he personally put in hours on the properties, he desperately needed someone with a greater flair for appearance and decor. It was some 30 years before such characters appeared. Life then became calmer, but I wonder at the providence that held back for all those years when all other spiritual necessities were permitted.

Hearing Brash speak of the prophetic word which God gave him about revival in Britain, inevitably brought to mind *the prophetic words of Smith Wigglesworth in 1936*:

'There is a revival coming that at present the world knows nothing about. It will come through the churches. It will come in a fresh way. When you see what God does in this revival you will then have to admit that all you have seen previously is a mere nothing in comparison with what is to come. It will eclipse anything that has been known in history. Empty churches, empty cathedrals, will be packed again with worshippers. Buildings will not be able to accommodate the multitude....'

These were precisely the kind of words that Brash used. Smith Wigglesworth was of course a Pentecostal, and he was prophesying over David DuPlessis, another (at the time, very rigid) Pentecostal who, after World War II, was to have a major part in bringing the Pentecostal testimony into the mainstream churches.

It was more than prophetic words that linked Brash with the Pentecostals, however. Brash himself at some point embraced the Pentecostal testimony. Quite when this happened I am not sure, but certainly for the last five years or more of his life this Canadian Presbyterian minister whose favourite mentor was Dr. Graham Scroggie, found his spiritual home in a Pentecostal church that was a remarkable and dynamic product of the 1930s revivals associated with the Jeffreys brothers.

Whilst there was always an unresolved tension in some of his doctrinal statements about the gift of the Spirit (Graham Scroggie was scarcely a supporter of the Pentecostals), there was never any doubt in Brash's mind about the fact that the presence and power of the Spirit was all-important. This was most significant for the College, for it meant that in its most formative years there was always room for pentecostal and charismatic worship, gifts and anointings. Always a place for people to seek to be filled with the Spirit.

This unquestionably was part of *the revival ethos* of the College and made the College fertile for all that belonged to the development of revival vision. It *gave a powerful note to the praise and worship life of the College, and a depth to its prayer life.* It is very doubtful if the College would have become so revival centred or fulfilled its founding vision, without this emphasis.

This concern for the testimony of the Spirit was always balanced, however, by the *equal* concern for diligent study of the Scriptures. *Perhaps the most important achievement of Brash's principalship was that he allowed the College life to be balanced on these twin pillars of the Spirit and the Word.* Here lay its spiritual strength. Here was the source and sustenance for the spiritual vitality that became characteristic of so many students.

At a time when it was common to accuse Pentecostals and charismatics alike of little knowledge of the Word, Brash and his colleagues provided a clear reminder that the accusation was not always just.

Principals are called to be men of vision and also leaders of teams and, alongside his unusual characteristics, Brash typified some essentials of real leadership. He was a man of very big heart with extraordinary humility. He was secure in God's call and God's care, and found no difficulty in giving members of staff all the room they needed to develop their own teaching and gifts. His support and appreciation was always there. He used to say, 'Tops make their own groove as they spin round.' Certainly at times we felt we really *were* spinning a bit too fast, but at least we were allowed to do it in our groove and pursue our own thing within the bounds of equipping the students.

The only thing he asked in return was that he should be allowed to spin in *his* own groove ... and *of course he spun quicker and wider than anyone else*! His groove included the setting up of a printing press and the hiring of printers. It never made a profit, but he was *convinced of the power of the printed word*! His groove also included experimenting with the early efforts at computerisation. In particular, as the College found itself unable to keep up with the accumulation of properties, his 'top' found itself spinning in the area of his own small property empire, housing many students over the years. We kept clear and left him alone. *He was God's man.*

Bound up with his ability to allow people space to develop

their own style, was an ability to recognize where his own gifts ended and others began. Not only to recognize where they began, but to happily remark, 'Over to you!' This was where his humility was expressed again and again. He was so *delighted* at the expression of other people's abilities and gifts, and his readiness to take a back seat was never soured by a disparaging remark.

Another feature of his style of leadership was his readiness (even *over*-readiness) to communicate. Everybody knew what was going on. Decisions were, in the main, *corporate* decisions. The 'up' side was, that everyone felt a part of things; the 'down' side was the plethora of meetings! But the principle of 'share and go together' was a very important one. And at least we all *knew* what he was up to! Everybody could always have their say.

Brash lived to see the denominations blessed by an outpouring of the Spirit, but not to see what was always uppermost in his mind – widespread conversions of large numbers of people. Indeed it has yet to be seen. What he *did* live to see however, was all those students who went out into the churches with their *own* vision for revival and a heart to pray and work for it. To this day, there are so many of them giving a lead to earnest intercession for the promised outpouring. In this way 'the flame' was to be passed on....

44

'OVER TO *YOU*!'

When Harry eventually reached the finishing line someone wrote, 'What a glorious race he has run!'

I'm sure *he* did not look at it like that.... He just did what he had to, one stride at a time. He listened for clear directives from his Coach at the start of the day, then took off into the heat of the action ... and just kept on going, with the vision ahead growing brighter and clearer as he neared the finishing line....

He was well aware that at the end of the track, all God required of him was to be obedient, to be faithful and to finish well!

So it was with the original marathon runner of the fifth century B.C., who had to combine the qualities of soldier and athlete ... winning personal battles along the way, whilst slowly moving towards his final goal. The ancient Greek notion of discipline over mind and body not only produced long-term fitness, but character-building qualities of courage, patience and endurance. '*Perseverance is not a long race – it is many short races, one after another*' (Walter Elliot).

Christianity, however, is *not* a spectator sport. Oswald Chambers called it, running 'today's race.' Selwyn Hughes, 'fulfilling one's spiritual destiny.... The greatest thing anyone can do in this life,' he says, 'is to fulfil their spiritual destiny.... Nothing is more important than doing the work of God. We can opt for the average, or we can pursue excellence.... Has God given you a clear direction concerning the path He wants you to go? Then *go for it* – and never give up! Doing the work of God *faithfully* is the excellence He is looking for!'

Gladys Aylward of China, put it another way. 'Don't worry about your education. God won't ask you for certificates. He'll only ask you if you've been faithful to your call!'

Demos Shakarian in his book *The Happiest People on Earth*, describes his excitement as he discovered *his*. 'Here was my job – the work assigned to me by God Himself.... God had called me – me! – to be a helper, and from that moment on, the wonder of my appointment would never leave me.' 'Friends,' he went on to say, 'I believe God has a particular gift for each of His servants, some special ability we're to use for His Kingdom. I believe, if we find that gift – and use it – we'll be the happiest people on earth. And if we miss it, no matter how many excellent things we do, we'll be utterly miserable.'

But how can you know your call? C. T. Studd, that brilliant sportsman and soldier who gave up a fortune to become a pioneer in Africa, was an 'all-or-nothing' man like Harry. He held the secret. '*Mean business with God.*'

In his small booklet *The Chocolate Soldier*, he wrote a scathing little poem on 'chocolate soldiers', who are all talk, but don't mean business with God. 'Who merely go to *see* battles and coolly urge others to fight them.' They are the ones, like David's brothers perhaps, who had not been trained to hear God's voice or God's directives. They are the ones who, through disobedience or lack of attention to God's voice, become *padded Christians*. They just don't mean business with God. The tragedy is, that they are so used to obeying the demands of their own voice, when God comes to call them, no matter what He does, they just can't hear!

In Harry's terms, 'We *must* have a disciplined spirit ... for in the battle between *will* and *emotion*, emotion nearly always wins. *We must be firm with ourselves, if we are serious about heaven.*'

C. T. Studd painted a similar picture:

> Mark time, Christian heroes,
> Never go to war;
> Stop and mind the babies
> Playing on the floor.
>
> *Chorus:*
> Round and round the nursery
> Let us ambulate.
> Sugar and spice and all that's nice
> Must be on *our* slate.
>
> Wash and dress and feed them
> Forty times a week,
> Till they're roly-poly –
> Puddings, so to speak.

'*Real* Christians revel in desperate ventures for Christ,' he says, 'expecting from God great things and attempting the same with exhilaration.... God never was a chocolate manufacturer and never will be. God's men are always heroes. In Scripture you can trace their giant foot-tracks down the sands of time.... Whilst others were learning pretty theories, David had been alone with God in the wilds, practising on the bears and lions... The result? He *knew* God and did exploits.'

The exciting fact is, so often God seems to see potential in the most unlikely candidates. He did not choose the most obvious candidate of Jesse's family in 1 Samuel 16:7. Instead he said to Samuel, 'Do not consider his appearance or his height, for I have rejected him. The Lord does not look at the things man looks at. *Man looks at the outward appearance, but the Lord looks at the heart.*'

David was a very young, unknown shepherd boy, but God saw his heart, then called him and trained him to hear His voice alone and to fulfil his own spiritual destiny.

266

Gladys Aylward was a little parlourmaid from London with no money, but a great heart for China. Through her obedience and faithfulness, God was able to train her to do exploits and she, too, achieved greatness. When only in her 20s her passionate prayer had been, 'O God! Here's me! Here's my Bible, here's my money! Use us, God. Use us!'

Harry, too, had to overcome many obstacles and limitations in *his* race, but he was faithful to his call. With all his gifts, he was incredibly highly strung at times. As a young student and only child, he was often shy and reserved. Unconventional to the point of idiosyncrasy on occasions and, at a time of extreme stress in the early days, not far from breakdown. He battled against illness in Canada, under direct spiritual attack and major setbacks in Taplow and Birmingham. He had little of this world's goods and money at a minimum. Disappointments when let down, sometimes by people whose vision was small. In his excitement for God's best, he could over-enthuse at times, as he raced through life at 100 mph – but, like Dosie, he never ever gave up.

As a man of integrity he took all his needs very simply to God and held on to God's faithfulness. In fact, he had to wait years for his wife, but when she came on the scene she was worth waiting for! He hung on for victory like Sir Winston Churchill, during World War II, who thundered out, 'Never give up. Never, *never* give up. Never, never, *never* give up!'

Jesus chose very ordinary uneducated men to be His disciples, who had nothing but a heart for God. They became firebrands with the Gospel and turned the world upside down! God is *still* choosing His team – an army of ordinary people trained to win.

'*He always wins, who sides with God.*'

Harry's burning call was to train ordinary people to become

267

leaders. Young men and women disciplined and trained to hold their own pace in the race and carry the torch to the finishing line. In the end he earned high praise from his (then teenage) grandson, Andrew:

'Grandpa was an Abraham kind of man.'

He said himself, 'Each of the great heroes of the faith in Hebrews 11 were commended for the same qualities. Their faith, their faithfulness and their perseverance. Not for the fact that they were perfect, because they weren't!'

It may be tough nowadays, as we reach for the 21st century. The whole concept of faithfulness, integrity and commitment are seemingly out-of-date. People let us down badly, but we have God's word on it that *He* will not. He will never ever let us down. '*God is faithful*' (1 Cor. 1:9). His word is true. His promises are certain facts. Harry's secret, like Hudson Taylor's, was to 'hold on to the faithfulness of God'. In these days we have to hang on to that fact for dear life ... find our call, train for it. .. and keep on going! That's the rule of the marathon. It may be tough, but there's Glory at the end of it ... and many exhilarating times on the way. Serving the Lord is always an adventure!

In the film 'Chariots of Fire', Eric Liddell, that incredible missionary sportsman said, 'I believe God made me for a purpose – and He made me fast!... So where does the power come to see the Race to its end? From within.' Harry could have re-iterated the words of Bill Taylor of World Vision, '*My passion is to finish well.* To encourage the younger generation to run the race well, to trust in the truth of Scripture and the Christ of Scripture and *to finish well*!' Yes, that is the aim of the marathon runner.

One of Harry's fellow Principals looked back on the life of his old friend and said, 'It was no ordinary life, but a wonderful testimony to what God can do with a man who has a vision and follows it through!'

The message is clear. Revival is certainly coming. Are we ready for it?

Now is the time to prepare. Harry and Dosie gave themselves to lay the foundations and carry the torch but it's *our* responsibility to be out there on the track and running with it.

A COMPLEMENT TO THE
BIOGRAPHY

HIS LEGACY

As Others Saw Him

Over the years, Harry encountered many students and friends who encouraged him, and in turn were encouraged and inspired by his life. A biography is not big enough to include all the fascinating stories and events that filled that life and made such an impression on others. Both he, and his wife Dosie, touched many lives.

In order to understand more fully the man, what made him tick and most importantly, the God whom he loved and served, this section includes challenging, inspiring and humorous excerpts from his life, taken from a wide range of personal letters and articles contributed by friends, family and colleagues. As with the biography, the purpose behind this selection of letters, anecdotes and remembrances is not to elevate one man, but to glorify God, and to show how He can use anyone who is totally given over to Him to affect the lives of countless others.

Canada
We start in Canada in the 1930s, as Harry lay on his back, immobilised in a Vancouver Ward.

Arnold Hart-Davies, a friend from Knox College, wrote of a visit to the hospital:

'June 25th, 1934 – I called on Harry Bonsall one day and had a very happy visit. He is slowly and patiently recovering from all the sickness that has been his lot, and is a great man in prayer. One cannot help realising this after visiting him.'

At the time, Harry wrote regularly to *Judson Merritt*, a friend from student days, with up-to-date news of his Intervarsity friends. At the end of one letter, he added... '*myself, awaiting orders.*'

Then the orders came (see *THE VISION*), and Harry was on the move at last, armed with all kinds of references:

'...Mr. Bonsall's health is somewhat impaired and he is on a vacation. He is a young man of splendid ability and excellent character. During his short pastorate he rendered our Church first class service and has always been loved and admired, not only by his people but by his brother Presbyters. Our prayer is that God may soon restore him and bring him back to his work.

J. R. Frizell
Clerk of Westminster Presbytery'

Britain: Early Days

After All Nations Bible College was forced to close due to the outbreak of war, Harry had one sole student who came to him for Bible teaching.

Derek Porter remembers:

'Harry was a great man of God with such vision and faith, especially for Bible training to be available throughout Britain. As a young believer, called to be a missionary, the intensity of his faith-filled prayers enthused me – and in later years thrilled me as I saw the results of a life of prayer.

'In the end my young American wife and I spent 40 years in Nigeria with SIM ... and through the years that followed I kept in touch with Harry Bonsall, whenever there were urgent matters for prayer! He never failed to encourage me.'

Ernest Nunn was another friend from early days in the Friends Evangelistic Band (1940):

273

'Mr. Bonsall came with his mother, a remarkable woman....
He was not at all well at the time, but even then his mind was
so alert and concerned with the work of God's kingdom.

'He was a great listener, who always had time for people.
But what amazed me, was the way he seemed to come
forward with suggestions and encouragement to see things
that were quite beyond our vision...

'He was a man who lived close to God, with very little of
this world's goods ... and if anybody knew what it was to trust
the Lord for daily needs, the Bonsalls did!

'Brash Bonsall had such a wonderful appreciation of the
value of the Word of God.'

Colchester 1941-45

David Morris was an Army Officer in Colchester, and former
Principal of All Nations Christian College (1959-82):

'I loved your father and thought he was one of the "choice
saints" of this century. The fact that he was a Christian
eccentric, endeared him to people – there are too many
stereotyped, rather drab believers around!

'Early in 1946, Trenna and I lived in a caravan, just
outside Colchester. I was a Staff Officer in the garrison there,
and Trenna had been de-mobilized. We tried to find all the
Christians and gradually had a small group in the caravan for
meals and prayer, etc....

'It became a recognized way of making contact, if you
were in a strange place, to whistle, "Wide, wide as the
ocean..."

'I had gone on a trip to find other Christians and was
whistling away, when a window high up on the barracks
building shot open, and a return whistle floated down! A
minute later, a tough regular Sergeant appeared. He was a
staunch PB (Plymouth Brethren) and relied on his Scofield

Bible for spiritual needs. He at once told me that he had seen posters in the town saying that an evening Bible School was due to begin and the topic was John's Gospel. We rounded up all the known Army saints, and Trenna and I went along.

'We found a hall with chairs (being Army folk, we got there early!) and waited. The expected time passed. Then suddenly the door burst open, and a middle-aged man, wearing a black gown and grasping more books than his arms really had room for, rushed to the front.

'He put a spare part of one arm to his eyes and said, "To prayer". He prayed as if he really knew God ... ranging far and wide in his requests, and just as quickly said, "We're going to study Pastoral Work tonight."

'Immediately my new Sergeant friend jumped up and said that they didn't have pastors in his Assembly, and that he had come to hear John's Gospel ... and that he'd fight to his last drop of blood to stop anything to do with pastors! The lecturer, who was of course, Henry Bonsall, was not in any way put out by this onslaught. He merely replied that this was what he thought God meant him to lecture on – and lecture he would! There ensued a verbal battle about pastors, John's Gospel, Sunday Schools and Assemblies, which Henry Bonsall won – with an approximate score of 7 to 3!!

'Eventually a lecture began, on Organising a Sunday School, with elaborate cross-references of scholars – all kept in filing boxes. I can't remember any more about this event, but I did realise that here was a "man of God", the like of whom I had never met before!

'I only saw him once again in Colchester. The town was crowded on a Saturday morning and I was pushing through the people on the pavement, when I was aware of a man running down the main road, clasping many books, going towards the station. I recognised the lecturer and pushed out to join him in his race for the train. He said nothing, but

repeatedly burst out with, "Must pray, must pray, must pray".
He ran on and I hope he caught his train – but again I realised
that *this was a man who walked (or ran!) with God, not only
in the pulpit, but in every event of his life.*'

Gilbert Kirby, later Principal of London Bible College, was also
there:

'I was Minister of Halstead Congregational Church in Essex,
having been ordained there in June 1938... but I was a fairly
unusual member of my denomination in those days, as most
men in the ministry had been indoctrinated with "theological
liberalism". Imagine my joy when I discovered that I had a
near neighbour just a few miles away in Colchester, who
shared my theological views and also ministered in a
Congregational church. He was none other than Henry Brash
Bonsall.

'We arranged to meet and he invited me to his church,
where we soon found we had a great deal in common. I also
realised I was in the presence of a man of considerable stature
and academic ability. He was a visionary, and one day in
Colchester High Street, he unfolded to me his dream of
founding a truly evangelical Bible College somewhere in the
Midlands, possibly Birmingham. To me at that time it all
seemed somewhat remote from reality ... a pipe-dream. He
even hinted that I might consider joining him in the
enterprise!

'The years passed and we lost touch to some extent. I
moved to a pastorate in Ashford, Middlesex, and later
became General Secretary of the Evangelical Alliance.
During that time when my travels took me to Birmingham, I
called upon my old friend. Little did I think at the time of that
kerb-side conversation in Colchester, that 50 years later we
were both destined to become College Principals; Harry

heading up the Birmingham Bible Institute, with myself the retired Principal of London Bible College.'

All Nations Bible College (1946-52)

It was a bit of a shock for soldiers coming back from the traumas of war, to find themselves behind a desk once again! Senior student, *Ken Le Mottèe* (1948-51) reminded others that:

> 'The wide scope of the College Syllabus means a considerable volume of work, determination and diligence, particularly for those of us who have not been accustomed to mental concentration!'

Fellow student *Bill Worboys* apparently arrived from the services with only one shabby, old, navy suit. His wife Molly remembers his delight when a favourite aunt saw his plight and took him out to an exclusive men's store for a replacement.

> 'Why don't you send that old suit to the cleaners,' she said.
> 'You can't go out preaching for the Lord looking like *that*!'

Bill left the store that day feeling 'ten foot tall'!

Doug Abrahams (1947-49): 'The impact of your father's ministry on me, was heightened by the fact that I left school at 14 (1934), was in the Army when war broke out and demobbed in 1946. I had never sat in a lecture room and knew nothing of missions ... certainly nothing of Bible School....'

Bernard Collinson (1946-48), who came to All Nations after six years in the British Army with the Field Ambulance Service ('Normandy landings and all that!'), watched the Bonsall team in action.

'In those early days I was very impressed with their quality of life. Brash and Doris walked with God.... Their composure in the midst of a busy, busy schedule, proclaimed it. There must have been so many frustrations following ANBC's move to Taplow (starting difficulties, lack of adequate funds and accommodation, lack of private transport – only one student with a car, plus less than efficient communications) but I never saw Brash or Doris lose their calm.'

An Overview

Looking backwards – looking forwards
Some years later, *Edward England* (then Publisher and Director of Hodder and Stoughton) in his book 'An Unfading Vision' (1982) described the current attitude, preceding and during the 1960s:

'Fifteen years ago there were few publishers in Britain who would publish a charismatic book. There was almost a conspiracy among Christian publishers and booksellers to keep quiet about this fresh recognition of the Holy Spirit ... worried by what they saw as similarities to old-style Pentecostalism, with its prayers which bordered on ecstasy and lack of ministerial formality.'

In 1984, *Colin Whittaker* presented a book on 'Great Revivals'. In the flyleaf of my father's copy he wrote:

To Brash Bonsall,
With appreciation of your outstanding teaching ministry to the Body of Christ in these exciting days, when Revival is beginning.   God richly bless you.   *Colin Whittaker*

278

Yes. Preparation for revival was his 'trademark' – at a time when a fresh recognition of the work of the Holy Spirit was *not* popular in some established Christian circles. How did he cope with this challenge ... and how did it affect his ministry?

LET THE STUDENTS TALK

Let's pass the pen to the young men of All Nations in the 1940s...
.

From South Africa, *Vincent Rudman* (1949-52) writes:

'One cold and frosty, late December afternoon in 1949, I knocked on the door of All Nations Bible College in Taplow near Maidenhead, then a small town situated on the banks of the River Thames. Having worked my way over from South Africa on a cargo boat, I was not in a position to provide an arrival date, as the boat had traded its way up the west coast of Africa through rough and stormy weather, taking over 21 days to reach Southampton.

'After a moment's delay the door opened and a tall man stood in the doorway. "Good afternoon," I said, "Is this the Bible College?" But before replying to my question he asked, "Are you from South Africa?" As I nodded, the realization dawned on me that this man was sharp. In only a few words he had sized me up. He grabbed one of my suitcases and said, "Do come in."

'This was Henry Brash Bonsall, Principal of All Nations Bible College, whom I learned to respect as a man of great integrity, kindness and sincerity.

'Everybody, including students from Poland, the Ukraine and Georgia, loved and respected him very much in spite of the language problem, and his leadership was an inspiration to us all, not only in the classroom but in all aspects of College life.

'His interest spread throughout the student body, including their activities outside the classroom. There was a woodworking shop and a printing room, to which he was a regular, if not daily

279

visitor. Students really appreciated this kind of interest and it flowed freely and naturally from our Principal. Clearly, he was the right man in the right place!'

Lectures
'If the pupil has not learned, the teacher has not taught.'
'In the first place your father was born a compassionate gentleman; in the second, a remarkable teacher. He made things really come alive and stay alive! As a student I was impressed by the way he regarded everything he did with such urgency and thoroughness.

'There were five lecturers at All Nations when I joined them as student ... and during the early part of my course, I had the privilege of New Testament Greek lectures from your father. We got on famously, until the College appointed another full-time Greek lecturer. For some reason or other, one could no longer look forward to lessons in New Testament Greek!

'His lectures on the Person of Christ were the most interesting and fascinating imaginable and I was overjoyed to hear they were to be published in book form. I now have four volumes of *The Person of Christ* and I can assure you that I regard them as the most valuable books in my library of 800 volumes. There are numerous sermons on practically every page. Your father was a past master in drawing spiritual lessons from the ordinary events of Biblical history.

'I do not believe the students had any difficulty whatsoever in following Mr. Bonsall in the classroom – with the possible exception of speed! (In Greek he had so much to say, he pounded ahead at the rate of an express train.) Some students complained, others gave up taking notes and just listened. He got through a vast amount of instruction in 45 minutes and when he actually dictated for the purpose of taking notes, murmurs and audible sighs of relief could be heard from some quarters of the classroom when the lecture was finally terminated!

'His teaching techniques were of the highest standard, and as

280

a theologian he taught with a minimum of words, helping his students to grasp basic truths quickly and easily, whilst leading us to think and reason for ourselves. As far as I am concerned, he was a top-notch lecturer and a born teacher and I just loved him for it.'

Taffy (Tom) Pratten (1946-48): 'One day he gave us a stream of interesting stories one after the other, then coming to the end of the lecture, he dashed off a boardful of references from Genesis to Revelation, fleeing from the room, with his gown flying ... leaving us students (some of whom were slower than others) reeling with shock and completely "at sea"!

'His phenomenal knowledge of the world, people and cultures, was coupled with intricate understanding of a wide variety of professions and trades, so whatever the subject – tracking in Canada's north, or maritime navigation – he had that ability to communicate the feelings and fears of every participant in the drama. The result: lectures and sermons were rich with illustrations, many from his own travels and experience of life. Just as Jesus taught through parables, so Brash's anecdotes and stories aimed to implant a truth in the mind and heart of the hearer.'

Fred Marlow (1948-51), Head Student: 'We knew him truly affectionately as "Brash", bordering on the eccentric and very close to genius. His entrance into the lecture room was tempestuous, his gown flowing behind him and his chin resting on a pile of books which he rarely referred to!'

Alan East (1949-51): 'The same tempestuous procedure was repeated regularly in lectures in the temporary lecture hut. Students would be sitting expectantly awaiting the Principal.

'After a few minutes delay (and at the last minute) the door at the back would fly open and in he would storm with massive strides, his academic gown billowing out behind him as he mounted the dais. Then the flood of teaching would pour over us.

281

Any cries of help would receive scant regard and all that would change would be the metaphor!

'"Pin the ghost" he would command, leaping around in front of the blackboard, hammering in imaginary nails ... meaning "Make a concise summary of my salient points!"'

Fred Marlow and Bernard Collinson: ' "My anecdotes are the 'clothes pegs' for my teaching" he used to say, and he encouraged us all to *"Write it down"* – to build up our own private fund of stories and anecdotes, indexed and labelled ready to pull out at the right moment. "If you ever read a book without a pen and notebook nearby," he'd say, "You're wasting your time."'

Noel Stanton (1951-52): 'What an exciting, loveable man, whose inspired lectures, punctuated by anecdotes, were the most interesting of the syllabus!'

John Pickett (1949-51). 'No wonder his own study was not a tidy place! His books were at least two deep on the shelves and most of his desk was covered with papers, but he knew exactly where everything was!'

Bill Flagg (1949-51): 'His lectures were very vivid and usually started with "Gentlemen..." My second lecture on Calvin in Geneva was illustrated by Brash stamping around the platform portraying Calvin in the inn, with everyone saying, *"You must! You must! You must!"*'

Alfred Lau (1946): 'One of Mr. Bonsall's special subjects in Church History was the persecution of the Christians – during Nero's reign, or the Reformation. He just loved history and lived it as if it were the present. Somehow he could put himself into the position of those heroes of the faith, to present them vividly before our eyes. In today's world, where values are changing, it is hard to find a man like the Rev. Brash Bonsall. Covering his footsteps will be close to impossible.'

Arthur Caiger (1948-50), Head Student: 'H.B.B.'s Systematic Theology lectures were such an uplift. One fellow student turned to me and said, "Listening to H.B.B. and his biblical exposition is just like sitting in a marquee at the Keswick Convention!"'

Bert (Jim) Metcalfe (1949-51): 'Brash was a fine gentleman, saint, scholar, teacher and preacher. I remember how he pictured Biblical prophecy in stages, like a series of peaks. One got to the peak of one mountain, only to find a new peak lying ahead ... then another ... and another!'

Brian John (1949-52): 'His wealth of stories and illustrations stand out. Sometimes they were fantastic. Much more interesting than the subject matter in hand! If he felt the story didn't quite match his point he'd say, "*Catch the ghost*" (i.e. forget the story but get the point!).'

On the Funny Side
Lectures were obviously highly entertaining and unpredictable!

Ray Giles (1949-52): 'Students getting ready for foreign fields needed a sense of humour to keep them going in tough circumstances and B.B. certainly set them a good example! Many practical jokes were played on him and he took them all in good part – adding to the liveliness of his lectures.

'One day lectures were in full swing, when he was interrupted by the shrill blast of an alarm clock coming from somewhere beneath his feet. His eyes swept the room but saw nothing. The clock was happily concealed in the six inch platform he was standing on! Shortly after this, the ringing stopped and H.B.B. carried serenely on. A few minutes later it started up again: Ring

ring! Ring ring! Ring ring! His action was the same. Smilingly he waited for a break in the noise, then carried on teaching. After a few eruptive peals of sound the alarm eventually gave up – but BB never tried to discover the culprit.'

Life in the Fast Lane
'Don't put me off my drive!'

Bernard Collinson (1946-48): 'His ability to work with and under the authority of Principal Poole-Connor, was a tremendous testimony. Rev. Poole-Connor was a fine and saintly man, but elderly, traditional and cautious. Brash was much younger, unconventional and venturesome. Both men had vision but *Brash lived in the fast lane and urged everyone to join him there!*

'When Brash became Principal the twice weekly sessions began, introducing building, gardening and printing. During these sessions Brash would be seen working on his plot of land, clad in old clothes and heavy boots. Even when his academic responsibilities were heaviest, he found time for practical tasks. This illustrated a true balance in life and sent a powerful message to us students.'

Ted West (1948-51): 'He seemed to be a man who was in a hurry with life – but then he would be, knowing how much there was to be done! He was an extremely fast worker and wouldn't want to waste a moment. Once I was in charge of a gardening party. Brash, the Principal, came to me, asking what I would like him to do. I was quite embarrassed to be giving orders to the boss, but asked him to begin a new row of digging, as some half-dozen students were already part-way through the row we were on.... In no time at all he was at my elbow, asking what he should do now? He'd finished his row on his own and was eager for more! Indefatigable indeed!'

Fred Marlow: 'His trips to the garden were an experience to watch! Almost every garden tool imaginable was piled into a wheelbarrow, which he pushed at great speed. He would then dig at twice the speed of any student for about two hours, then rush back at the same speed.'

Ray Giles: 'Brash Bonsall's rapid action was also seen at the breakfast table, when all the students took it in turns to be "butlers". Naturally, the Principal's porridge was served first, but B.B. would consume his porridge at his usual high speed, and be waiting for the next course before all the students had received their first!'

Alan East: 'The sedate Miss Housego would partake of lunch at the next-door table in a composed and dignified way, engaging in reflective conversation. Not so H.B.B. A few deft strokes with the knife and then a flurry of forkfuls to clear the plate – followed by restless impatience waiting for the slow coaches to catch up!'

Ted West: 'Before we could recover he would be pounding through the meal keeping up a running commentary on all and every subject, with a graphic grasp of detail on each student's particular problem and interest at the time. How he never got the desperate indigestion or ulcer trouble that nearly floored me in those days, I shall never know!'

John Pickett: 'Grace before meals for Brash came in a variety of sentences, languages and styles – Greek, Latin or whatever. Once we were all taken by surprise as he pronounced, "Bene dictus, bene dicat," and sat down!'

Bryan Baxter (1949-52): 'Another time he swept into his lecture in such a rush that instead of the usual opening prayer, to our delight he shut his eyes and said "Grace!"'

285

People

Jack Armstrong (1949-52): 'Almost everything he did fast, except when he was listening to someone.'

Noel Stanton: 'Brash was an unforgettable, spirit-filled man, full of energy and vision. He loved Jesus and he loved his students.'

Bill Flagg: 'Another thing that inspired me was his ability to become profoundly interested in whatever topic challenged him, (i.e., the purchase of a guillotine for the All Nations print room!). Soaking in new information like a sponge, he became a semi-authority on every subject that interested him ... and was equally keen that everyone else should join in with their own particular skills, passing them on to others in the process.'

Fred Marlow: 'One mealtime Brash sat next to a student named Harry and, in his usual style, he asked Harry what his father did for a living.

Harry's father was a 'wheel-tapper' on the railway-line (checking all the wheels along the train with a long-handled hammer, when the train stopped). I think Harry was just a little embarrassed, as generally this was considered quite a menial task, but, by the time Brash had finished, the whole railway system hinged on this one operation!'

Jack Dawney (1950-52) *The Man in the Boiler Suit:* 'His humility really impressed me. It was my first day at College. I cycled into the yard through the back gate ... and there in front of me was a man in a boiler suit, stoking a fire. I really thought he was a workman and asked where I could find Mr. Bonsall.

'"I *am* Mr. Bonsall," he replied. That really took the wind out of my sails. Fancy the Principal stoking fires!'

Leslie de Smidt, the first post-war student at All Nations, made an entry in the Student Minutes, on stoking the boiler:

'The Principal is of the opinion that overalls are unnecessary. He himself has done the job and is convinced that it can be done without dirtying oneself or one's clothes!'

Harry had a heart for people, particularly the disadvantaged. Remembering his Japanese friends in Canada, his heart went out to one lonely young German, who was brave enough to join up just after the war.

Alfred Lau: 'It was not easy for me, as a German, arriving in Britain just after the war ... finding my way into British society with all the collective guilt of the holocaust, but the love shown to me by my first Principal, took away any feelings of loneliness. He had a transparent openness and integrity about him. The fact that I grew up in the lower department of the Hitler Youth Movement before I became a Christian, made no difference to him. In his eyes I belonged to the great family of the Lord Jesus Christ, where there were no racial or national barriers.

'I only had a very limited permit to stay in Britain, but I was sure God wanted me to stay and study for the ministry. Prepared with prayer, we dared to visit the Home Office in London. Mr. Bonsall and I went alone, praying in the train and again before entering the building. The secretary took our petition and left the room.

'"*Now* is the decisive moment," he said, "Let's pray as never before!"

'We prayed – and believed – to the extent that when my extension of stay was granted, it was hardly a surprise! The quality of this man of God stood out to me. Back on the busy London street with thousands of people milling around he pulled out a huge London map and said, "If we don't praise God now for the answered prayer, He may never be as generous to us again. Let's pretend we're looking at the map!"

'So we gazed up at the map, in the hustle and bustle of London and thanked the Lord there and then, with deepest gratitude. I shall never forget it. For me as a German, such practices were unheard of, but that was the start of a practical prayer life for me. Expecting the miracle – then thanking Him on the spot.

'Not long after this, Germany held a very important international conference on missions – and Lutheran Bishop Martin Erdmann, invited my friend Rev. Bonsall to be the British representative. H.B.B. insisted on giving his "address" in German and wanted to learn the language within a few weeks. He bought all the necessary books to teach himself, but particularly asked for my help with pronunciation.

'I couldn't be fast enough! Every few seconds he would say, "Next page." He was very impatient – and I, far too slow a teacher! He had a tremendous grasp of grammar (which was no wonder, as he was an excellent Greek scholar) but when it came round to the pronunciation, we had real trouble! I shall always remember how his moustache twisted and turned when he came out with "Schwarz" (or "black") in German. At that time he was tall, but very thin, with a most expressive face, and every muscle would move as he tried to imitate my pronunciation of this very difficult word. Even the word, "Er" (which is 'he') was almost insurmountable! And over the next 35 years, whenever I visited him in Birmingham, he would greet me in flawless German with, "I still remember your parents' address, Tannenstrasse 42."'

Jack Armstrong remembers how he loved to preach. ' "Always have a sermon ready," he used to say, "even if you're woken at midnight." Here is one he gave for emergencies. The A.B.C. of the Gospel:

    A 'All have sinned and come short of the Glory of God' (Rom. 3:23).
    B 'Behold the Lamb of God that taketh away the sin of the world' (John 1:29).

288

C 'Come unto me all you that are weary and burdened and I will give you rest' (Matt. 11:28).'

Jack and Ivy Armstrong also recalled some of the 'Principal's Points to Remember':

1. *A good life is made up of quality decisions.*
Take the scripture, 'Don't let the sun go down on your anger.' If you are too upset to pray with your wife before you say goodnight, make a quality decision not to sleep until you have sorted it out and said 'sorry'.

2. *God will meet you on your level.*
Ask God for boxwood furniture and you'll get it, but ask Him for oak furniture and that's what you'll get!

3. *There is always God's part and man's.*
Oliver Cromwell said, 'Trust in God and keep your powder dry!' Just so, in Acts 12, God's part was to shake the prison and set Peter free. Peter's part was to obey the angel, 'Put on your clothes and follow me!'

4. *Don't give the devil a foothold or else he will make it a stronghold* (Eph. 4:27).
The more you do it, the easier it will be. The less you do it, the harder you become. Illustration: Normandy landing in 1945: 'The first objective was to hold a foothold for 24 hours on Normandy beaches, then the Allied Forces would be able to fan out all over Hitler's Europe and conquer it.' This is just what happened.

Fred Marlow: 'When I was offered a lay pastorate after my three years at All Nations, I felt that this was second best, but your father said to me, "Half a loaf is better than none."'

John Kessler (1946-48): 'In one lecture Brash assured us of the value of taking our holidays on time. One student shot back, "But, sir, when do you take *your* holidays?" to which he replied without batting an eyelid, "Do as I say, *not* as I do!"'

Bill Flagg: 'You have heard of the phrase "Strike while the iron is hot". Charles H. Spurgeon once said, "Some wait until the iron is hot *before* striking. Others make it hot *by* striking." Your father came into the latter category!'

Prayer
Ray Giles: 'Above all he was a *man of prayer*. When I first met B. B. I was only 10. I remember his vibrant personality and, more than anything else, his sudden suggestion, "Let's have a word of prayer". We did ... and I never forgot it! B.B. was still a man of prayer in 1949 when I enrolled at the age of 24. His prayers were like mini sermons, full of theology, yet with praise or intercession in view. He was totally uninhibited in his prayers. They weren't formal or stereotyped (in fact you never quite knew what was coming next). He would use some well-known story or place and build it into his prayer ... like "the marshalling yards at Hamm, in Germany!"'

Bernard Collinson: 'His prayers were quite specific. He remembered people in context and prayed for them by name. His prayers included the cook, the gardener and the French au pair girl, just as they did the members of the tutorial staff.'

Bishop Bill Flagg: 'Coming straight from the farm as a raw young student, Bill vividly remembers his "lovely smile and encouraging manner" ... and on his return visit to the College just after being ordained, I was a little embarrassed and quite amazed at his fervent prayer when he got round to my name. "*Lord, make him a Bishop*!" If ever an unlikely prayer was answered, that was it!'

John Pickett: 'When I called to discuss something with him, he always had other people and their concerns on his mind, and we'd soon be on our knees – sometimes even before my concern had come into his conversation!'

Bernard Collinson: 'Before opening day at Taplow, 7th June 1947, when the Rt. Rev. Haye, the Lord Bishop of Buckingham was to be present, Brash prayed, *"O Lord, may there be no pussy-footing to the Bishop!"*'

Ron Waine (1946-48): 'H.B.B. was a true man of prayer. He could pray any time, anywhere, indoors or out, in the midst of a crowd, or privately in secret.'

To illustrate this point John Kessler's wife, *Margaret*, remembers Brash meeting a lady in Colchester High Street one day. She obviously had a problem, as he asked how she was ... listening intently to her reply. Suddenly, to the amazement of the passers-by, he said, 'Let's pray about it' and dropped to his knees on the pavement!

Ron Waine: 'He was never tempted to engage in "vain repetitions". His heart was filled with a long list of urgent prayer needs. One of his prayers I remember, ended ... "fourteenthly, Lord ... and lastly, Lord ... in Jesus' name. Amen."'

Doug Abrahams: 'Brash was a man in touch with God. As far as revival was concerned, Brash hoped for and expected more than the humdrum of average church work. Yes, your father gave us a spirit of expectancy ... for the supernatural. In fact I arrived at College in the middle of a revival (summer '47). Old student, Dr. Joe Church, had just been visiting us with his team from revival in Rwanda, followed by Dr. Edwin Orr, who was himself researching revival and writing many books on the subject. Then Oswald Sanders said to me, "The man who has seen revival is hungry till he sees it again!" and your father's message to me was

291

"You must *be* filled with the Spirit and *stay* filled with the Spirit."'

Fred Marlow: 'My most significant moment with Brash was one morning during my final term. I was Head Student and we always went to his study to pray before lectures started. As your father prayed I began to realise that I didn't understand a word he was saying! It wasn't Greek, I don't think it was Hebrew, and it certainly wasn't English! I told my friends.

'There was an awesomeness in that study that I had never experienced before. I remember feeling that I had no business to be there. Indeed, your father seemed quite unaware that I was in the room.

'I came out and said nothing, which I now regret. It was not till years later that I understood the significance of praying in the Spirit and the awesomeness of God's presence.'

Marriage

The right wife for his students was top of the priority list on Harry's agenda for prayer! From time to time, he would rather enjoy reciting this little couplet, with a twinkle in his eye:

> 'The eyes that over coffee look so sweet
> May not look so tender over shredded wheat!'

Ted West: 'One of the most challenging and devastating memories of Brash, was his way of greeting a new student on arrival, or at his first interview – down on his knees, praying for his future wife and family! It was quite overwhelming. He maintained that next to your personal salvation, the devil would attack your marriage and your family most vigorously. If he could just destroy those relationships, he had effectively destroyed your testimony, abroad or at home. "There are many important things in life," he would say, "but none more vital than the three Ss: *S* for Salvation, *S* for Sanctification, and *S* for Sweetheart."'

Ruth: 'It was rather awesome for my future husband, Murray, to discover that my father had started to pray for the person I would marry before I was born. That's really thinking ahead!'

Ron Waine: 'We were an all-male college in those days, and H.B.B. was so concerned for our relationships. This was a strong element in his care for us as students. His words to me were: "If the enemy can't get you to marry a *non*-Christian he'll try to persuade you to marry the *wrong* Christian." You might say H.B.B. was responsible for first introducing me to my wife ... then followed a sequence of events which merit another romance novel!'

On one occasion, according to the Principal, things got a little complicated when several of the men felt that they all had specific guidance about the same particularly attractive young lady!

Tom Pratten remembers:
'Once your Dad told me that he had always wanted to be a missionary, but illness held him back. At All Nations Bible College he said he felt that he was only doing second best for the Lord. But we know otherwise! Just look at how God went on to use him in such a remarkable way. He may not have been an overseas missionary, but he was a great one at home!'

Noel Stanton would agree: 'Brash was a pioneer, determined to create leaders.'

These happy and fulfilling years at All Nations led on to an unexpected change of course, after a difficult period of spiritual warfare.

Moving on from All Nations, Harry would now make the significant move to Birmingham.

BIRMINGHAM in the EARLY DAYS

Mrs. Joyce Kingdon, who later joined Harry's staff, with her husband Bassee, as lecturer at Birmingham Bible Institute (BBI), was a fellow-teacher at Eversfield Preparatory School: 'I first met Mr. Bonsall at Eversfield in autumn 1952, when I was teaching the six-year-old boys and he had a class of seven-year-olds. My memory of him stands out. He gave himself to that class of small boys with as much dedication as if he had been educating university graduates! He had such enthusiasm combined with such old-world courtesy.

One evening he arrived at the supper table to tell us, quietly and joyfully, that he had led one of the boarders to the Lord. Later, 22 out of 24 boarders made a profession of faith.'

Flo Green (WEC team): 'Mr. Bonsall was like a father to me in those days. I would go into the library to ask his advice up a ladder, in the midst of all his books! He had great strength of character and was such a man of prayer, that after only a few minutes he would start ... "Let's have a word of prayer." Not only would he pray for me, but in a very short time would embrace the world in his prayer (still up the ladder!). And what can I say about Mrs. Bonsall ... the heart of the home and a tremendous woman of faith. I don't think I ever met anyone with such faith, not even in WEC. Whenever you children were ill she never called the doctor, but laid hands on you for healing from God ... and He always touched and healed you. It was her faith and prayer and loving attitude which embraced all she came into contact with.'

Harry's unconventional way of doing things was another world to some more conventional experts, trained in the usual handling of funds! Finances were tight, to say the least.

294

Norman Gidney CBE, a businessman and family friend, remembers that feeling ... and more!

'I first met Mr. Bonsall soon after he came to Birmingham from All Nations Bible College – and my personal experience of him was one that I hold in my memory very dearly indeed. As I am a financial man, he wanted me to work with him in planning the development of the BBI, but I found that after two or three meetings with him, the only plan that he was prepared to consider was one of reaching out in faith and in being on his knees.

'Now this I will always acknowledge is an important and noble strategy, but because I felt that he was taking chances that were unrealistic, I found it quite impossible to accept the responsibility for what he felt he was being driven to accomplish!

'However, as I got to know him better and got to love him more, it became quite clear to me that the things that a financial man, albeit a committed Christian, would be afraid of, he reached out for with a great courage of faith and actually possessed. So, whilst I couldn't find a comfortable way of working with him in an orderly financial structure, I came to enormously admire the courage of his faith and the great success that he achieved in the prosecution of his objectives.

'Somehow Mr. Bonsall had a relationship with God ... and through the eyes of faith, he knew what he should pray for. This made his working with normal, organisational people like myself very difficult, as he was viewing spiritual matters from a plane that we simply did not understand. For him, prayer was like a contraflow of communication, which involved as much time listening to God as in talking to Him. For he believed that whatever a man's academic achievements or energy of ministry, he would never be greater than his own personal prayer life.'

Ruth talks to *'Auntie Kay' Duddridge* (one of the 'Midland Gypsies', at 93 years old): 'Sometimes, in those early days, your mother and I would visit the terrible "slum" housing areas nearby. We two rebels got on like a house on fire and would have lots of fun in the Bull Ring market. On one visit, I only had 6d, and your mother not much more. "You go first," she said to me, "I'm not cheeky enough!" So I approached a butcher from Worcestershire, who had a very cheap stall on Saturdays and Wednesdays. "Sixpence-worth of bones, please!" His reply was to cut up some mutton, jointing it and leaving most of the meat on the bone. "I like serving you," he said, "you know exactly what you want!" BBI and WEC lived on that soup for 10 days, and got so much meat off the bones, that they made rissoles with it!'

BBI Students Pick up the Pen

A Maintenance Officer's Testimony

'"Three weeks is enough for me!" The work at BBI seemed colossal. How anyone could carry on under such circumstances was just beyond my comprehension. To me it was quite impossible, but I'd taken my eyes off the Master.

'At this point I was challenged at Hockley Pentecostal Church by a sermon and prophecies that talked of "refusing the challenge" ... turning back to an easier life, but outside God's will. They prayed for me ... and from that moment, my outlook completely changed. I took up the challenge, and it wasn't long before things really began to take shape.

'Student workers came to help me; fellowship was great; encouraging words on every side. Everything my hands touched prospered. I found myself being truly blessed ... and ended up with a lovely wife!

'The fellowship throughout the College was tremendous! I can only look back and say again, "Yes, three weeks was enough for me to get sorted out!"'

The Dutch connection: Anneke Companjen, Harderwijk, Holland.

' "You have been accepted and we will reserve a flat for you", said the letter from BBI. This is what we had been praying for. Some clear direction as to where we would be studying before our wedding, just a few days away.

'BBI was one of the Bible colleges we had applied to ... and the one that appealed to us most. Brother Andrew van der Byl was a good friend of ours who had brought us both to the point of dedicating our lives to the Lord and it was through his ministry that Johan had just spent a year in Vietnam, working alongside Dr. Stuart Harveson and his missionary team (1968-9). After one year of separation, all we wanted to do was to be together and train for the next step. Andrew had already met the Bonsalls in England and we knew of their vision for families at BBI.

'It is many years now since we left College, but we are constantly reminded of things Mr. Bonsall used to say or do, or teach us. We learnt from him that *"there are no short-cuts in getting to know God. The long way is the short way in the end,"* he would say ... and now that Johan is leader of a team himself, we are often reminded of our Principal, getting up long before dawn every day to pray for his students – past and present.

'One memorable Saturday afternoon in 1976, we made a return visit to England and went to have a cup of tea with the Bonsalls. After being missionaries in Vietnam for several years, we had been evacuated following the communist take-over in 1975. Subsequently, we had joined Brother Andrew's organisation 'Open Doors', where Johan served as Director of Development in Holland. Brother Andrew had just asked Johan to leave the Dutch team and become his personal assistant, so we were earnestly praying for guidance when we visited the Bonsalls. But they didn't know it.

'We felt we really needed to hear a clear word from God, as working with Andrew would mean a lot of travel abroad – and

297

we had a young family.

'No sooner were we sipping our tea, than Mr. Bonsall began to ask how Andrew was. He kept coming back to Andrew's well-being and the issue of Andrew needing 'a Timothy'. We had our answer that afternoon! But still we never told the Bonsalls any details of our situation. Next day we went to worship at Hockley Pentecostal Church.

'There we met Mr. Bonsall again – and of course, he had come walking. As soon as he saw us, he said, "That was God speaking yesterday afternoon, not me." We sure were aware of that!

'Now, twenty years later, Johan is still working very closely together with Brother Andrew in his international ministry of "Open Doors". God has confirmed the guidance we received that Saturday afternoon and we are so grateful. We pray that their vision of a college for revival will be fulfilled.'

A steady stream of more than thirty Dutch students at BBI would come and go, enriching College life – and going on to work all over the world. One or two, like *Evert and Nelie Schut* (1979-80) have gone on to join Brother Andrew's Open Doors team. Harry loved those students ... and one wrote of him, '*He was the most lovely man I have ever met in my life. I will never forget him.*'

MORE STUDENTS ...

Audrey Herbert (1957-60), now freelance writer and artist, was a pioneer at BBI, being one of the first three girls! She writes: 'I knew nothing of Bible colleges but I felt a strong call to train, so applied to the first one on the list! I had high hopes, but my heart sank in despair when I realised that without qualifications, there was not the remotest chance of getting there. Then out of the blue, I heard about another Bible college ... for young people like myself who simply had a "call" to serve God. It was here in
298

Birmingham, that I first met H.B.B., or "Brash", as we students affectionately named him ... definitely "a man for his time"!'

Audrey's call had came through the ministry of Gladys Aylward[1], that courageous little lady from London who had earned her passage to China earlier in the century. But after Audrey's interview, she was shocked to find that she was expected to provide her own fees for three years. 'I thought they would be paying *me*!' she exclaimed.

'Needless to say, I returned home to Yorkshire full of exuberance at the prospects before me. But how could I possibly collect enough for my first term? My application for a grant was turned down. The only other option was "coil-winding" at the General Electric Company factory at £5 or £6 a week. Like my missionary heroine Gladys Aylward, I was determined to earn my way. Soon I was earning £10 a week. Then I graduated to 'piece work'. An average turnover was 40 to 50 a day, but I was so full of enthusiasm I began to turn over 100 a day, to the consternation of the other girls! I couldn't wait to embark on my new adventure for God.

'One evening, just before I left for Birmingham, I happened to be at a Youth For Christ Rally. In spite of all my efforts, I still didn't have enough money for college. At the end, I was talking with a group of young people, when a complete stranger approached me. "Are you Audrey Herbert from Redcar?" This young man then told me that he had been in a prayer group somewhere in town, where someone had prayed for God to supply all my needs for Bible College. He took out a cheque book, asked how much I needed and proceeded to write out a

---

1. Gladys Aylward, 'The Small Woman' missionary to China, was heroine of the film *Inn of the Sixth Happiness* (played by Ingrid Bergman), friend of the Bonsall family and visitor to BBI; later to appear on the television programme *This is Your Life* with Eamonn Andrews. Alone, she led more than one hundred children across the mountains into safety during the Japanese invasion of China in 1941.

cheque. God had told him to pay for my first term's fees. I was absolutely flabbergasted! This was only the first of many wonderful incidents in which people of God were moved to support me ... and not only me, but other students at BBI with me over the next three years.

'In September 1957, I suddenly found myself at 27 Elvetham Road, – thrown together with thirty men, two other women and the Bonsall family. We all felt like pioneers in an exciting new venture for God!

'It was hard work and tough discipline that got us through those early days. We were all in this venture together, both students and staff. Along with studies every morning, came "chores" to help with the maintenance of our large home. There were the occasional personality clashes and emotional involvements from time to time, and we all had to sort them out together. On top of all these practical things, we were now plunged into an intensive course of lectures on Biblical Theology, Church History, Christian Doctrine, Social and Pastoral Psychology and many other subjects relevant to the Christian ministry. Those early days were daunting to say the least, but we were full of faith and enthusiasm and accepted the discipline and intense routines.

'H.B.B. was a "spiritual giant", as far as we students were concerned. His vision for world evangelism and worldwide revival was like a burning flame. It set all our hearts on fire every time he lectured to us. Time and again through the exposition of the text, he brought God's Word to life as we had never heard it before.

'It was "Brash" who first introduced us to the art of *Rocket Prayers*. Over and over he pointed to some Bible character who used this way of instant communication with God in tough situations.

'We soon got used to "Brash in action" when dealing with us students, or anyone else for that matter. On the spot; on the telephone; in the middle of some busy street, he'd stop. "Let's pray about it now, brother." Head bowed (to the embarrassment of those around him) he would bring the problem to the Lord. The amazing thing was that in no time at all those prayers seemed to be answered and the friend or student would carry on rejoicing!

'As far as I was concerned, in those early days Ma and Pa Bonsall were my "spiritual parents" in a spiritual family ... there in my life, to build up my faith at a time when I needed them most. That family has grown larger year by year and is still growing. Mr. and Mrs. Bonsall were father and mother to us all and their ministry will live on forever in our hearts.'

Audrey was one of the first of many, representing many nations and many walks of life: from the army, the navy and the airforce; doctors, policemen, journalists, gang leaders, hippies, teddy boys, ex-convicts, farmers, nurses, teachers, hairdressers, engineers ... a dentist, a bouncer-cum-boxer, a Chinese restauranteur, a former 'Buddhist' martial arts expert, and so the list goes on ... BBI was quite a mixture!

"Those beautiful days at BBI..."
Joyce Halsall/Dunlop (1961-64): 'BBI was a happy time. Brash was never too busy to bother with us students, and we had lots of fun and often at the expense of the staff.'

John and Elizabeth Hollins (lecturer and staff – late 1970s): 'During the short year we knew him, we learnt a very great deal about how to be an inspirational leader and teacher of young people. *He had such a great love for the most mixed-up students.*'

'He was the most meek and humble person I ever met.' (*'Derek'*)
'Always an encourager to me.' *Moses En* (1983-86)

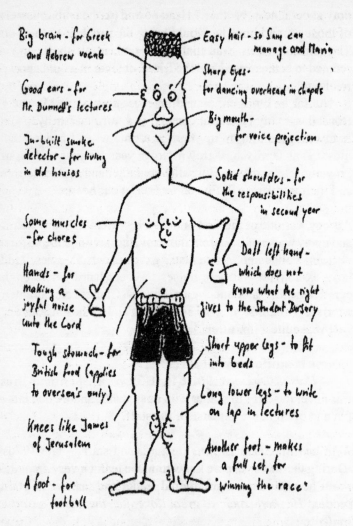

The ideal BBI student

Cartoon: Martin Zaske

A Complement to the Biography

Ron Bailey (1966-69): 'As Married Students Council representative, I got to know our Principal well and I don't feel I'm exaggerating when I say that he combined intellect close to genius, with the simplicity of a child. I never met, or expect to meet a man who was a more perfect example of the injunction "In malice be children, but in understanding be men." I never heard a word of criticism from him or a trace of bitterness. His gifts were great. His heart was greater.'

One student remembers: 'It was his keen interest and care for every student that sticks in my memory. He knew me as a person and prayed for me by name daily. This did not end when I left College. Only days after my dad died in 1982, Mr. Bonsall wrote to me by hand, including many things he remembered about my home and family. It was this personal touch that meant so much to me.'

Mike Hill (1985-87): 'It was 1984. I was going through a very rough time personally. I had written to several Bible Colleges ... received all the usual "blurb". But with BBI though, came a simple letter of encouragement typed out by Brash.

'1985. Another letter from Brash. He knew I was discouraged. Would I consider coming to BBI, where I would be loved and taught? When I came to Open Day, I could see that *BBI was actually more about people than property*.... And what a lot of different people there were!

'At dinner I remember watching Brash, this quiet and gentle man, eating his dinner, as I tried to make up my mind about BBI. Suddenly, he turned to me and said, "Mike, I want you and your family to attend an interview this afternoon at 2.00 p.m." Panic! "Yes, sir," I said.... The outcome. We joined BBI in the Autumn 1985, after an intense period of dramatic panic, being made to hang on tight as the Holy Spirit took control of our situation! They call it "Living by Faith". I just call it "Living by Amazement!" '

Over the Top?

John Fee (1970-74): 'His "all-embracing acceptance" could lead him sometimes to the occasional use of hyperbole ... or politely, "seeing the best in people!" H.B.B. was great at picking on some particular point of achievement in someone of whom he was speaking and, waxing eloquent, emphasising it with expansive enthusiasm. This could lead to introductions to people that were not always "cringe-free"!'

Richard Dugdale (1962-63) describes this same enthusiasm: '"*Above a hundred,*" he always wrote triumphantly, when speaking of College numbers.'

In the same way *Rev. John Peck* (lecturer) also describes his experience when about to take evening classes on the minor prophets and the Pauline epistles. 'I remember being led to the lecture room by the Principal, who then went over to the grand piano, sprawled across it, and proceeded to introduce me in embarrassingly glowing terms.... It was not till later conversations, that I saw behind that image the power of an incredibly agile scholarship. *He's got a mind like a sponge. When you squeeze him in the right place the information comes out!*'

Matthew Hill (1952-62): 'Mr. Bonsall's great love of books and the value he placed on them stands out to me. He tried to pass this sense of value on to us. Time and time again in a lecture he would hold up a book large or small, old or new, saying, "*Master this, master this.*"'

John Fee: 'We all laughed at his delight in gory stories, often from Greek mythology, or Caesar's civil wars! We also laughed at his frequent tendency to start with a story then diverge from one tangent to another. But he was always interesting and always going somewhere of great spiritual value. My personal assessment of the value of his story-telling ... I have never heard anyone with such a fund of stories so finely-tuned to the precise detail of the spiritual truth he wanted to convey. As far as his speaking ability is concerned.... There are many good speakers in this world. Many brilliant ones. Rare to find though, are those who combine such a deep spirituality with the clear teaching, lively illustration, warmth of appeal and understanding of the human condition as he did. You could warm to the Jesus that he preached and taught. And I did!

'The greatest feature of BBI to me.... We were taught to love the Lord by lip and by life. I remember your dad saying to me as I was about to take on my first pastorate, *"Just live the life!"* He did.'

Ian Mason (1987-88): 'He was unique – there will never be another.'

Stuart Pascall (1968-71): 'Our Principal saw potential in everyone.'

John Fee: 'Entrance qualifications for BBI. Basically – none! This could be good or bad, depending on your point of view! I was personally impressed that you could come in with degrees, doctorates or nothing ... and study, so to speak, on the same level. Many non-academics found in practice that they just "grew on the job". Mr. Bonsall's all-embracing acceptance met many people "where they were", and helped them to grow. I suppose in this policy there were mistakes, but he would say: *"He who never made mistakes, never made anything!"* '

Letter to Harry from H.M. Prison:

'Dear Sir,
'I have just read your advertisement in "Renewal", and the Chaplain here has recommended me to write to you, the reason being that I have a burning desire to serve the Lord. As you can

see by this letter I am currently serving a prison sentence for theft and I am afraid to say that nothing in my past life could act as a recommendation to spend a life living in Christ. Now though, I have had a new life given to me and I want to make up for all I've done in the past.

'I can't begin to put down on paper how much the Spirit has altered my life and maybe it would be futile to attempt to do it, as I know that there is a stigma that surrounds ex-prisoners. I know that the Lord preached forgiveness, but as yet I have not proved that I am worthy of being forgiven. I suppose this letter is for advice. I want to know what I must do to be able to dedicate my life to Christ in a positive way.

'I am only 20 years old and I feel Christ's hand upon me. I know my past is somewhat sordid ... but I have got Christ on my side, so I am able to go through anything that is required of me to fulfil my calling in life.

'If you could just write and advise me of my best course of action to get myself started I would be very happy, as my release is drawing very near and I would like to know where I stand. Please thank your students that came to share with us here. Although I only spoke with a few of them briefly, I was very impressed with their sincerity. I look forward to hearing.

'Yours faithfully.'

Honestly ...

Stuart Pascall, Head student: 'I learned a whole lot at BBI at an academic level certainly. The often rambling genius of Brash, and the wonders of the *Person of Christ* (Vols. 1 and 2); the clipped tones of D.B.P. ('Dippy') Smith as he worked us through the rigours of the History of Israel and the ability of Mrs. Kingdon to make the dullest periods of Church History seem even vaguely interesting with her smiling face and encouraging tones!

Even more importantly for me, personal spirituality was

greatly enhanced by the good friends that I was privileged to make ... although there were times when I seriously questioned whether I had any spirituality at all! Some things drove me to distraction at times! I just wanted to go to the pub and not evangelise – to meet people in the street for a conversation about the weather, about the Beatles or Birmingham City ... without feeling I had to make a report on it, so that the student body could pray about it! ... to experience normal relationships without the tacit assumptions that they were an integral part of God's directive will for my life!

'Having said that, it would certainly be true to say that the biggest single influence on my life was exerted by that surely most remarkable of all Bible College Principals, Henry Brash Bonsall. The memories of the man are legion and the stuff of which legends are made!'

More, on the Funny Side ...

Stuart Pascall continues: 'As senior student, I joined Mr. B. every week for an early morning meeting in his study, but one week he was unwell, so he conducted the meeting from his bedroom ... sitting propped up in bed in striped pyjamas but wearing his ubiquitous dog collar. Trying to concentrate on prayer for the student body is not easy when wondering, "Does he wear that all the time, whatever he's doing?!"

'Before long I was co-opted onto the "Bonsall Chores Team", with a firmly fixed memory revolving around the demolition of one of the chimney stacks at number 6, which was in a somewhat precarious state of repair. It was a windy and cold winter's day, and we were instructed to meet Mr. B. by the side of said building. When we eventually arrived, there was no immediate evidence of "the man", but there was a rather long and rickety-looking ladder leaning against the side of the house. We were in the process of deciding that none of us was brave, or foolish enough to ascend the ladder, when a voice hailed us from above!

On tracing the source of the voice we located Brash at the very top of the ladder, almost in the clouds it seemed, exhorting us to follow in his footsteps. It was from this seemingly impossible height that "The Prin" spent the next couple of hours pulling the structure apart, lobbing bricks at those below, and exhorting us not to let them break when they fell to the earth because "they may well be useful for another project!" Yes, he saw potential in every one and every thing. Don't throw it away, it may be useful!

'Time fails me to tell of the many other easily recorded incidents and the life of this student of the class of 1971. Of such things as ... the plaster falling from the coving in the lecture hall and Brash, almost decapitated by falling masonry, carrying on without missing a beat, whilst the room filled with dust ... of collected birds' nests stored among the books in "The Study" ... of the fervent, faith-inspiring prayers for £40,000 to purchase the Church across the road and of the assurance that "When the money arrives I shall walk across the road like a good Presbyterian to make the announcement" ... of the time, when I was asked to take H.B.B. to preach in Derby, when he had his leg in plaster and, as I led the service for him, finding my leg being pulled back, as Brash tried to attract my attention from behind the pulpit by hooking the crook of his walking stick around my ankle and pulling! Or, of the desolate conversations among the male section of the student body about the bad news (at least as far as some were concerned!) when a proud father announced that his elder daughter was engaged to be married to a man who would take her from the site, to work in Ophthalmics in some far away land in the shadow of the Himalayas!!

'In spite of my earlier misgivings about life in a BBI regime, these were good days and I learned so much from H. Brash Bonsall. He helped me to understand eternal security: he showed me the richness of the Word of God in everyday language and the importance of illustrative language in preaching: he helped me to learn what it means to live by faith and, perhaps above all, he taught me the importance and possibility of significant prayer. For these, and for so many other things, I shall always and eternally be grateful!'

Don Wootten, one of the first students (1953-56) later to return as lecturer, remembers: 'One warm afternoon at Pakenham Road ... lecture in full flow ... French doors opening onto the lawn ... cries floating in from the garden, as small son Tom fell out of an apple tree ... H.B.B. flew from the room, caught Tom, ran back, never missed a word and carried on with the lecture!'

Hilary Virgo, The wig: 'One girl sat perkily in the back row of Mr. Bonsall's lecture wearing a bright red wig. Her hair was blonde. Mr. Bonsall was obviously distracted but never uttered a word ... in fact he went on lecturing until she took it off at the end, when the whole class erupted in laughter at his relief!'

Ian Mason: 'I came to BBI through summer school in 1986 and I said to Bob Dunnett, as we went on a local walk with a very steep climb up a hill, "I don't think I'll go up the hill – it's too difficult." Bob replied in his gentle persuasive way, "Wouldn't you be ashamed if the Boss (H.B.B.) went up the hill and made it in his 80s, but you did *not*?" Yours truly climbed the hill – pronto! ... Whenever I felt like grumbling about chores, I would think of our servant Principal, in overalls doing chores with the students and would tell myself, "*If Mr. Bonsall can do it, then so can I*!"'

Tom Lori (1970-73): *The case of the falling hammer*. 'In 1970 I had the somewhat dubious privilege of being on Brash's personal chore team for the reconstruction of the "stable loft". On one occasion during the afternoon chore period, our beloved Principal climbed the loft staircase (still under construction) to view progress on the loft above. Having satisfied himself that all was well, he decided to personally fix a final strengthening member. Finding a hammer to hand, he found no nails, so I volunteered to fetch some. On my return, as I started up the staircase, he looked out from above and inadvertently dropped the hammer on my head. There was a lot of blood ... but it really looked much worse than it was!

'I remember so well his hasty descent, with a hand on my shoulder and "A word of prayer, brother, a word of prayer!" I was really touched by his genuine concern and gentleness and the speed at which he got my head patched up! A few days later I received a gift from him. It was a copy of his recently published book, *The Person of Christ*, Volume 1, with this inscription:

' "To Tom Lori,
' "In grateful memory of hazards and hardships experienced in the erection of the stable loft staircase at 8 Pakenham Road on the afternoon of Friday November 5th 1970, when we worked on it together.'
' "Signed, *H. Brash Bonsall*."

'This book I treasure together with many fond memories of his good humour, tolerance, spontaneous prayer and deep godliness. I remember too, his wise counsel during periods of stress in my personal life and his undivided attention when we most needed it.'

Alex Blower (1963-64): 'I remember seeing him in overalls and dog collar, painting the fence. He could go from lecture room to boiler room, get his hands dirty, then to prayer, or interview, or study. He was "all things to all men", equally at peace and at ease with everyone. "*Always be part of the answer,*" he said, "*not part of the problem.*" '

David Smith (1978-81): 'One memorable afternoon, Phil Mayo and I were detailed to help Mr. Bonsall in the cellar bringing up some carpets, etc. for furnishing a flat in Wheeley's Road. Anyway, we duly followed Mr. Bonsall down the cold, damp and dimly lit staircase into the bowels of the house ... more reminiscent of a scene from Dickens! Mr. Bonsall would point, and we would carry – often he'd carry as much as we did, which didn't seem right somehow, but, nevertheless, however much we protested, or managed to persuade him to give the particular item to us instead, he'd pass it over and pick up something else. In the end we gave up!

The one thing he did, that I'll never forget, was such a small thing, but it caused complete hysterics at the time! Phil and I picked up a huge roll of Persian carpet, after brushing off as much of the white powdered damp as we could – and underneath was a rather large beetle, glistening in the yellow light. It made us jump a bit when it started to head for cover. But after our initial shock we became quite curious and started to look at it more closely. We invited Mr. Bonsall to have a look, at which point he came over and said, "Bless it, Lord!" ... and then, without more ado, sent it on its way with a speedy dispatch! We just stood there open-mouthed! He walked off and carried on with his rooting about ... while we stood and stared at each other – and when he finally ascended to the hallway above, we roared with laughter for quite some time!'

Gordon Croft – first resident tutor (1957-58): 'I had just finished at London Bible College and was wondering what my new appointment might be like. With some trepidation I approached Pakenham Road looking for BBI and your dad. Knocking at the front door, I was met by someone in blue overalls with a paintbrush in his hand, whom I thought might be the decorator – only to discover that he was, in fact, the Principal! This was an amazement to me and it was not too long before I found that I, too, had a paintbrush in my hand – painting the kitchen sunshine yellow!'

Secretaries

Harry called his personal secretaries 'the nerve-centre of his work' and in his office, without a doubt, they certainly were. Unshockable and ready for any crisis! With his incredibly active agenda, massive correspondence and perpetual production of articles and literature, this was no mean feat.

Ada Housego at All Nations was one of the first in a line of first-class secretaries; followed by *Anne McCudden, Elizabeth Timms, Mavis Towers, Rachel Hare, Christine Carr, Virginia Perry, Joanne Eades* and many others who joined the team at different times.

John Peck, evening lecturer, particularly remembers 'The Study':

'Brash broke so many stereotypes! You might so easily have categorized him as an eccentric, absent-minded academic, but in fact, he was a man of so many practical interests, he was able to juggle them with astonishing efficiency!

'I shall never forget his personal study. He had referred to an article that had aroused my interest and said he had a copy in his study. So together we went to get it. He pushed open the door of his study (I say 'pushed' because behind the door there was a pile of books in the way). Facing me was a wall covered with shelves of books, but at the far left-hand corner their orderly arrangement was disturbed by a pile, rising from the floor, of miscellaneous papers, books, boxes, typewriters, tape-recorders and other less-clearly identified objects ... all more or less precariously "perched" on top of each other. There seemed very little floor space left.... Directly in front of me was a large desk. The top was completely covered with more piles of books and papers, together with a reading lamp. Right in the midst of all this was his secretary who looked up briefly from her typing to greet us....

'One would imagine that finding anything not immediately

obvious to the eye would be almost insuperably difficult; but B.B. went straight to the desk, muttered, "It should be about ... here," and choosing unerringly one of the piles of paper, flipped briefly through the middle of it; exclaimed, "Ah, here it is!" and drew out a copy of the article. The speed and efficiency seemed to be miraculous! My memory of that room is still vivid, 40 years later!'

Liz Timms (student 1965-67)

'Annie McCudden and I worked very closely together with Mr. Bonsall, especially over the writing of his books. We never forgot the day he was to present his first completed manuscript of *The Person of Christ*, Part I to his publishers (Christian Literature Crusade) in London. He was due to catch the 10.00 a.m. train, so Anne and I arranged to meet him in his office at 4.00 a.m. to do all the last minute changes. I arrived first, to be met with a new sheaf of notes. "Overnight, the Lord has changed the last chapter," he said. "It has to be re-written and re-typed!" We gulped in horror. By the end we could hardly speak in our anxiety to finish in time. It was an amazing operation. Typing, checking, packing, with Mrs. B. standing at the ready to ferry him to the train. Anne and I collapsed in a heap on one side of No. 28 door as H.B.B. slammed down the steps on the other! It took us all of 5½ hours. The time was 9.30 a.m. and we didn't recover until the afternoon!'

Anne Keart also worked in his office for several years. 'I never knew anyone so appreciative of anything done. He always made you feel you wanted to do even better!'

Bill Williamson (1991-92: S.I.M., Chile) *The Story of a Stencil*: 'It must have been about 17 years ago that I called at the BBI office to repair their stencil duplicator. I was not a Christian at this time (1979) and must have casually mentioned this to Mr.

313

Bonsall, who was in the office at that point. I was working quite happily on the machine, when Mr. Bonsall suddenly told the other BBI workers to stop what they were doing and join him in praying for me – on the spot! I was somewhat taken aback, as you can imagine! For several years I had been searching for God and didn't want to say anything to stop them praying for me ... I think I mumbled some sort of 'Thank you' and left for my next call. After 25 years in secular work, I never had the slightest thought of training at BBI, but that day in 1979 was the first link in the chain that led me on, with my wife Jean, to serve God overseas. My personal experience with Jesus, through BBI, ended up in a home for abandoned children in Santiago, Chile!'

TO PRAYER!

'More things are wrought by prayer than this world dreams of.'

Mavis Towers (1971-74) remembers: 'One day I was in Mr. B.'s office, when I distinctly heard the Holy Spirit saying to me, "There's a man of God standing before you," and I remember thinking, "I know that already!" Sometimes it was hard to tell when Mr. B. was just talking or praying – conversation and prayer intermingled. He did both so naturally.'

Evert Schut (1979-1980): 'We were walking to Hockley Pentecostal Church, discussing all kinds of items. Suddenly I noticed, still walking, that the tone of his voice had changed only a little bit. Then I realised that he had started to pray aloud to the Lord about one of the things we were talking about! This made quite an impression on me, because praying to the Father in Heaven, was as natural to him as talking to one of his students.'

John Fee: 'His "Arrow Prayers" seemed to cover everyone and everything in the process of life. Once you'd got on to Mr.

Bonsall's prayer list, you'd had it! He had a phenomenal memory for personal and family details – and, it seemed, about almost everyone with whom he came into contact. Although he certainly had an amazing mind, I think that amount of detail can only have been maintained by prayer!'

Peter Conlan (1964-67): 'Brash was "a prophet for his day". He never dwelt in the past. His vision was solidly in the future.'

Tailor-made Prayers
The Ring. 'One young student was wandering up Pakenham Road, when something flashed and caught his attention. To his amazement it was an engagement ring. Being a young man of integrity, he took it straight to the local police station where it waited to be claimed by its owner. Some months later our friend returned to enquire about the ring, only to discover that it was still there! So much time had elapsed that he could now claim it himself. But what should he do with it? His first response was "Ask the Principal". H.B.B. was soon found and had no hesitation in his reply. With one of those to-the-point, "Mr. Bonsall" prayers he asked, "Lord, please find a finger to fit this ring!" This story was told at Harry's farewell, surrounded by his students and friends, young and old. But the final telling brought the house down, as a young girl next to the story-teller shot up with her left hand in the air and said, "Here's the finger!"'

Jonathon and Ann Booth (1971-74): 'We were enjoying a quiet stroll down New Street one Saturday afternoon. Suddenly Brash was there, grey-haired and suited as usual ... After a few pleasantries we were just about to say goodbye, when Brash uttered his famous "word of prayer" and without a pause for breath, launched into a prayer of blessing upon our lives. We managed to get our eyes closed while he was in full flow and, as suddenly as he started, we heard an "Amen". We looked up and

315

he was gone, already ten yards down the street waving goodbye....'

Melting Moments. (*Joyce Halsall*): 'I was on my way back from holiday in the Lake District with two friends, when I bumped into your parents at a service station on the road to Keswick. I was holding three ice cream cones. Your father very quickly broke into the inevitable "word of prayer". It was a hot sunny day and, as the prayer lengthened, the cornets shortened ... ice cream trickled down my arms and dripped off my elbows. By the time we reached the "Amen", the evidence had virtually disappeared!'

'Let's Get to Prayer!' (*Ruth*): 'A young ex-Cambridge graduate with a unique healing ministry, was to visit the Bonsall home on several occasions, to minister to my father in this respect. Richard was an academic with a personality that rather matched my father's. On one memorable occasion he came to pray for him. I remember the occasion vividly, as Murray (my husband) and I, my father's secretary and my mother, were all in our sitting-room together, when Richard began to talk at length and with authority on the subject close to his heart. My father was nearing his 9.00 pm bed-time. To our embarrassment he seemed to be dropping off to sleep. Every so often Richard would ask, "Mr. Bonsall, did you get that point?" To which he would surface and reply, "Yes, yes. Let's get to prayer. Let's get to prayer."

'An hour or so later, Richard finally asked him for a résumé of his treatise, to be sure he'd got the message right! We were all feeling very hot under the collar at this point, but, to our utter amazement, my father suddenly sat bolt upright and said, "Of course! Point 1 ... point 2 ... point 3 ... point 4 ... point 5 ... point 6 ... point 7." In no more than five minutes, he had given a precise summary of the 60 minute talk. 'That's what you said wasn't it, Richard? Now, *let's get to prayer*!' We were just staggered. In spite of all appearances to the contrary, 'Mr. Bonsall' had obviously been listening intently to what *he* felt were the salient points – whilst dozing off in between!'

That little story illustrates the point made by *George Rabey* (1956-59), an early BBI student who later became General Secretary of the Unevangelised Fields Mission Worldwide, 'All of us knew and loved Mr. Bonsall as he was on our U.F.M. Council for 25 years. When he spoke, his opinion was always worth careful consideration ... and he seemed to have a gift for summing up a discussion!'

Madeline Stanley (Nottingham Bible Institute): 'Mr. Bonsall had a unique ability to get the main points of a lecture across, brought to life by his illustrations. From the student angle, your brain can only take so much in at one time! It was only when you were quietly meditating afterwards that the in-between bits would come back to complete the picture.'

'HE'S MY BROTHER!'

Rev. Duncan Campbell was God's man when revival came to the Scottish Outer Hebrides in 'The Lewis Awakening,' 1949-53. It was said of him that 'people meeting him were introduced to new spiritual dimensions and could never be the same again'. Duncan visited the Bonsalls on several occasions, once in the early 1960s, when he brought with him two young women from the Faith Mission, Brenda Charles and Jean Wilson. He was very much a Highlander and in some ways a mystic, but there was also a very gentle side to him – a kind of child-like innocence ... He once said, 'When the next revival comes to England, it will start in the Church of England.' Well, we shall see!

(*Dosie*) 'It was lovely talking about that revival in the Hebrides. Whenever he came to visit he always made a bee-line for us. He very much enjoyed coming!'

(*Ruth*) 'As a young girl, I remember him in our home, as a wonderful warm and gentle man that you felt you wanted to hug!'

Rev. Geoff Grogan, who as Principal of the Glasgow Bible Training Institute followed in Andrew MacBeath's footsteps, vividly remembers his first meeting with Harry.

'I first met Harry about 30 years ago, when I deputised for Andrew MacBeath at a gathering of College Principals in London to discuss missionary training. He was one of the most regular attenders at the Association of Bible College Principals conferences, and even at that time he was regarded as a senior member of the group. As the only non-Principal present I was feeling a little awkward ... and I remember with gratitude, his warm brotherly attitude to me. I was so glad of such a welcome and felt a warm bond with him ever afterwards.'

Margaret Habermann (Principal of Romney House Theological College, Cambridge) was another member of the Association of Bible College Principals, who also used to meet H.B.B. at their conferences. She writes:

'My most vivid memory of Mr. Bonsall was at Scarisbrook Hall Christian School. The Headmaster had been telling us all how the massive and magnificent Hall (on which the previous owners had just spent a quarter of a million pounds) had been acquired by the school for a paltry twenty four thousand pounds!

'As my husband and I went for a walk to digest this remarkable piece of information, Mr. Bonsall was doing the same ... just ahead of us. Hands clasped behind his back, head thrust forward, he was walking at a smart pace, muttering repeatedly, with increasing volume,

'"Twenty four thousand pounds – the price of a country cottage! Twenty four thousand pounds – the price of a COUNTRY COTTAGE!"

318

'It was not an envious exclamation ... but a triumphing in God and His wonderful ways.... I can just imagine him now exclaiming in wonder as he contemplates the glories of heaven!'

Richard Bennett (who beams out across five continents on Trans-World Radio (TWR) and the Far East Broadcasting Association (FEBA)), first became friends with Harry at Dr. Edwin Orr's annual conference on 'The History of Revival' at Oxford University.

'In Brash, I found a beloved brother with the rare combination of a scholarly mind and a flaming heart ... may Mr. Bonsall's vision of "Revival in our Time" live on.'

Roy Hession (evangelist and author), with his wife Revel, occupied the top floor of No. 4 Oxford Road before Harry arrived in the early 1950s.

'This has been a beautiful time. I am so thrilled to see the way the Lord's hand is upon you in extending your borders. England needs BBI right in the middle of the country and it is thrilling to see how the work is progressing.

May the Lord mightily encourage you and give you strength and energy to go *right through to the end*. Our love to you both from us both. Yours, Roy.' (1977)

George Verwer, in conversation: 'In the early days of Operation Mobilisation, Brash was a most important person to me ...a key person when I came out with my ideas, as so many thought they were quite "way out" and unrealistic, but Brash didn't. He listened to me and grabbed hold of my ideas with enthusiasm!'

Colin Peckham, Principal of the Faith Mission Bible College, Edinburgh:

'Harry's care and thoughtfulness were always evident. I once had to speak at a meeting in the heart of town, that had nothing to do with his own cause ... and instead of directing me across the strange city, or sending a student with me, he came himself! I deeply appreciated his love and concern. Always refreshing, always interested in you, always with a vision of some aspect of God's work, he would speak to the Lord as if he were holding a conversation with someone in the room: "And now Lord, there are six reasons why we think this project should be tackled. The first is ... the second is ... the third is ... What's the fourth again, Lord? I've just forgotten, but You know it, Lord, and many more reasons besides. Yes, Lord, we believe we're safely in Your will. Just lead us out in victory Lord, and we'll give You all the glory!"

'His enthusiasm was infectious, his resourcefulness amazing and his scope and interests wide. In fact, Harry was a most lovable, kind, energetic, thoughtful and inspiring man of God.'

Mary Peckham (née Morrison) worked alongside Duncan Campbell during the time of the Hebrides Revival.

'Harry Brash Bonsall is a man whose whole-hearted interest and concern for the cause of Christ went far beyond the field of his own activity. He was involved in every project that came to his notice ... not only in word but also in action.

I will never forget his concern when my fellow-worker and I arrived at the College in Birmingham on a scooter. We had travelled from Leicester at his invitation to address his students. He was horrified when he saw that we had no helmets – and forthwith, he purchased two and presented them to us! That was the kind of man he was – unique in his personality and ministry – a living example of perpetual motion!'

'A PEEP BEHIND THE SCENES'

For us four children, living with Pa was a positive and colourful experience. Already, we have incorporated many personal memories within the main body of this book. There are so many more left unsaid.

Charles (Bonsall): 'I think it was true to say, that my father had half a foot in heaven. He once said, *"If a boat is in the harbour, it isn't possible for God to steer it. You have to be out there going somewhere. At that point God steers!"*

'Like Abraham, he was a man of faith, who never seemed to take the safe option. I remember him always categorising, filing and recording, putting everything into little boxes where he could get his hands on it! A man of such drive, who did not want to slow down in what he was doing, but would stop whatever it was at the drop of a hat if someone needed help. A great listener. He wouldn't mess about wasting time. He would *go* for it. Speed was the essence. As an old man he once said, *"I want to do hard physical work,"* and that's what he did. Never drove, always walked or cycled.... Cared about keeping his body fit. Exercise was important to him. Hard physical work. In my mother's case she did it till she nearly dropped, because she *had* to. He did it because he *wanted* to. He knew how important it was.'

Charles vividly recalls Pa's great love of books – of all varieties, on every possible topic. How he would suddenly "go mad" on one particular subject, searching for all the books he could find on that one theme, be it some personality or era in history, like Churchill and Hitler, Charlie Chaplin or Dale Carnegie. *'Don't put me off my drive,'* he'd say. When he had researched and taken notes to his satisfaction, he would then move on to 'new pastures'!

It was the same for music. His records were a constant companion as he worked, and at one period he organised a series of musical soirees in the long lounge of No. 28, inviting thirty or so friends at a time. A highly knowledgeable speaker then entertained the guests with enthralling stories of Tchaikovsky, Beethoven and others.

Charles also remembers his father saying: '*I'm fed up with too much religion! I've had enough of it ... but not enough of Jesus.*'

Rachel: 'Pa made pipe-dreams become reality. His motto was *"Adapt to change"*. Any new venture – he went with it. He read up on all the latest in technology and forged ahead. He wouldn't stick to the old, but grabbed for the new. He kept on asking me, even when he was in his eighties, "Have you started to use a computer yet? You must learn how to use it!"

'He invested £5,000 in a 'Variatyper', before anything else. It was his priority and in order to be able to buy it, he went around the demolition sites, picking up what had been left behind. He built a truck like a big trolley on wheels, painted it maroon, and named it 'The Wells Fargo Express' in white letters. Then, one afternoon after lectures, he put on his overalls, rounded up a support team of students and set off to the building sites with, "Come on, Gang! There's at least £2,000 of demolition timber here!"'

Tom: 'Pa's Sayings on the Lesson of Life:

1. Aim at nothing and you'll hit it!
2. Don't wash your dirty linen in public.
3. The lust for power can be one of the worst of sins.
4. Reading a book is like eating a fish. Eat the fish and leave the bones.
5. On the phone, "I'll just say Goodbye before I start, in case I get cut off in the middle!"
6. Don't forget to look after No. 1, so that you can look after Nos. 2 and 3.
7. Do your best and leave the rest!'

For others, it was a similar experience.

John Morrison (Glasgow): 'I never met anyone to touch your parents, before or since .. just like family.'

Phemie Muir (Gamrie, Scotland): 'When they came, it was like a visit from angels. They were so lovely.'

Gita, BBI student (1976-78): 'I have never met anyone like them. So simple ... yet so deep. They always sat at our table and ate what we ate. One day I asked Mr. Bonsall, "Why?" I shall never forget his reply: "Because you're my family!"'

Parents to a Multitude
Marshall Holdstock, BBI student (1957-60): 'For Jean, your father has a special place. He had "married" people before, but Jean was the first person he gave away, as her father had died a few years before. He was awfully nervous and rushed Jean to the altar in no time at all! Those were the kind of family ties your parents had for us early students.'

Rose: 'Your Mum and Dad's kindness was outstanding. I was delivered to them in a state of inner turmoil and complete misery – and they not only provided a bed-sit and a hearing ear, but also a paid job as warden to a house full of foreign students!'

Lodger in the House
Many lodgers, from different parts of the globe, filled the top floor of No. 8 over the years. All of them were drawn into our family in one way or another; university students and professional people, or those with a particular need.

Penny Howell, (summer 1989) was one of these. She wrote:
'Heaven provided your dear mother to care for me in the summer of 1989, when I came back disorientated, after exciting and

complicated experiences in New York! I can't imagine anywhere more suitable and secure to have lived. I had an enormous amount of work to do and would have studied far too late. But at 10 pm every night, your mother came up to stop me overdoing it and have a time of prayer. While I was there, her correspondence with Margaret Thatcher was in full swing.

'Saturday morning trips to the market filled the house with boxes of the most unlikely vegetables (and I very often got the spin-off from this for my own little kitchenette up aloft). I never quite understood your Mother's kitchen, but its products were most tasty and she was so hospitable at weekends. I would find little cakes to brighten life up. It was an unforgettable summer, sharing a little of Bonsall family life and the huge work done at BBI.

'A frequent daily treat – watching the early evening news with your parents (and the dog!) usually accompanied by cake and ice cream.

'Both your mother and I belonged to "Intercessors for Britain". Every day I'd drive back from school, my head spinning with the day's problems (including the involvement of some girls in the occult). Your dear mother would invite me into the kitchen, where we'd analyse everything and pray about it. She did indeed have a lovely face. And your father was very amusing about the many air letters arriving for me from a certain mutual friend in Israel. He would always announce the arrival of the distinctive letter and then your mother would tell him off for examining other people's correspondence!!'

Guests from the North
Brenda Charles and *Jean Wilson* (Blanshard) from the Faith Mission in Edinburgh, came down to visit BBI with *Duncan Campbell* in the 1960s. He loved to visit the Bonsalls.

Brenda: 'I stayed in your parents' flat and they treated me like a daughter. I shall never forget your father bringing me a large mug of his special early morning tea.[1] I was amazed that the Principal of the Bible College bothered to do that for me ... it was a mark of the man's humility. I still remember their tremendous enthusiasm as they shared the vision of the College, with your father telling us about all the materials he was collecting from demolition sites for future use in building-work: doors, shelves and loads of second-hand stuff. They weren't just prayerful, but also very practical. Always looking ahead.'

Jean: 'I can still remember your father's eyes dancing with delight as he talked about all God's provision, and took us on a tour of the buildings, with newly acquired accommodation and growing student numbers. Humanly speaking he was surrounded by large financial needs, resident student pressures and some very real problems ... but it was his calm trust in God and projected vision that rose above it all.

'I saw Harry Bonsall as a man of great spiritual stature. He had a very busy timetable, but he made time for people. Whether the time was long or short, he had a restful spirit in your presence, and he gave himself in sharing the deep spiritual longings of his heart for BBI – and the world at large. In contrast, he sat listening so intently to Duncan and the experiences we had of God's work in revival. He so hungered for more of God. I thought, "Here is God's man, in God's place!"

'The complete loyalty and oneness of purpose your parents shared was very special, and fellowship over lunch was a treat! (Particularly your father's "Instant prayer menus". "Lord, send us revival...", "Lord, these girls *do* need a scooter helmet! Amen."). So was chatting with your mother on the settee afterwards. She was so gracious and quickly drew people into the inner circle of her family with plenty of humour and wisdom. I

---

1. Apart from his delight in 'demolitions', one of my father's specialities was different blends of tea in large pint mugs of all shapes and sizes.

am grateful for all I learned of Christ Jesus from them when we came to stay.'

Far from Home

... Students from Singapore, a family from Portugal, a doctor and his wife from Brazil. Others from Nagaland and Japan ... Harry and Dosie knew what it was to be lonely and homesick.

Toshiko Kosumi, (Japan 1990s): 'Mrs. Bonsall was so special for me. I could tell her a lot of things, good things and bad things ... and she always prayed for me. Even though I could not meet Mr. Bonsall, I could know him and his vision through Mrs. Bonsall! *BBI was, is, and always will be the College of the great vision of Revival.*'

Alex and Renie Elsaesser (BBI students and Printing Manager from the USA):

'So many of us are indebted to you both for where we are today. You became our family away from home and helped us in all our adjustments to this new and 'strange' land of England. I remember saying to Renie, "If I ever went to Bible College, I'd go to a place like this." Lo and behold, you said, "It looks as if the only way you can stay in the UK is to become a student!" I said that our motives were not the best! You said, *"Leave the motives to God!"* We did – and I've never regretted it!'

Frank Cheung (served as pastor to the Amsterdam Chinese Church in Holland; BBI student, 1986-87; then senior pastor to the Chinese Overseas Christian Church in Birmingham):

'I first met Mr. and Mrs. Bonsall in my Restaurant in 1967 and straight away they encouraged me to go to BBI to study! Mrs. Bonsall favoured sweet and sour pork and I taught her how to make sweet and sour sauce and fried pork!

'I learned a lot from Mr. Bonsall on how he always used his

time so well. He taught me how to deal with the difficult circumstance and pressure of work. He told me, *"When you face the Sun, the shadow will always fall behind you."*

'That is how I learned to fix my eyes on Jesus instead of my circumstances, and to cast all my burdens on the Lord, trusting everything to Him. Straightaway, my burden became lighter, so that I could carry on to serve the Lord.'

Marjorie van Halem 'Dutch Maggie', BBI student 1976-78): 'Mrs. Bonsall loved to have us Dutch students on "chores" at No. 8 – not just for one term only, but for as many as possible. Chores! This surely was a satisfying job! How amazed I often was, that in the midst of her "challenging" kitchen (and it was a challenge after a visit to the market, with boxes of vegetables, fruit and fish everywhere), Mrs. Bonsall was always able to find what she was looking for!

'After this very exciting chore for six terms, I have grown very close to Mrs. Bonsall, as we peeled onions and made beds together, sorting through millions of bags of second-hand "10p" clothes ... and pouring endless cups of tea. *Never a dull moment at the Bonsalls!'*

Kees and Riet Blom (BBI students from *Holland*):
Kees (Dutch Merchant): 'I first came here fourteen years ago, leaving Riet and the children in Holland, because the Lord had called me out. I really felt lost, but Mrs. Bonsall invited me in straight away for Sunday lunch. She welcomed me just like part of the family ... and we have felt like that ever since! I loved going with her to the wholesale market; seeing her in action; watching her bartering. How many friends she had among those traders! They loved to give her things or chat with her. I learnt so much from her, the way she gave as a servant. In our minds, she will always be a lovely lady with a heart for everyone, who really embraced us and cared for us as foreigners in this country.'

The Team

Riet (Chiropodist): 'Mr. and Mrs. Bonsall, whom we loved so very much, to me were like one! The way they lived was a true example to us of how to live the Christian life. I was chiropodist to them both and we had many, many talks together. What a privilege that was! One of their gifts was that they never gave you the feeling you were too much trouble. They always had time. We learnt from them how to pray for everything and everyone – and expect to see the answer.'

Josie Philips: 'Mrs. Bonsall was not one to push herself forward very much, as she seemed to prefer to "beaver away in the background", but she had a very keen perception of needs ... and one sensed a deep love and understanding between them. With God's help she was the secure home on earth for your beloved father, and I am quite sure that without that devotion to each other, your father would not have achieved what he did in his lifetime.'

George Rabey (early BBI student, in a letter to Dosie): 'Mr. Bonsall was a wonderful man whom God used in a remarkable way. I do not say that lightly. For me, he was a man of prayer, concerned for every person the Lord brought within his orbit ... but I shall always remember the two of you as a team, working so closely together over the years.'

Dosie Makes Her Point (letter to John Major, December 1991)

'Dear Mr. Major,

'I am a member of 'Intercessors for Britain' and pray for you daily. You certainly have had a difficult first year in office and it is very wonderful how you have come through. I am sure an ever more difficult year lies ahead of you and needs God's help and guidance as never before.

'Europe is the vital question and then there is the General Election! In all these matters God is Sovereign and we neglect Him at our peril. Man proposes, God disposes. We are basically a Christian country – all our laws are based on the Bible. Today we are reaping the penalty of disregarding Him. I believe in the keeping of the Ten Commandments, which would solve most of our social problems. "Six days shalt thou work and rest on the seventh day" – would boost the economy and cut out the need of tranquillisers. Why educate children on how to use protection? Teach them the straight commandment, "Thou shalt not commit adultery" (Exod. 20).

'Our most precious possession is our Christian heritage – we do not want to be ruled by atheistic countries, nor told how to bring up our children by them. God has promised this country a very powerful revival – men and women will know the fear of God and will be brought face to face with Him (as in the Welsh Revival) and there will be a great conviction of sin and crying to God for mercy throughout the land, followed by a time of great blessing. Our hope lies in God – the Creator of the universe.

'I am praying that He will speak to you personally as to what He wants you to do at this time – not influenced at all by men, however much it makes you stand out of the crowd. Providing we walk in obedience to Him, we will have a time of great prosperity in the nation.

'I myself have trusted the Lord for almost 60 years and found Him faithful.

'Yours sincerely

'Mrs. Doris Bonsall'

Stuart Pascall (BBI Student) remembers:

'Because I was of a fairly practical bent, with a training in the motor trade, it was not long before I was co-opted onto the Bonsall "chores" team, with particular responsibility for *The Car*! The vehicle in question was a rather elderly Rover, model

75 (I think) or perhaps 90. My initial introduction to the car showed that it had had a good innings and that it was by now clearly showing the cumulative results of a rather Bohemian existence, evidenced by the fact that the driver's door catch was broken and the sole means of insurance against sudden death around any left-hand bend was a piece of stoutish string attached to the driver's door-handle, with the other being tied to the handle of the door on the passenger's side! This once stately gentleperson's car had come, in these its later years, to a life which consisted of a series of emergency measures designed to keep it running, courtesy of visits to local scrapyards, interrupted by manic forays into the wilder regions beyond Edgbaston. The locals had long since become used to the sight of a grimly determined Mrs. B. aiming at the apex of the next bend in the road, whilst beside her sat the tall behatted Mr. B., lips moving in what was probably a constant invocation of the Almighty with sincere requests that the angelic beings be allowed back into the vehicle just this once more!'

Every year 'the Car' would take the Bonsalls to the Talbot family farm on the annual July pilgrimage to Keswick. Old friends and family haunts in Lancashire were very dear to Harry.

Elizabeth Talbot: 'It was always a red-letter-day when the Bonsalls came to our home. Their car was so heavily laden, especially at the back, that the springs almost seemed to touch the ground. Since he was a small boy, our young Brian (now a minister himself) remembers them getting up at 4.00 am to pray. This seemed to continue till 8.00 am ... and Brian's bedroom was next to theirs. He could hear them praying, but couldn't make out what they said, and kept wondering, "Whatever can they find to pray to God about for all that time!"

'One day our youth leader gave all the young people in our church a questionnaire. One question was: "Who has been the

330

greatest spiritual influence on your life?" Our other son, Steven, was 14. Without hesitation, he answered, "The Reverend H. Brash Bonsall" (the youth leader told me this) and Mr. Bonsall only came to our house once a year. What a tribute!'

On the Bus. Harry had no inhibitions where matters of eternity were concerned and one day, student *Roy Browning* (1963-65) happened to be travelling in the same direction. 'I was on my way to preach somewhere one Sunday evening and was sitting upstairs, near the front of the bus. Brash got on at the next stop and sat near the back beside a West Indian lady. He was soon in animated conversation, which I could hear. First he showed her some family photographs; then very simply, he moved into personal witness about the Lord. He got off before me so had no idea he was overheard (though I'm quite sure the other passengers would have got the message!)'

The Way to Evans?
An evangelist to the core, Dosie never missed an opportunity either, and one day she had a lot of fun making the most of it!

'Excuse me. Can you tell me the way to Evans?' one portly lady asked her as she was walking along Birmingham's New Street. Quick as a flash Dosie replied, 'I'm so sorry I can't – but I'll tell you the Way to 'Eaven!" and she did, without a moment's delay.... The family had a good laugh about that one when she came home!'

QUERNMORE BOOKS
(Bonsall Publishers Ltd!)

'He was not afraid to think and write the unconventional ... and certainly part of his greatness lies in those thoughts and writings' (DeWayne Coxon, President of Jordan College, Michigan).

What the Readers Say

Vincent Rudman (ANBC) writes from South Africa:

'The Bible student who prayerfully sets himself the goal of achieving an in-depth knowledge of the New Testament and its history, need go no further than the acquisition of the four volumes on *The Person of Christ* by the Rev. Henry Brash Bonsall, late Principal of the Birmingham Bible Institute. These volumes are a masterpiece in thought, arrangement and explanation. Rich in illustration, they make study a delight. Almost unobserved, precious pebbles of sound New Testament doctrine are set in a crystal-clear matrix of Biblical history – the truth of Jesus Christ in four volumes, taught and written by an evangelical theologian of the twentieth century. This is the Rev. Henry Brash Bonsall's contribution and gift to the Church of Jesus Christ.

'Apart from the Scriptures, I can think of no better source of getting to know the suffering Lord. In his books he makes the way of salvation quite clear to anyone who would accept and believe, taking care not to deviate one step to the left or the right in his clarification of the great and fundamental doctrines of God's plan of Redemption. These volumes on *The Person of Christ*, together with his *Historical Introduction to the Bible* should maintain their rightful place on all bookshelves of preachers, Bible schools, institutes, colleges and universities.

'Never was there a dull moment in the classroom, never is there a dull moment when looking up some part or other of these four books.

'Harry Brash Bonsall's voice echoes through the pages of his books; a clear voice in the modern wilderness of theology, but his legacy to the Christian, evangelical church will continue ... because it is inspired by the Holy Spirit. In fact he was much more aggressive in his championship of Truth than is discernible in his books. I can still hear his voice ringing out in the classroom in defence of the true gospel of Jesus Christ, challenging all modernists to stake their claims on the Scriptures, for what they claim to be the truth. He sowed the Word and we trust that by God's grace and the power of the Holy Spirit we may yet see the flame of revival sweeping the countryside, all the way to Land's End and back, through the cities of Britain. The Lord knows, we need it urgently....'

'...THEIR CHILDREN'S CHILDREN'
(Psalm 103:17)

David (at 24)

'It was only really after my grandfather died that I realised just how special he was. What an amazing man! Someone who was able to take huge leaps of faith; who believed in prayer with a passion and who did not lead his own life, but let God lead it for him. I am so privileged to have been born into a family that not only prays together, but had a wider family of grandparents with whom we could pray too. I knew that if I had an exam, an important rugby match or even if I didn't, Grandpa and Grandma would be up at 5 am praying for me before I had even started my day.

'My fondest memories of Grandpa, however, are much more personal ... walking the forty minutes to church on a Sunday morning with my brother and sister, holding Grandpa's hand. He'd be wearing a buttoned-up trench coat and satchel bag, strapped in swashbuckling style diagonally across the outside. As we walked the familiar route, he would test our general knowledge, particularly History and English Literature. He was especially concerned about our lack of understanding of the Hanoverian period, which was perhaps a little harsh, considering I as the eldest, was only 11 years old! No doubt he would be intrigued to know that I now have a History degree.

'I also remember the excitement of being allowed to sit next to Grandpa at the College lunch, where he would rise

333

unceremoniously to say grace with a simple, "Thank you Lord, Amen," and then plough into the fare before him. These were always fascinating times because you never quite knew who was going to be at the table. Guests would come in from around the world and Grandpa would always quiz them about the situation in their own country, invariably finishing off by praying for them.

'Looking back, I wish I'd had the chance to know him as an adult, because I'm sure we would have had some terrific talks. I would have loved to get to the bottom of what he thought about different subjects, particularly on how to follow the Christian walk with the total commitment he had. I guess at some point in the future we probably will.'

Andrew (at 22)

'As I write these words, I see a small photograph of Grandpa which sits on my desk. True, he's younger there than when I knew him, but it's unmistakably "him": warm, dignified and purposeful. Ever since my mother gave me this photo some five or six years ago, the memory of Grandpa has become a regular source of comfort and inspiration to me, because Grandpa embodied something special. When he died, I was fifteen years old, with many of the usual mid-teen physical, emotional, and spiritual "crises" (they still crop up occasionally!). However, as I look at this photo I realise that he was one of those rare people whose presence or simply whose *memory* is enough to shed light on any daunting challenge. A number of times in recent years, I have struggled with difficult personal situations, only to think of Grandpa and therefore of the God he served with all his heart ... the result being a tremendous sense of "You know, everything really *is* going to work out; you really *are* going to make it." Grandpa made it. He and Grandma and the Lord made it together, as a wonderful team.

'I never had the chance to know Grandpa at his most active, although that seems incredible given the brisk speed of the walks we used to share together ... on the way to church, or round the Birmingham reservoir. We would pester him to ask us general knowledge, History or Bible questions (not that he needed much encouragement!). This was always a special, personal time for us and showed his great desire and willingness to pass on some of the things he had learned of life. Those were very happy days; times in which I came to love and respect him in a way which will last my whole lifetime. He *invested* in us, having prayed for me since before I was born (and proclaiming at my birth the arrival of "a very important child", as Brash is one of my middle names!). He and Grandma were "constants" in my life, as they continue to be ... in a different way. Of course, I wish they were still here, especially so that we could have great, lengthy discussions on those subjects about which he enthused and which now excite me also. However, as my life unfolds, with its many distractions and attractions, one of the greatest encouragements is to look back and see the unfolding of another life ... a life spent investing in things that will last forever. He was a man who, despite many of the same distractions, made it – and, as a friend of mine would say, "looked good when he got there".'

Carrie (at 20)

'I have very fond memories of my grandparents – and particularly remember those long walks to church. At the age of eight, I figured that 1 out of 10 was a pretty fair average for general knowledge questions – and happily left the rest of the answers to my two brothers! But later on, when I reached my "A" levels, it was a different story. Studying Church History and the Reformation was hard work and I was worried about the exam, so Mum handed me some of Grandpa's photocopied lecture notes. They were fantastic!

'A few nights before the exam I had a dream. There was Grandpa in his long trench coat, striding briskly ahead of me on the same route to church that we had walked so many times before. In my dream, I remember running up to him, waving his notes in the air and calling, "Grandpa! Grandpa! I'm using your notes. They're *great*!" He turned round with a twinkle and a smile and just said, "I know – and it's going to be fine!" then just faded out of sight....

'A little baffled, but encouraged, I got up to revise the next morning. The exam went well the following day, and I'm happy to say – *I* was the one with a twinkle and a smile when I opened my exam results!

'Grandma was the administrator of domestic affairs and knew how to use every thing she had, especially in creating wonderful soups! She was a very down-to-earth person who always put other people before herself.

'On my seventh birthday she took me with her to the Bull Ring market. Almost every stall we stopped at, Grandma knew the owner ... and as soon as they heard it was my birthday they loaded me with piles of fruit and vegetables. "Wow!" I thought, "Grandma's *really* popular," whilst peeping over the growing mountain of fruit balanced in the box I was carrying. "I want to come to the Bull Ring *again*."

'My motives for returning were certainly mixed. Grandma's were not. She wasn't just "stocking up" – she was reaching people.

'I have always thought that the closer you are to Jesus, the more *you* you are. For Grandma and Grandpa this was true. Their whole personalities reflected the hours they spent in prayer.'

GOING FOR GOLD!

In September 1990, Harry finally reached the end of his race.

'Mr. Bonsall knew such a lot about heaven,' said *Shirley Cox* (1965-68, tutor 1973), 'and now he's there himself!'

Old friends, Professor F. F. Bruce and Kenneth Hooker, both followed Harry within days. The next month, it was Malcolm Muggeridge who joined the throng. One old friend who knew them both wrote to Dosie from Riyadh, Saudi Arabia, remembering:

'Brash Bonsall's wonderful life, his example, his dynamism and vision ... and the time that he came for lunch one day ... one of the most precious experiences of my life. Despite his incapacity, I could see Brash's mind was just as acute as when I first met him as a youngster 35 years ago.'

He continued:

'This morning in the English paper, I had other sad news ... Malcolm Muggeridge died yesterday. To my wife and myself, Malcolm Muggeridge was particularly kind. I think he was the same age as Brash and I place Malcolm and your husband on the same level; prophets and teachers raised up in the holy church for the edification of the saints. Both followed different courses in life and Malcolm only came to faith late ... but to me, that they have both died so close together in time, is, in a mysterious way, very significant.

'Two men, both of outstanding ability – one of whom, your husband, I knew only marginally, yet over a long period. The other, Malcolm, I knew more intimately ... but, in my pantheon to the illustrious dead, both of their names will shine.

'On the bald street breaks the blank day.'

'The death of your husband to me represents the end of my childhood; because it was as a child, I first knew of him and came under his ministry. The death of Malcolm Muggeridge to me represents the end of my youth and young manhood...

'My dear Mrs. Bonsall. You will excuse these ramblings, I'm sure. But this morning I feel like one of the sons of the prophets. Elishah and Elijah are both dead ... and now, who will go over this Jordan?'

Three years later, in October 1993, Dosie herself made that journey – and the tributes for both of them continued to roll in.

Miles Witherford, Hockley: 'She was a very dear friend and a very unique lady, who didn't have very much interest in things, but an overwhelming love and passion for people.... There will be many around that throne because of the life and testimony of Doris Bonsall.'

Pat Reynolds: 'She was like a mother to me and I thought she would last for ever.'

Beth Clark, Worthing: 'I can hardly believe it, Ruth. Your mum had her finger on the pulse of so many things and seemed so tireless. In that short space of time I realised what a woman of God she was. She made a lasting impression. Never have I forgotten her beautiful face, snow-white hair and sparkling, piercing eyes. To me she was unfading, undying, always abounding with life and vitality....'

DeWayne Coxon, President of Jordan College, USA: 'I was shocked today to see that my friend went to be with the Lord. He seemed so invincible, always active and creative.'

Audrey Herbert/Johnson, (BBI student): 'Even now, I can't think that he has gone before us. He seemed so ... immortal ... somehow. Just like Moses.'

Piers Crocker (archaeologist working in Australia): 'May I add my tribute to those hundreds you will have received at this time of great loss. Not just your loss, of course, but a loss for the evangelical community of the nation; a great warrior in prayer and in labour for the coming revival. Of his secret life, hidden with God, I cannot speak. I simply know that he radiated a

338

gentleness and, more especially, a spirituality which I have not experienced elsewhere. I look to him as one could look to Paul, as an exemplar who "followed Christ". It would be doubly sad, if there was not some record of his life to inspire others. Is a biography planned? I do hope that someone will write something in the future.'

A family friend: 'A very great man.'

David Harley (former Principal of All Nations Christian College): 'He truly was an amazing man and has made a remarkable contribution to the whole field of Biblical teaching in this country.'

Richard Dugdale: 'A glorious man, full of faith and prayer. Wonderful in his life and witness; in touch with God and caring for his fellow men. A man of letters, but at the same time a man of action ... a teacher and a missionary.'

David Morris (former Principal of All Nations Christian College): 'I loved him and thought him one of the "choice saints" of this century.'

Geoff Grogan, (when Principal of the Bible Training Institute, Glasgow): 'Who can measure the influence of Harry's life? His very long ministry for Christ, his teaching gifts and leadership of a most significant Christian training establishment for an exceptionally long time, his warmth of personality, his pastoral heart and most of all his great love for Christ, have all made a great impact on an ever-widening circle of God's people.'

TWO PETERS

Peter Horne (BBI Student 1968-1971/Head Student)
International Secretary of the Christian Literature Crusade

'A man who left his mark'

'Thirty years ago, when I was trying to decide which Bible College to apply to, I arranged to spend weekends at three of them. The first offered a top academic programme; the second was in a beautifully located country house; and the third was BBI, which didn't and wasn't. Yet the reason I chose that remarkable college in Birmingham was an unmistakable sense of the presence of God among the staff and students, and *that* reflected the ethos of Henry Brash Bonsall.

'I once asked him what he thought the biblical rationale for Bible colleges was. "There isn't any," he replied. "But look at how disciples were trained. For three years they lived, ate, studied and worked in the presence of Jesus, and by then they knew what to do." That was the experience he sought to give to his students ... and to make sure they got it, he rose at five every morning to pray for them. They were *very down-to-earth prayers*, if they were like the ones I heard, *but the result was hundreds of ordinary students who were ready to go anywhere and do anything, with a fire in their hearts which was not easily put out.*

'BBI students were a diverse bunch. In my first term I shared a room with a doctor, a physicist, a carpenter and a gardener, and found I had much to learn from all of them. People who would have been turned down by other colleges generally had a chance with Brash. *He could recognise saints who were still under construction*, like the two who got into a fist-fight over the doctrine of sinless perfection, and still have faith in them!

'What sort of man was he, that had this strange influence on people?

'He was a man of *vision*, who saw people not as they were, but
340

as they could be. At the heart of his vision was his life-long conviction that revival was coming, which was the reason for BBI's existence. After three years with him, most people had caught the message that God had something better ahead, and they would not be content until they saw it.

'He was a man of *simplicity*, who in spite of his degrees, could present theology in terms that a school-child could understand. This simplicity was reflected in his life-style – he did not need new cars, furniture or clothes until the old ones had given all the service they could. With all that he had to do, his life could have been cluttered, but it never *seemed* to be. *He demonstrated that great men could be ordinary men.*

'He was a man of *tenderness*, who always had time for students with problems, however trivial they might be. In the term I was head student I had the privilege of extra time with Brash to discuss how things were going in College, and I don't think I can ever remember him criticising anyone, whatever they might be saying about him.

'More than anything else, he was a man of *prayer*. Brash took Paul's injunctions to pray at all times and for all men, very literally. He knew the background not only of every student, but of every student's parents, and the details came back each time he prayed for them (sometimes maturing a bit with age!). No-one could get out of his presence without a "word of prayer" even if they were running down the street to catch a bus. In fact he seemed to talk more naturally to the Lord than to the person with him.

'His lectures were unique, and you never knew quite where they would end up; as different stories and illustrations came into his mind from different points in his life and ministry, the syllabus took second place. His "Systematic Theology" course did not always tell you everything you needed to know about theology, but it always told you something you needed to know about God.

'I often heard complaints about different aspects of College life. Things were not perfect, but on reflection most of the problems which I encountered in twenty years in missionary service in Japan had already been met in embryo in those three years. Brash's training was remarkably practical.

'Eccentric he may have appeared, but his insights were generally "spot on", as he would shoot a line about someone's future. It was he who first told me that administration was a gift of the Holy Spirit (1 Cor. 12:28 – not so obvious in the Authorised Version days when it was the gift of governments). "The governor was the one who sat at the back of the ship and steered it," he said, and to him it was "as plain as a pikestaff" that I had it. That word had a prophetic quality about it, and made it a lot easier for me to accept the role that the Lord eventually led me into.

'Today, as International Secretary of the Christian Literature Crusade, my responsibilities have widened, with involvement in the 50 countries where CLC currently works. BBI has given us a significant number of workers, who are normally recognised by certain qualities. As I travel, I keep my eyes open for BBI students in other missions also, and generally see in them a dogged pertinacity, and a sense that what they are doing is just part of the preparation for something far greater in store. *Brash created a hunger for God in those who knew him, so that they would never be satisfied with second best.*

'I pray that the same passion will dominate my life that dominated his, and that the things that rubbed off in three years in his presence will stay attached.'

Peter Conlan (BBI student 1964-1967)
Operation Mobilisation, Director 'OM Ships Project'

'A tap on the shoulder, some high speed questions, my name scribbled into his note book and a quick word of prayer, was my introduction to Harry Brash Bonsall. It was the 1964 Keswick Convention at the close of a marathon missionary meeting in the big tent and I, along with many young people, had stood in response to the challenge of world missions. As we emerged from the tent, a rather intense Mark Twain figure with a loose fitting clerical collar, tapped me on the shoulder and said, "*I saw you stand. What is your next step? You'll need training.*" He spoke so rapidly and with such urgency, that I thought he was lost and asking directions. Within a few months I began missionary training studies under his leadership at BBI!

'Thirty years on, my memories of Mr. Bonsall are still vivid. His passionate and often peculiar prayers, "*Lord, you have no doubt seen the headlines this morning....*". However, the main focus of his prayer life was always people. His memory for names spanned half a century. In my last conversation with him, just weeks before he died, he asked about my mother by name.

'He was a man of great vision, with a surprisingly down to earth grasp of the practical skills needed to get there. Even BBI was only a means to an end. His dream was to train and prepare God's people for revival – a sovereign move of the Holy Spirit, which he believed would sweep the nation and then the world. "Missions" was an important part of the vision, and BBI became for him the key training programme. Complaints about leaking taps, freezing dormitories and a social policy that some thought had been borrowed from the Inquisition (even married couples were not allowed to hold hands within two miles of the College!), were usually met with, "*It's all good missionary training*."

'Brash Bonsall fiercely resisted any dichotomy between sacred and secular or, as he put it, between "*horse sense and theology*". He was as enthusiastic about the latest printing equipment acquired for the College, as he was about the theological notes soon to be printed on it. His understanding of property finances and building maintenance was as astonishing as his grasp of New Testament Greek. The world renowned theologian, Professor F. F. Bruce, believed him to be one of the finest Greek scholars of his day.

'Whilst he may have been warm hearted, he was far from soft headed. He did not suffer fools easily, nor did he waste time. His famous *"just a word of prayer"* was used more than once to abruptly end a boring conversation! Loyalty was important to Mr. Bonsall. In the final term of 1965 when student and even staff unrest threatened the entire future of the College, a tougher side to him emerged. Yet still the dominant memory from those difficult days is Mr. Bonsall's humility and big-heartedness.

'More than once I experienced his big-heartedness. One night a fellow student and I broke College rules, by going out on our motor cycle after hours to take hot chocolate and Gospels to "down-and-outs" – homeless men sleeping rough in derelict buildings. We returned to the College hostel at 3 am, were subsequently reported and faced possible suspension. The next day I stood outside the staff room door awaiting the summons. Mr. Bonsall came to the door and whispered, *"Because you broke the curfew rules, I'll have to join the staff in a reprimand. But I want you to know, I wish we had more students ready to take these kind of risks to reach people with the Gospel. Well done!"* The staff issued their reprimand. Mr. Bonsall just nodded his head and smiled, before launching into prayer for more important things.

'I was soon to discover the same big heart and big vision in a new movement which had exploded across the UK in the mid 60s. Operation Mobilisation, with its dynamic young American leader, George Verwer, was attracting hundreds of British young people into what then was a revolutionary new idea – short term missions. Not every British church leader welcomed the arrival of OM. There were murmurs from some parts of the establishment of para-church activity, extremism and superficiality. Some mission leaders grimly warned that OM was "*no substitute for the real thing!*"

BBI, however, welcomed Operation Mobilisation. *Op. Mob,* as Mr. Bonsall called it, was like BBI on wheels! OM's commitment to "no frills" discipleship, prayer, faith, world evangelism and a 'God can use you now' philosophy found an immediate resonance at BBI. Mr. Bonsall became one of George Verwer's greatest supporters and close friends. Indeed BBI functioned almost as an unofficial OM base in the UK. OM'ers could always find a bed there. OM speakers were welcome and students encouraged to join OM summer campaigns. BBI council member, Alf Ridpath, even went with OM out to India. BBI was the perfect preparation for Operation Mobilisation.

'My dream had been to serve the Lord in India. While many of my fellow students were planning careers with the more "respectable" and established mission agencies, I was increasingly drawn to OM. George Verwer invited me to work with him for a year as his "gofer". This was not so much because he saw great potential in me, but rather because he was willing to take a risk! That first year with George, mostly in India, stretched to a further three years. Then along with others, I had the privilege of helping to pioneer OM's ship ministry and today serve on the leadership team for the ships.

'When I announced at BBI that we (OM) were "believing God" for a ship for world evangelism, Mr. Bonsall's immediate response was, "Pete, I think you should be praying for *two* ships!" And he did. As I write, the Doulos has just completed a successful visit to Shanghai, China, and our second ship, Logos II, an incredible period of outreach and ministry throughout the West Indies.

'The British Christian press in the 1960s were less optimistic than Mr. Bonsall. When the word got out that we were praying for a ship, a leading Christian magazine said, *"These OM young people have more enthusiasm than common sense!"* Since that article was written, more than 25 million people have visited the ships in 130 nations. One hundred million pieces of Christian literature have been distributed through the ship ministry and tens of thousands of people have responded to the message of the gospel. Thank God for a little too much enthusiasm, especially if it is mixed with the prayer of faith of men like Brash Bonsall!

'I have valued the friendship of both Mr. and Mrs. Bonsall for almost thirty years. Mr. Bonsall has been one of the major influences in my life. I still revel in his world of ancient classics, history and literature, that brought to life every lecture he gave and opened up entirely new vistas for me. I often quote him – *"the heart of the problem is the problem of the heart."* I remember the disarming and canny way he introduced his flow of brilliant new ideas – *"you can throw this out on its rubber neck if you like ..."*. I meet former BBI students all over the world who have been influenced by those ideas and who are in turn shaping the lives of others.

'Perhaps the lasting impression for me of Mr. Bonsall, was his absolute conviction that God answers prayer ... and when he prayed something new was going to happen. I'm not sure why he tapped my shoulder and prayed for me more than thirty years ago – but something happened and it changed my life.'

'OVER TO YOU, RICHARD!'

Dr. Richard Massey
Principal of BBI (1990 -)

Many times I sat in staff or committee meetings with Brash Bonsall and heard him say, in characteristic style: 'Over to you!' Never once did I anticipate that the *ultimate* 'Over to you!' would come to me! However, around May 1990, Mrs. Bonsall rang me at my London home to say that Brash Bonsall was thinking of retiring that year. Would I consider becoming Principal?

Needless to say, I was somewhat taken aback by the invitation. As Director of the Deo Gloria Trust for some three years, I did not anticipate leaving that interesting post. Work with Kenneth Frampton and the Deo Gloria Trust had begun when I left BBI in 1987 (having been Director of Studies since the early 1980s). Even earlier than this, in 1976, while I was still in pastoral ministry in Melton Mowbray, Brash Bonsall had first invited me to BBI as visiting lecturer, when Vice-Principal David Smith was unwell and needed some assistance with his lecture programme. So, in many ways I thought my association with BBI must be over, having enjoyed a fairly long connection with it!

However, when that phone call came, I sensed immediately that God was saying something and that the offer should not be quickly dismissed, so I asked for time. After a few weeks of prayer and discussion (with my wife Christine, Brash Bonsall himself and two men whose wise counsel I valued in the past – Harry Sutton of Leicester and Bob Dunnett of BBI), I strongly felt the call of God to accept this somewhat daunting appointment. Not for one moment did I anticipate that within three months of my acceptance, Brash Bonsall would be with the Lord! He died in September 1990.

It was strange, but somehow, accepting the responsibilities of the Principal's role seemed so much easier when Brash Bonsall was alive than after his death, probably because while he was alive all his vision for BBI remained active, despite his retirement ... and during his funeral service at Hockley Pentecostal Church I found myself thinking: '*Who* is sufficient for these things?'

Of course, the answer has to be that '*God* is sufficient'. The original vision of 'BBI playing its part in a revived and renewed church', is quite capable of ongoing fulfilment in the hands of a sovereign God rather than the passing endeavours of men!

In fact, the signs and potential for such revival at the present time seem remarkable. The great opportunities in Eastern Europe and the former USSR are almost beyond imagination. Similar stirrings are taking place in China and the Far East. Even the growth of the New Age movement in the West is a sign of the underlying religious longings of mankind made in the image of God. Implacable Islam at least makes religion a constant talking point in our western media.

Brash Bonsall's vision in this area of revival was not a complex or esoteric one. Doris Bonsall often spoke of it in the College's morning chapel after his death. Praying for large numbers of Christian converts drawn from all levels of society ... men and women who would need nurturing and, in many cases, training for leadership ... encouraging BBI to be ready for such a programme and fully committed to praying for such a happening. I feel very comfortable with this vision handed on to me and the College continues to maintain it. Bob Dunnett's wider ministry of a 'Prayer For Revival' network is also an expanding and continuing aspect of Brash's original vision for revival.

Although, at first sight, many might see BBI as less academic, in fact, a highly important facet of Brash Bonsall's early vision was to maintain high standards of evangelical and biblical teaching and to offer such courses, often in an evening, to Christian leaders as well as full-time students. He was well qualified as a classical and theological scholar, and from the beginning, BBI was teaching external London University certificates, diplomas and degrees in divinity. Some of these classes were held in the Midland Institute in the centre of Birmingham. I feel sure that Brash would have been highly delighted with the new directions the College has taken in achieving validation for its present courses from the University of Wales. These lead on to the award of BA (Hons) Theology, and are taught by a well-qualified staff.

A practical legacy handed on to me by Brash Bonsall lay in the areas of management activities and properties. If he had any faults, perhaps they lay in this area. His dogged determination not to retire whilst still active, led to his Advisory Council of Management growing old with him ... replaced after his retirement by younger professional men and women to guide the College forward. This was very harmoniously achieved with Charles Bonsall, son of Brash, becoming the new Chairman and others such as Bob Dauncey, a leading Birmingham solicitor and Mike Smith, a businessman, being appointed along with several others. Now the College has become a charitable company with an able Board of Directors, chaired by Mike Smith – and a steady programme of restructuring of the administration, with re-furbishment of buildings. All so much part of the 'handing-on' process, particularly in the areas of faith and prayer.

Brash Bonsall was a man of great faith and each year, the College has taken on some faith enterprise in its expansion or improvement. We would not want this decidedly spiritual heritage from the Bonsall era to be lost! Perhaps one major unfulfilled vision of the earlier era has been to see new buildings constructed to give better purpose-built facilities for the ongoing work of the College. This may yet be a faith-target still to be undertaken.

It is now some years since the 'Over to you!' call came to me and I feel that those past foundations have been carefully built upon, whilst *new* directions have been explored. Like all pioneers and founders, they are inimitable and unique, with strengths and weaknesses that inevitably influence the next generation who follow them. Brash Bonsall was certainly in this mould. On his death a close colleague of his said: 'The mould has been broken.' This is true, yet God is in the business of re-creating new vessels and instruments, taking the work and staff of BBI forward into a new era of programmes and service for His church.

Christian Focus Publications publishes biblically-accurate books for adults and children. The books in the adult range are published in three imprints.

Christian Heritage contains classic writings from the past.

Christian Focus contains popular works including biographies, commentaries, doctrine, and Christian living.

Mentor focuses on books written at a level suitable for Bible College and seminary students, pastors, and others; the imprint includes commentaries, doctrinal studies, examination of current issues, and church history.

For a free catalogue of all our titles, please write to
Christian Focus Publications,
Geanies House, Fearn,
Ross-shire, IV20 1TW, Great Britain

For details of our titles visit us on our web site
http://www.christianfocus.com

RUTH McGAVIN

Ruth (Bonsall) McGavin was brought up in a very unusual environment! Along with her love of music, literature and a special interest in people, she has travelled widely.

A hospital training was put to good use in Central Asia, where Ruth and her husband Murray, an eye surgeon, lived and worked for several years. They have three children – David, Andrew and Carrie – one of whom has played professional rugby (not Carrie!), following in the footsteps of Murray, a Scottish rugby trialist.

A Scottish MA degree from Glasgow University later led to a post for Ruth at Bedford School, where she was asked to set up an EFL Department, for teaching English to foreign students.

Murray continues to work in the prevention of world blindness, and together they are now setting up a Christian Trust, seeking to alleviate suffering and promote health and education in developing countries.